Everyone

The Steven

"COMPELLING . . . *THE STEVEN McDONALD STORY* is a real-life drama . . . the inspiring story of one man's struggle to survive. It is well worth reading. . . ."

—*Macon Telegraph & News*

"A HEARTRENDING, INSPIRATIONAL STORY . . . written in an upbeat tone that relates the McDonald family's tremendous spiritual strength."

—ALA *Booklist*

"INSPIRING . . . written with great clarity, detail and honesty . . . This story is one of tragedy and triumph. . . ."

—*Florida Times-Union*

"A first-person story that will make the reader proud of both McDonald and Patti Ann."

—*Abilene Reporter-News*

"A poignant chronicle of their lives before, during and especially after the tragedy . . . Both McDonalds are secure in their faith that eventually they will triumph. These pages demonstrate they have already. . . ."

—*Publishers Weekly*

A Literary Guild Alternate Selection

An Alternate Selection of the Doubleday Book Club

The Steven McDonald Story

STEVEN McDONALD &
PATTI ANN McDONALD
with E.J. Kahn III

POCKET BOOKS
New York London Toronto Sydney Tokyo Singapore

POCKET BOOKS, a division of Simon & Schuster
1230 Avenue of the Americas, New York, NY 10020

ISBN: 0-671-70648-9

First Pocket Books printing April 1991

10 9 8 7 6 5 4 3 2 1

POCKET and colophon are registered trademarks of
Simon & Schuster.

Cover photo by Theo Westenberger

Printed in the U.S.A.

Did you ever know you were my heroes,
Everything I wish I could be . . .

For: Our loving parents and families
Monsignor John J. Kowsky
John P. Fay
Jessie O'Rielly
Donna Critchlow
David Womack
Bobby Mohammed
The New York City Police
and Fire Departments
and the New York City Emergency
Medical Services Department

Foreword

John Cardinal O'Connor
Archbishop of New York

Steven and Patti Ann McDonald are two of the most remarkable and courageous people I have ever met. They are true heroes not only to family and friends, but also to those who don't know them and have only heard of them. They are role models not only to Catholics but to all who have faith in God.

They are ordinary New Yorkers—he, a cop, she, a housewife. But they are extraordinary too. Imbued with the spirit of forgiveness, faith and fidelity to each other beyond earthly measure.

This is the story of a young couple's struggle to regain the life they had hoped for. From his room in Bellevue Hospital, to the nation's leading rehabilitation center in Denver and back home again, they have attracted the attention and admiration because of their decision to say no to vengeance. In spite of the pain, anger and division of their plight, their conscious effort to conquer death and hatred with the spirit of life and love, enobles them.

Their faith in the goodness of human nature and the love and support of their family and friends have nurtured them. Today, Steven's tragic heroism engenders inspiration for others more fortunate and imitation in those equally challenged.

I met both the McDonald and Norris families at Bellevue the day after the shooting. Patti Ann, of course, was tremendously shaken, physically shaken. She was quietly moaning. I talked with her a bit and saw that Steven was in an extraordinarily precarious condition, on the verge of death at any moment. Yet he quickly gave the impression that he had no intention of dying, that—against all odds—he would live.

From that point, I became close to them. I offered to say a Mass in my own private chapel in our residence the next morning and both families came. For several months, I went to the hospital virtually every day—frequently late at night—and I never recall Patti Ann not being there. Together we said a Rosary and a few simple prayers. From time to time, I'd have Mass in their room—Monsignor John Kowsky, the police chaplain, would say it every night without fail. Steven was unable to speak.

At times, Patti Ann would come to see me alone, to talk about the intensity of it all. Months later, Steven was moved from Bellevue to Colorado for rehabilitation. After the first few days, I told Steven I felt everything would change once he would be able to speak again. It was clearly agonizing for him not only to be totally helpless physically, from the neck down unable to move a single muscle, but also to be unable to express himself. The anguish, the frustration of not being able to tell his wife he loved her, of not being able to do more than move his lips as we would pray together. He never lost his radiant smile, but there was always great pain in his eyes, coupled with ferocious determination.

During this period, I began getting letters from throughout the world, as far away as Australia, simply because people had seen my picture in the newspaper or on television. Convey our prayers to Steven and Patti Ann, they asked me, and they added—a great number of them—that this couple's acceptance of their suffering and the obvious clarity of their faith had given others courage. Steven and Patti Ann, at the same time, were getting many more letters, an avalanche of mail.

Patti Ann would call me frequently from Colorado and I'd call them, and—to the degree it was possible—talk with Steven over the phone. He began to recover some speaking ability, and some power over his diaphragm. This did, indeed, make a radical, dramatic difference. Now he could communicate, with difficulty, but clearly and articulately.

Patti Ann would return to New York periodically, and I'd see her then to discuss the situation from both a spiritual and a psychological perspective. Meanwhile, Conor had been born—to me it was remarkable Steven had been able to sit in a wheelchair for the baptism—and the baby became a focus of attention, and a tremendous gift to them. Steven's awareness he's transmitted new life—and that whatever his future might be, he'd live in their son—was enormously important. It was true for Patti Ann, too: whatever the future her husband had given her a son. There would be memories of what had been, and hope for the future.

Conor's baptism may have been a focal point for the city at large, but—to me—it was one of a continuing pattern of emotional intensity, faith and love that the McDonalds expressed. I went to Mercy Hospital as soon as the baby was born and saw the radiance of Patti Ann then. She offered to let me hold the baby and I refused.

"The man who should first hold this child," I said, "should be Steven."

That was difficult. And, equally difficult, was being

with Steven and Patti Ann when she began bringing Conor to Bellevue. Steven was still in bed and the baby was placed on him; he couldn't lift his arms. He wasn't sitting in a wheelchair. If the world had seen that moment—Patti Ann putting the baby on top of Steven—that would have been recalled as their most dramatic moment.

I'm not diminishing the drama of the baptism, when Patti Ann gave that extremely faith-filled reading. The public could see that; they didn't see the other occurrences. Did I anticipate the media would react so strongly? I couldn't do otherwise. Throughout the Mass, the emotion was building up; everyone who'd had a share in this couple's struggle—the mayor, the police—they were all there. When I was giving my little homily, I felt deeply stirred. And the climax, with Patti Ann overcome with emotion as she finished the statement, touched everyone. The reporters were clearly moved; no one said anything, but I don't think they would have trusted themselves to ask any questions. For quite a time, no one felt the need to break that silence.

I was there at the press conference after the baptism because Patti Ann had asked me to be. Usually, when they were being interviewed or the media was taking shots of them, I'd try to move off to the side. This was their moment, I thought. And on that occasion, I told her she'd be fine. "You don't need me," I said.

"No," she told me, "I won't do it unless you stand beside me."

Which was why I was there to embrace her when, grief-stricken, she finished describing Steven's forgiveness of his assailant. Understand that, although this couple is special, grief is part of my life. I'm involved in it all the time, and see this same reaction in so many instances.

For the nearly three years since Steven was shot,

I've tried to be there when they needed me. After Steven and Patti Ann moved into their house in Malverne, I went to visit and stayed for dinner. After the meal, we talked for a long time about their relationship. Steven says he remembers this as an extraordinary moment, but it wasn't. When requested to witness a marriage by a couple, I still give my own premarriage instructions. I spend twelve to eighteen hours with each couple I marry, over twelve sessions, talking about communication in marriage, the problems of adjusting to a new life together. So I just took for granted that Steven and Patti Ann would have these problems. There was no question in my mind about that.

Given the circumstances of Steven and Patti Ann's life—with the whole world caring for them—they would have had difficulty resuming their life together even if Steven's injuries hadn't been severe. The attendant publicity, and not simply the bullet in the spine, had profoundly affected them. These were simple, honest people. He was a good, straight-forward, humanitarian policeman, always doing things with and for kids; she was a very simple, pretty, working wife who'd just become pregnant. They expected to live out their lives in relative seclusion.

And, then, *boom!* They're facing the eyes and ears of the world. Not once. Every day. There was a complete loss of privacy. Patti Ann couldn't go into the subway without people saying, "There she is!" There were days when she'd avoid going out at all, a direct correlation, it seemed, to the amount of publicity that surrounded her daily life. Famous people were coming to see them: actors and actresses, football and baseball players, a call from the President of the United States to name but a few. And this wasn't a complicated, sophisticated couple, from an environment where learning to handle such attention is part of growing up. People have been fooled because Patti Ann's a natural in life and on television, photogenic with natural poise. They turn a television camera on her, and she speaks freely, without pretense. She began to be seen as an accomplished public figure. Colleges and schools would give her, and in absentia Steven, honorary degrees and awards. This doesn't happen in real life to most young, married couples.

At the Mount Saint Vincent College commencement in 1987, where she received the Elizabeth Seton Medal, Patti Ann told me she wouldn't give her acceptance speech unless I was there. I was trying to wean her away from that need, and for the very reason she talked about that June day—that she had to resist letting herself be a victim, that she had to resume some kind of normalcy. I deliberately got to the college late, intending to sit in the back of the auditorium, thinking that sooner or later she'd spot me and that that would be sufficient. I knew she'd be nervous before she began—she always was—but she'd inevitably live up to everyone's expectations for her.

Quietly, I settled into my seat. Unfortunately, the college president spotted me and called me up on stage, so my arrival had precisely the opposite effect I'd intended. I lost the opportunity to be an unnoticed interested observer.

When Steven returned from Colorado and could get around in a wheelchair, I went to fewer and fewer affairs honoring them. Only when they personally and strongly asked, would I go. They were supporting each other in their love and courage.

Clearly Steven and Patti Ann are still a very young married couple. There's no question they were deeply in love when they married, and they're deeply in love now. When we spoke together on "Face to Face with Cardinal O'Connor" on WCBS-TV, N.Y., the week before Christmas 1988, Patti Ann was subdued, uncharacteristically quiet and reflective. Towards the interview's end, I asked her what was on her mind after her two-and-a-half year trial. "I love my husband more now," she told me, "than I did when we got married."

Confront your mutual desires, I've advised them, those desires which are difficult, if not impossible, to satisfy. One is young and vigorous, the other incapacitated. Will that always be the case? I don't think so.

The tenacity of their determination will one day allow normal marriage relations. They haven't given up on that thought for a moment. There are periods of discouragement, I'm happy to say, because otherwise they'd be automatons, or plastic people. One point I've made to them—one I make to anyone in particularly tragic circumstances—is that the normal problems of life continue. When you have an underlying, enormously tough situation—as Steven and Patti Ann do—there's a tendency to attribute all the ups and downs to it. They had to realize that, I've told them, and they had to understand the reverse. Steven's situation *is* always there, and they can't kid themselves about it; it *will* penetrate and permeate every facet of their daily lives.

"You'll find days," I told her, "where you'll just be screaming internally. And you're going to be thinking, 'I can't scream at Steven. He's a helpless invalid.'

"You've got to scream at Steven," I advised Patti Ann.

"That's the normal outlet. And you have to be prepared for him to scream at you. You can't say to yourself, 'After all I've done for him. I wait on him hand and foot. I take care of him constantly. My whole life is focused around him, and he doesn't appreciate it. He screams at me as though I'm a servant or something.'

"He's got to be able to scream at you," I said. "You've got to be able to scream at him. There are other instances where you're going to have to try to work it out on a conscious level, and this is one of the reasons to talk, to communicate. So you don't *just* scream at each other."

This is crucial. And this is what Steven and Patti Ann McDonald have to face. For God knows how long.

I have also advised the McDonalds about how to deal with the inevitably waning celebrity. How do they cope with the knowledge that, five years down the road, another police officer will be injured and capture the public's attention as they have?

I've tried to prepare them for that in little ways.

They frequently come to my 10:15 A.M. Sunday Mass at St. Patrick's Cathedral, and in 1988, they came to my Midnight Mass at Christmas. Steven had longed to come to that Mass since he'd been shot. There were all sorts of designs and plans for him in 1986, when he was still at Bellevue, but it was impossible; his health was too unstable. In 1987, he'd returned from Colorado in November and was able to attend. I'd made a very big thing of that Christmas Eve, with a television camera focused on them, and they were seen by a national audience. In 1988, I'd simply mentioned in passing that they were in the cathedral. And now, when they come to the 10:15 A.M. Mass, I rarely mention their presence.

Coping with less notoriety is something I discussed with Steven and Patti Ann early on, and continue to do so. The day will come, I've said, when another policeman, another tragedy with a great emotional drama about it will occur, and that will take front page.

Steven and Patti are prepared for that, I think.

Some say their faith makes them special. But I've seen that faith before, in other police families, and I've seen it since: for instance, in the families of the victims of the Lockerbie, Scotland air disaster. A peculiar set of circumstances put Steven and Patti Ann on the front page and kept them there. The mayor went running to Bellevue Hospital, the media poured in because the mayor was there, and then they saw Patti Ann. She was an instant star. And then they saw Steven. He was a profile of courage.

It made for, and it makes for, a magnificent love story.

The Steven McDonald Story

Prologue

For a Wednesday night in the Bronx, the streets were damn quiet. The cop walked quickly, his heavy leather soles brushing the pavement. *Swip, swip.* The sound held in the chill November air like feather brushes on a snare.

Ahead, on the opposite side of Beach Avenue, light splashed across the sidewalk from a doorway. Galvin's Beer Garden. In front, a sedan idled. The bright entrance held the cop's attention. I could go for a beer, he thought. He shook his head quickly. Almost seven more hours to go, he reminded himself, don't even think about it.

Shouts interrupted the cheery laughter and music. "Hey! . . . What's going on! . . . You can't . . ." From his place in the shadows, the cop saw two figures backing into the street. His hand went to his hip, fingers closing around his revolver. He ran towards the pair. Did they have guns? He couldn't tell.

"Stop!" he yelled. "Hands up! Quick!"

The taller man turned, surprised at the voice, so close, just six feet away. The cop saw a glint of metal in the tall one's hand, then an explosion. His right shoulder was torn by a .35-caliber slug.

The cop fell to the sidewalk, still holding his pistol. The short guy ran to the car, telling his buddy to get moving. But the tall one hesitated, moving towards the dazed, fallen cop. Two feet away, he aimed at the cop's head, and fired again. The bullet somehow missed, ricocheting off the concrete and flying into the street.

The tall one turned and ran, and the cop struggled to one knee. The shoulder was numb, his back ached, he had trouble breathing. The Galvin's crowd spilled onto the sidewalk, then ducked back into the bar as the cop emptied his revolver at the fleeing suspects.

Behind him, the cop could hear the siren of a radio car. The driver, Ray Garrick, braked next to him, and leapt out, asking what had happened. "Oh Christ, I'm shot, Ray," the cop sputtered. "Holdup men. There they go in that car."

Garrick hesitated, and again the Galvin's crowd gathered outside. The cop needed a doctor, Garrick knew that, but the bad guys were getting away and no other cop had responded. The wounded cop, spitting blood now, told him to start the chase.

"Can you walk?" Garrick asked.

"Damn straight," said the cop.

"Well, hop in, and we'll catch them," Garrick told him. This was the hoodlums' second robbery of the night, Garrick said. They had already cleaned out Leonard's Bar, on Kingsland.

In the passenger seat, the cop struggled to reload his

gun, while Garrick sped through the Bronx streets, gaining on the getaway car little by little. Garrick fumbled for his gun; the other cop pushed it back in its holster.

"You do the driving," the cop told Garrick. "I'll do the shooting."

The cop found, by steadying his right arm with his left hand, he could rest his shooting hand on the car door.

Garrick pulled behind the sedan, and the injured cop, leaning out the window, fired four times. The bad guys returned the fire. The siren screamed like a fiend and bullets skittered off the fenders, singing in the wind as they flew by the officers. The wounded cop aimed a fifth time, and the bullet tore into the sedan's right rear tire. With a squeal, the car swerved into a curb, and crashed.

The holdup men staggered from the wreck, hands in the air. More patrol cars arrived. The wounded cop collapsed.

That wounded cop was my grandfather. The year was 1936.

That incident was told and retold in my household as I grew up. My mother was six when her father, James J. Conway, won the Police Combat Cross that night. She's never forgotten the cops who came to get her, her sister, and her mother from their apartment, and escort them to the noisy, frightening chaos of Fordham Hospital, where doctors were probing for the bullet that had pierced Grandpa's lung.

She's never forgotten her father's bravado, trying to bluff his way through the pain, and the fear. "I was puffing on a cigarette when the doctor was cutting," he'd say. "Just as he managed to get it out, he warned me, 'Look out where you're throwing those ashes.'"

And she's never felt safe again. When her father left the house, when her husband went on patrol, when I put on the uniform, she'd wonder, Will I relive that night?

But, to me, Grandpa's story was always one of magnificent courage, selfless bravery. He was on the streets to serve and protect the people of the city. Whenever I heard the story it inspired me. I didn't pay any attention to the part about the pain.

If I had, I might never have become a cop.

But, as I sit here today, a machine pumping air into my lungs, arms and legs strapped to the chair, unable to breathe and walk, to touch and hold, I still know I made the right choice.

I was a good cop. Someday I'll return and be a better one. I believe that. I have to.

. One

New York, July 12, 1986

Do I ever imagine what life might be like if that day had never happened? If Steven had never gone to work? If he'd never been shot?

All the time.

We'd be happily married, I'm sure of that, and living in an apartment in Manhattan. We'd be working parents, I expect, trying to save enough money to buy the kind of house we have today.

Steven and I would be doing what most young couples do. We'd argue. We'd go to dinner. We'd walk around hand in hand. On the weekend, or whenever the urge hit us, we'd go out. We'd hug. We'd make love.

Our lives would be normal. Uncomplicated. We wouldn't worry about wheelchair accessibility. Or which nurse was coming with us. Or who our driver was scheduled to be. We wouldn't be wondering if our appearance somewhere was going to cause a scene, or if we were going to be surrounded by people who wanted to meet us, or shunned by people who didn't know us.

We would have had more children. At least one more. I wanted children, that sense of family, the simple life. Nothing too extravagant, nothing too big. Something like our mothers and fathers had.

Something like the average American dream.

But I don't know what average is any more, and I don't know what normal is any more. Priorities have changed; I've changed as a person. I'm trying hard to hold onto my optimism, but sometimes it's so hard.

In the end, though, I realize I love Steven very much. I'm twenty-seven. He's thirty-one. We have our whole lives in front of us. I can't see myself living that life without him.

In the end, I come back to reality.

Yardley, Pennsylvania, 4:45 P.M.

The weekend of July 12 had seemed like a good one to be out of town.

I was starting the third month of my pregnancy and feeling exhausted. Steven was scheduled to work a 4:00 P.M. to midnight shift on Saturday. He was going to a Friday night New York Mets baseball game with the other three guys in his anti-crime unit from the Central Park Precinct. I'd be asleep Friday and Saturday when he got home. And Sunday we'd all be going to Mom's.

When was I going to see him? Even though we'd only been married eight months, I was beginning to feel like the typical police wife, in bed when he was up, out of the house when he was home. Steven suggested that instead of staying by myself, I visit Julie.

My sister Julie—there are six Norris children, and Julie is the second oldest, four years ahead of me, the third—had moved from Long Island to Yardley, Pennsylvania, a suburb of Philadelphia, at the start of the year. Her husband, Kenny McGuire, an executive in a brokerage house, had found a new job there and since she'd left, I hadn't spent much time alone with her. The trip wasn't a bad one, just a little over two hours, and I'd get a ride back with them. Our youngest sister, Katie, was celebrating her birthday that weekend—my mother was having a party Sunday afternoon—so Julie, Kenny, their kids and I would return to New York that morning. That was the plan.

The weather in Pennsylvania was overcast, and Julie and I spent the early part of Saturday shopping. I found some Halloween decorations on sale, and bought them, although more than two years would pass before I'd get a chance to put them up. There've been lots of small ironies like that.

By the time I got back to Julie's, I was exhausted. Kenny took the kids to church. Julie changed, and went to work at a nearby restaurant where she was waitressing. I climbed up the stairs to the bedroom. Moments later, I was sound asleep. No dreams, just dead to the world.

At 4:30 P.M., the phone began ringing.

I didn't even hear it.

Minutes later, Julie, Kenny and the kids all returned. For a moment, the house was noisy, and I was half-awake, but confused. Why were they home now? They'd said they wouldn't be home for another hour. What happened? Then Julie *shushed* the children and had Kenny send them out again. I came downstairs as the front door was closing.

Julie asked me to come into the family room. She had a strange, worried look on her face. What could be so bad?

"Patti Ann, I have something to tell you," my sister said. "Sit down. Something's wrong."

My father, I flashed, *he's had a heart attack!*

"Steven's been shot," Julie said quietly. "Mom called. She said he's alive, and that the police are going to come here to take you back to New York."

Steven? I thought. *That's impossible! He hasn't even begun his shift yet, has he?*

"No," I said to Julie, shaking my head, "no, they have it all wrong."

"A teenager shot him," Julie continued.

"A teenager?" I said incredulously. "Where did he get the gun?"

You see, teens with guns weren't a part of my life. My suburban upbringing didn't have room for that stuff. I'd grown up in white, middle-class Malverne, on Long Island. I'd gone to Catholic schools. Our big teen crisis had occurred when a couple of girls smoked marijuana in a bus bathroom on a class trip to Washington, and the rest of us hadn't told the nuns right away what was going on, or tried to stop them in the first place. I wasn't aware of what was going on in Steven's work. Kids shooting cops didn't happen, kids carrying guns didn't happen, and I was happy in my ignorance. Steven shot? This just couldn't be.

The phone began ringing again. First, the New York City police called. Oh God, it must be true, I thought. Then my mother. The doorbell rang. The Pennsylvania state police were there. Was I ready to go?

Hardly.

Outside was a cruiser. Later we'd pick up escorts—two more cars, plus motorcycles. For now, though, we were alone. Julie and I got into the back seat. I still hadn't spoken to anyone other than her. Ken fielded most of the calls, and all I knew—all any of us knew—was that Steven was shot in the arm, and that he was "stable."

Stable? What does that mean? He's okay, right? Stable meant, to me, he's okay.

With lights flashing, the patrol car pulled away. There's nothing to worry about, I told myself. Relax. Everything will be fine.

Please, God, I prayed.

Malverne, New York, noon

A few more years on the force, I probably would have called in, asking for the day off.

I felt lousy that morning, and when I called Patti Ann in Pennsylvania to tell her, she said, "Steven, just don't go in."

"Nah," I said, grumpily. "I'm going in. I'm going in."

The anti-crime unit—Sergeant Peter King, who was our boss, Bob Lally, Tom Culhane and myself—had gone to Shea the night before to see the Mets. One of the guys got ahold of some friend's season tickets, and we'd done a day shift, then driven out to Flushing. Maybe it was the beers we drank, maybe because the Mets lost . . . I just know I felt like staying in bed. But I had an attitude about the job, that I'd make my mark by being on time, and not take sick days. I'd heard enough stories, and knew enough people, who called in sick every time they didn't feel well, and sometimes when they did feel well. What was going to be the difference between myself and those guys was showing up for work on time. I'd been on the job four days short of two years, and taken one day off. And that had been to cook dinner for Patti Ann who'd been having a bad time at the magazine where she worked. Being in anti-crime after less than two years meant my career was moving along pretty good, and I didn't want to do anything to slow it down. July 12 was a day to work, not to rest.

At least I didn't have to clean our apartment up. When Patti Ann was home, I tried to keep everything neat: no dirty dishes in the sink, the bed made. I can do all that when I finish my shift, I thought. Patti Ann won't be getting back until tomorrow.

The drizzly rain that'd been predicted had already started to fall, and I decided to drive the Firenza into the city. Usually I'd take the train, then grab a subway ride from Penn Station uptown. Police officers are permitted to ride the subways free off-duty. Not that the city's losing anything in that deal. On a train, we are expected to take police action even as passengers. I always expected that that'd be where I got shot, even killed, by one of the skells, the lowlife riding those cars.

I didn't think it'd happen in Central Park.

Halfway to the city, as I was passing Shea Stadium on the Grand Central Parkway, Belinda Carlisle's "Mad About You" came on the radio. I loved that song. "Mad about you," I began singing, "lost in your eyes . . ." A month or two earlier, I'd been watching

"American Bandstand" on a Saturday afternoon when Patti Ann was out, and had seen Belinda Carlisle perform. I was getting ready to leave for a 4:00 P.M. to midnight shift, but I'd quickly written the lyrics on a sheet of paper and left the paper on the kitchen table so Patti Ann couldn't miss it when she got home. I was mad about Patti Ann, and the song expressed that as well as anything I'd heard.

"Mad about you," I sang again, "lost in your eyes."

When I pulled into the Central Park Precinct lot, I was still humming the song. There was a parking space right next to the station house. This is going to be a good day after all, I thought. I met Sergeant King inside the ancient brick-and-stone barn that serves as the precinct headquarters. Both Culhane and Lally took the day off, which Sergeant King and I had expected. They had weddings, or anniversaries, to go to, and the sergeant and I knew we would be working by ourselves. In our anti-crime unit, there were no formal partnerships. Over the three months I'd been a part of the anti-crime unit, I'd worked with each, most regularly with Culhane. But the sergeant and I felt comfortable with each other.

At 4:00 P.M., we took our coffee, memo book, a copy of the afternoon *Post,* started up the green unmarked Plymouth Grand Fury, and began our patrol. I was driving, the sergeant recording. Any call that came over the radio for us, it was his job to write it down. There wasn't much. We headed for the bandshell where 72nd Street crosses through the park, then turned onto a paved footpath that wound its way up a small hill, passing the site of Mayor "Gentleman" Jimmy Walker's old casino. We tried to stay off the main roads as much as possible on patrol, because, frankly, that was where the action was. But not this afternoon. Even the drug dealers hanging out next to the Sheep Meadow, a stretch of lawn seven city blocks long and three blocks wide, seemed to be staying indoors.

Sergeant King and I talked a bit about the game, the day's news, Patti Ann being out of town, and how quiet Central Park appeared to be that evening. Its 843 acres would be closed to car traffic, as the park was every weekend between May and October, and the overcast, soggy skies were going to cut down on the number of joggers, bikers and hikers. With luck, the bike thieves and purse snatchers—our two biggest problems—weren't going to have much to prey upon, and maybe they'd decide to stay away too.

"Sarge, let's go uptown," I suggested.

"Fine with me, Stevie," said Sergeant King. The other guys called me Mac, or Mic-Dee, but the sergeant, he always called me Stevie.

I turned off the footpath onto Central Park's East Drive.

Central Park, New York City, 4:15 P.M.

In anti-crime, you wear your own clothes—"out of the bag," we'd call it—and each cop tended to dress for a role. Mine was the upwardly mobile yuppie, the West Sider who used the park for recreation and relaxation, especially on weekends and summer evenings. Reeboks or Topsiders, chinos or Levis, and a Polo or Izod shirt, the kinds with crests and alligators on the chest, that's what I'd put on, with the shirt untucked to hide my handcuffs and .38-caliber snubnosed Special. My shield—badge number 15231, which had been my father's number before he was promoted to sergeant—would hang on a chain, around my neck. If I was making a collar, I'd pull it out to identify myself.

Which is not too likely to happen today, I thought, looking around.

The East Drive was as empty as the footpath had been. I cruised slowly, no more than seven miles per hour, past the lake, and the Loeb Boat House. The few parkgoers we saw—an occasional jogger or bike rider—would give us a glare. I had to laugh. Even in uniform, when I was riding in a marked patrol car or one of the small three-wheeled scooters the precinct had, I'd get that look. The park's closed to vehicles, it would say, even *yours.*

The glarers would never think that you were there to protect them. Then, when they were robbed, they'd demand to know where you were.

The Metropolitan Museum of Art with its modern glass wing was on our right. Across the drive, in a small grove of trees, a young girl named Jennifer Levin would be killed the next month by Robert Chambers, a guy she'd met at the East Side bar, Dorrian's Red Hand, she hung out at. The case would be big news in the city, partly because it had happened here in the park, and partly because both the girl and the killer came from private-school, white, middle- to upper-middle class backgrounds. But because it would happen in the park, I'd think later, it became more celebrated than it would have in just about any other location, like my own accident.

At 88th Street, we reached the reservoir. When I

was riding a scooter, I liked to look for celebrities who'd use its perimeter as a jogging track. But there were no celebrity runners this afternoon. As we passed the 102nd Street fork, where the drive curves steeply downhill, towards the Lasker Swimming Pool and the Conservatory Garden, both Sergeant King and I quickly came alert.

On our left, standing at the inside edge of the roadway, were three boys. They looked like young teenagers. They were black. They fit the profile, I thought, the one I'd picked up from the crime reports back at the station house, the one that strongly suggested these were bike thieves.

"DTs," one of the three mouthed to the others. Street slang, for detectives. Our plainclothes and car hadn't fooled them, any more than their affected nonchalance fooled us. You boys might as well wear bandanas over your noses and mouths, I thought. You outlaws aren't going to find any stagecoaches today.

"Go down to the bottom of the hill," Sergeant King said quietly. I pressed the accelerator.

I tried to remember what I knew about the bicycle thefts.

For three months, since I'd joined the unit, I'd been reading and filing the "61s," the criminal complaint reports for the precinct. Anti-crime relied on these reviews, which gave us the information that suggested the crime patterns that we tried to anticipate. The 61s told us what the crime was, what the perps looked like, where and when the crime took place, and whether there'd been a weapon involved.

Since April, we'd seen an increase in bike thefts, and the thieves, typically, had been small groups of black or Hispanic boys, around five-and-a-half feet tall, who'd surround a single rider—often midway up a steep incline and usually on a blind curve—force him or her off the bike, and ride it out of the park at the nearest exit.

Usually, the kids didn't need to use a weapon. If they fit the profile from the 61s, they could easily intimidate just about anyone riding an expensive bicycle in the park to give that bike up.

Two months earlier, in May, that pattern had broken.

Then, the anti-crime unit, all of us, were on East Drive, around 65th Street, the southern end of the park. We'd spotted a group of a half-dozen kids, walking along a path by the road.

"Should we keep an eye on them?" I'd asked Sergeant King.

"Yeah," he'd agreed.

We'd given them some room, and had begun to follow as they'd made their way across the park to the West Side. At Strawberry Fields, the hilly garden dedicated to John Lennon, the boys had stopped. Strawberry Fields borders the park's West Drive, near the 72nd Street entrance. Getting out of the park from there was simple.

A bike—two kids were on it, making it hard to build any speed—had approached the bunch, and they surrounded it. One of the kids had pulled a black handgun.

A gun? I'd never seen one used in a crime before. And by little kids? I couldn't believe it.

Get off the bike, they told the two.

Sergeant King had ordered Mark Carlson to take the Grand Fury, and come back down the drive from

West 77th Street, to cut off that escape route. Now, seeing the gun, he'd realized he couldn't wait any longer.

"Police," the sergeant had screamed. "Don't move!"

Two of the kids had froze, and the sergeant and Culhane had grabbed them. Then Carlson and I had taken off, and had collared the rest. We had never recovered the gun, but had gotten a confession that there had been one.

One month ago, I'd seen what the possibilities were. Now, as I drove slowly down East Drive, I forgot.

The lesson hadn't taken.

Less than one hundred feet from the spot where the three boys were loitering was a short driveway leading to the staff parking lot for the Lasker Swimming Pool. The rain had kept the swimmers away and closed the pool, and there was plenty of space in the lot. I pulled in, and shut off the engine.

Sarge and I would split up, we decided. He'd return along the drive, and I'd follow a footpath leading from the pool. The path ran roughly parallel to the road, but twenty feet below it. It curved through the oak and maple underbrush.

I've got the long way back, I thought. I broke into a slow jog.

The path curved by the pool, and into the woods. As I came around a bend, I saw three figures peering up towards the roadway. The boys had moved. They were on the other side of the drive now, and below it, next to the path I was on. They were watching the road, their backs to me. They're waiting to see if we come back, I thought. I pulled out my shield so they could see it, and stepped into view.

"Fellas," I said, "I'm a police officer. I'd like to talk to you."

Then I yelled up towards the drive. "Sarge," I shouted, "I've got them down here." I couldn't see him, but Sergeant King was slightly shorter than me. If he was on the other side of the drive, looking for them, he'd miss us completely.

The three boys said nothing, just stared defiantly at me.

"What are you doing around here?" I asked. "Where do you live?"

Again, nothing.

All three, even the oldest, were at least a foot shorter than me. Intimidating to a bike rider, maybe. But I didn't feel threatened. Nor by the fact they were black. I'd had black friends all my life—in Queens growing up, in the Navy, in the department. Black skin didn't worry me. I wasn't their enemy.

I kept my .38 in its holster. Then I noticed a bulge under the pant cuff of one of the younger boys, next to his ankle. Suspicious, I thought. I bent to pat it.

Head down, my peripheral vision picked up the older boy turning, reaching, then turning again. I started to rise. Then . . .

Boom! Boom! Boom!

A cannon was exploding in my ear, smoke and gunpowder filling my nose. Remember the old TV series, "Victory At Sea"? With the scenes of battleships firing their broadsides? I was there, my head in the barrel of the gun.

Bullets cut into me. One went into my neck, shattering, its fragments in my spine. Another nicked my eye, smashing into my sinus. A third hit my arm, destroying an artery.

I could feel them inside. But . . . no pain.

Where was the pain?

I felt detached, my body numb with pins and needles, my mind outside, away, watching. Sergeant King had gotten to me, I could see that. He was crying, leaning over me, screaming into his portable radio, "Member of service shot! MOS shot!" The boys had run.

I was losing consciousness. Patti Ann appeared. I could see her, see what I was losing. "God, don't let me die," I prayed.

Then I fell off.

Yardley to New York City, 6:00 P.M.

As we got closer to the hospital, I knew something was up. These cops would not open their mouths. First I, then Julie, would ask them about Steven.

"I have no information to give you," they'd say. "I know nothing."

I felt like shaking one of them, screaming, "You've got to tell me!" Instead, I made them stop at every toll booth. I'd rush to the ladies' room. My nerves wouldn't let me keep anything inside.

We were headed to Bellevue Hospital, where Steven had already been transferred from Metropolitan. Not that I knew any of this. Nor did I know that Steven's parents, and brothers and sisters were already on their way by helicopter. Or that my parents were driving. Or that the New York television stations were broadcasting the story, with pictures of Steven being carried into the medical emergency rescue van, an emergency medical technician pumping an ambu-bag by hand, forcing air into Steven's lungs, keeping him alive.

I knew nothing.

My mother heard about the shooting from Steven's father, I learned later. She didn't even recognize his voice when she picked up the phone in her kitchen. She'd met him at our wedding and never seen him again. Actually, our families barely knew each other.

"Is Patti Ann there?" he'd asked. "This is David McDonald, Steven's father. He's been shot. But he's alive."

Mom was stunned. She couldn't think clearly enough to call me and she didn't know what to do next. She dialed my sister Deirdre, ten months younger than me and living nearby in Rockville Centre with her husband and their two children. When Deirdre answered, Mom told her about the call.

"He's on the TV!" Deirdre screamed in horror. "He's on the TV! Don't tell me that's Steven! They're taking a police officer who's just been shot! They're saying he's twenty-eight . . ."

No name had been released, Deirdre told Mom. She decided to call Steven's parents again. His sister Dolores answered, saying the rest of the family had left, in a helicopter.

"For where?" asked Mom.

"Bellevue," Dolores said.

My mother didn't want to call me until she had more information. So she called the Central Park

Precinct, explained who she was, and told them I still didn't have any idea of what was going on. "He's being transported," the lieutenant on the line told her. "He's alive. But we can't tell you what his condition is. Where's your daughter?"

Mom gave them Julie's number, but said she wanted to call first, to break the news to me. The lieutenant agreed, and Mom phoned Julie. That was the call I'd slept through. On her second try, she reached my sister at the restaurant.

"Where's Patti Ann?" asked Mom.

"Back at the house," said Julie. "Upstairs. Sleeping. Why?"

"Listen, Julie," said Mom. "I don't want to tell Patti Ann this on the phone, but Steven's been shot."

Julie, usually so calm and deliberate, began to scream.

"Julie, Julie, get yourself together," Mom said, "because you're going to have to tell her. It's better, face to face. We don't know how bad he is. They're going to send someone to pick her up. I don't know how they'll get her, but they'll call. I don't want Patti Ann to hear this on the phone, or on the television.

"Sit her down, and tell her."

Julie said she'd try. My mother hung up, she told me, and she and my father headed for Manhattan.

Our drive dragged on. At the New Jersey state line, and again at the New York border, we switched cars. Still, no one would say anything to us.

The last patrol car took us to the emergency room entrance at Bellevue. There, for the first time since Steven had become a cop, I got a sense of what this brotherhood of police officers was all about.

Outside the door, in the admitting area, down the halls, by the elevators stood hundreds of cops. They wanted to give support, to donate blood, to be of whatever help they could.

Everywhere I looked, there was a police officer. And I understood.

This was the Blue Wall I'd heard about so many times. And every cop was a brick in that wall.

Metropolitan Hospital to Bellevue Hospital, 6:00 P.M.

When a cop's shot, the entire system responds.

As I lay unconscious on the dirt next to the Central Park footpath, blood flowing from my neck, face and arm, officers from Central Park Precinct and all surrounding precincts were responding to Sergeant King's call. The problem was, they'd say later, that the sergeant was so distraught he couldn't tell anyone where we were.

Two uniformed officers, John McAllister and Dennis Robberstad, from the "two-three," the Twenty-third Precinct which borders the upper east side of the park, picked up the sergeant's cries on their radio as they cruised on patrol. McAllister, twenty-four at the time, and Robberstad, twenty-six, had gone through the Police Academy together and were best friends. They worked well as a team, although they were both only a year longer on the job than I, and that may have saved my life.

Turning into the park at 110th Street, they heard King describe the perps. "Three blacks by the pool," he shouted. McAllister thought he saw them, in the overgrown near-wilderness in the park's upper east side. He steered the car onto a narrow asphalt bike path, and crept through the woods.

"Through the trees," he'd say later, "we saw someone lying in a puddle. Carefully, we got out. No one else was around, and the guy didn't have a uniform. Then we saw the sergeant, and his shield. We began to run."

McAllister first noticed my neck. The blood was pumping out, he said, the worst wound he'd ever seen. Robberstad immediately applied pressure to it, and the two of them carried me up the hill, and laid me in their back seat.

"We found the cop," they radioed. Bellevue was eighty blocks south, too far to risk. Instead, they headed for Metropolitan Hospital, a few blocks away. As far as the public was concerned, Metropolitan had fallen on hard times, due to budget cuts. But cops in upper Manhattan had tremendous respect for its emergency room, and its skill with bullet wounds. Metropolitan was the best choice, under the circumstances. Robberstad sat in the back, pressing on my neck. King and McAllister were in the front. How's he doing? McAllister asked.

Not good, Robberstad said as they pulled up to the emergency room entrance. I can't find his pulse.

Metropolitan tried to stabilize me, putting me on an intravenous feed, and shoving an air tube down my throat. But the emergency room staff didn't expect to accomplish much. After they'd x-rayed me, and seen that the bullet had penetrated the spinal cord, one doctor told McAllister that it was hopeless.

"He's dying," the doctor said. "He's not going to make it."

At the Twenty-third Precinct house on 102nd Street, Patrolman Eddie Wagner heard Sergeant King's cries for help over the radio. He and his partner, Kenny Nietert, were about to start their 4:00 P.M. to midnight tour, and their radio car was parked outside. "The sergeant was screaming and hollering," Wagner told me later. "I couldn't get what he was saying. Then the central dispatcher came on. 'There's a cop down,' she said. 'A cop down.' "

Wagner and Nietert first thought King said he was at 110th Street and Fifth Avenue, bordering Central Park. As Wagner raced uptown, King came on again. This time Wagner thought he heard 102nd Street, or 105th. He braked into a U-turn, and—sirens screaming—headed downtown on Central Park West, against the traffic. Seconds later, King was on again. This time he could be understood.

"105th inside the park!"

At 106th Street, Wagner steered into the park. Instead of going directly to the crime scene—it would have been counterproductive since he knew other cops were already there—Wagner and Nietert pulled onto a path off the East Drive, and drove slowly along the border of the Harlem Mere, the lake dominating the park's northeast corner. Ahead, they saw a boy approaching. Wagner and Nietert stepped out of the car. The boy was looking over his shoulder, and walking quickly, almost anxiously. But what caught Wagner's eye was his appearance. The boy was soaking wet.

"As soon as he saw us," Wagner said later, "he hesitated, then came towards Kenny and me. 'I just got mugged,' he told us. 'Three kids did it. They stole my gold chain, and threw me in the lake.' The boy described the muggers as two blacks and an Hispanic, and said they carried a silver gun. He told us they ran towards the 106th Street and Fifth Avenue exit.

"That's dumb, I thought. Run out there? Where all the cops are?"

After the boy described his attackers, Wagner and Nietert put him in the back seat of the cruiser. Wagner was suspicious, and nervous. Neither he nor Nietert had frisked the boy. While Nietert radioed the robbery report into the two-three, Wagner carefully pulled his .38 from its holster, placing it on the seat next to him.

"What's your name?" Wagner asked.

"Shavod Jones," the dripping boy replied.

Detective Brian Mulheren had been having a decent Saturday for a change, he'd say later, when he heard the 1013 code: officer in distress.

"Please, I thought," he'd tell me, "not another one." Just two weeks earlier, Patrolman Scott Gaddell, who was only twenty-two, had been executed in a shootout in an alley in Queens. Gaddell and his partner had gone into the backyard of a house there, trying to execute a warrant on a guy wanted for possession of drugs. The guy came out firing, and they answered it. The guy had a 9 millimeter pistol, which holds more ammunition than our .38's. Scott was reloading, and the perp came up, put his gun next to Scott's head, and killed him.

What's this one? Mulheren would remember thinking. The twelfth cop shot already this year? And there are still five months to go? To Detective Mulheren, it seemed something terrible was happening every Saturday.

Among the street cops, Mulheren was kind of a legend. He was a tall, clean-shaven, almost severe-looking Irishman, and some used to say that, because of his intensity of purpose, in another, earlier century he would have been a monk. The detective was a close friend of both Edward I. Koch, the mayor of New York City, and John Cardinal O'Connor, the archbishop of the city's Catholic archdiocese. Mulheren was one of the officers responsible for coordinating and making sense out of every crisis the department ran into, whether it was working with the Fire Department at the scene of a blaze, or arranging for the funeral of a slain officer.

To cops like myself, it seemed that Brian knew every mover-and-shaker in the city. Not that he'd ever heard of me before that Saturday. Our friendship would come later.

Brian had just finished a hamburger at Melon's, a pretty chic place on the East Side, and was heading his black, unmarked Lincoln Town Car to, of all places, Bloomingdale's. "I don't know why," he recalled. "I never do. But that was where I was going." Instead, he switched on his flashing red light, and headed up Third Avenue.

"I got to the hospital pretty quickly," Brian remembered. "One of the perps was sitting in a radio car outside. In the emergency room, they were working on Steven. He was alive, but he wasn't conscious."

Brian's first job was to alert the city leaders. Mayor Koch was in the Hamptons for the weekend, and

Police Commissioner Benjamin Ward was out of town too. First Deputy Commissioner Richard Condon arrived, and began sorting out the details. And Brian contacted Deputy Mayor Stan Brezenoff, to represent the mayor.

A priest was needed, Mulheren knew. Monsignor John Kowsky, the police chaplain, another good friend of Brian's, and—perhaps most important—a veteran of two wars who'd delivered countless last rites on the battlefield, was the logical choice. But he'd gone fishing this summer weekend. Mulheren wracked his brains, then called Ken Fisher, the city fire dispatcher. Fisher said he'd send Father Julian Deacon, the fire chaplain.

Meanwhile, Brian was trying to find out my background, so my family could be notified. That information—address, phone number, next-of-kin—is listed on a ten-card, on file at the precinct house. I'd just gotten around to changing mine, putting our new address at the apartment in Malverne, and Patti Ann as the person to notify in an emergency. With her out of town, Brian was getting nowhere.

"When I realized where she was," Brian remembered, "I knew we had to get the Pennsylvania and New Jersey police involved. And when I found out the size of the family, I began sending helicopters to both Suffolk and Nassau counties to get them."

By the time my parents, brothers and sisters, uncles and aunts, and in-laws were accounted for, Brian had dispatched a fleet of vehicles.

The news Brian was hearing, however, was no better than what McAllister and Robberstad had been told. A resident in neurosurgery took him aside. The damage to my spine, he told Brian, left me unable to move, and unable to breathe.

"The officer," the doctor stated flatly, "is not going to live."

Brian refused to concede defeat.

"Maybe he won't," Brian said, "but we're going to Bellevue, because that's where the spinal cord center is. If we're going to give him any shot, we might as well give him a shot down there."

My father and younger brother Thomas were sitting at the kitchen table in the family home in Rockville Centre. Mom was upstairs, cleaning the bathroom. The radio was on, and the program was interrupted by a news bulletin. A plainclothes police officer has been shot near 110th Street and Fifth Avenue, the announcer read.

My father shuddered. Four nights earlier, I'd come for dinner, and we'd talked about the bike thefts. Where are they happening? he'd asked. The upper end of the park, I'd told him, especially around 110th and Fifth. A bunch of kids, I'd said.

"Don't forget," he'd warned that Tuesday night, "a ten-year-old can pull a trigger just like a twenty-year-old."

My father looked at Thomas. "That's Steven," he said. "No way," said Thomas. My father then called the Central Park Precinct.

David McDonald, my father, had been on the force for twenty-five years before retiring in 1976. He'd been shot at, he'd lost a partner, and he'd attended more funerals than he wanted to remember. He knew the routine. When the desk man wouldn't help, he asked for the nearest lieutenant. "That shot police officer," said my father, "that's my son, Steven. What's going on?"

"He's responding to treatment," was all the lieutenant would say. My father realized his intuition had been horribly accurate. "Where are you?" the lieutenant demanded. "We want to pick you up by helicopter."

With that, my father would say later, he knew it was the worst, the worst it could be. He told my mother, Anita, as gently as he could, knowing her darkest nightmare was about to be realized. First her father, now her son. She'd even married a cop, and never could be sure if he was coming home.

"I'd been looking over my shoulder for years," she'd say later. "I'd go to sleep at night, saying thanks to God for keeping us together another day."

Now she broke down, keening my name over and over.

"Steven," she wailed. "Steven. Steven. Steven."

The Nassau County cops arrived at my father's door. The helicopter was two blocks away, they said, in a field. Waiting.

The medical emergency rescue van responded to Brian's call, and pulled up in front of Metropolitan's emergency entrance. The press had begun to arrive, and the TV cameras caught the urgent rush to get me in. I was still out, kept alive by the hand-pumped air the technicians were supplying.

The van—which looked like a school bus with an operating room inside—headed slowly crosstown to the Franklin Delano Roosevelt Drive. There was no traffic. Brian had requested every street we'd be travelling on, including the drive itself, closed.

In the back of the van, attendants hovered over me. Slowly, I regained consciousness, half-consciousness really. There's a tube down my throat, I realized. Sirens were screaming, I could hear. People were moving around me, in what seemed like a frenzy. But they were unfocussed, blurry.

"You're going to be all right," said one shadow. "Rest easy."

I didn't think so. My body was numb, as if it had fallen asleep.

I'm all messed up, I thought.

I fell off again.

Bellevue Hospital, 9:00 P.M.

By the time Julie and I got to Bellevue, everybody in New York, it seemed, had a better idea what was going on than I did. A department spokeswoman, Alice McGillion, had told reporters about Steven's injuries, and that three boys, including a fifteen-year-old named Shavod Jones, had been arrested. Jones, McGillion told the press, had shot Steven with a .22, which he'd thrown into the Harlem Mere, a lake less than one hundred yards from the Lasker Swimming Pool. Then Jones had jumped into the lake himself and claimed he'd been mugged for a gold chain, she said.

Why had Steven confronted the boys? the reporters had asked.

"That's their job," McGillion had said. "They're anti-crime police, and they are supposed to intercept people who they think are going to be committing robberies. It's all instinct and obviously, since one of these people had a gun, they had good instincts."

Did the boys know Steven was a cop? the press had wondered.

"I don't think there was any question he identified himself as a police officer," McGillion had assured them. "It was absolutely proper procedure."

The police even told the press I was pregnant, something my mother and father still hadn't told our neighbors.

Julie and I knew none of this as we climbed out of the cruiser.

A group of officers led us through the emergency ward entrance. In the crowd outside the trauma room, I spotted my mother and father. I was startled. Their faces looked as if . . . as if someone had died.

"Why is everyone here?" I demanded to know. "What's going on? I want to know."

"Calm down," my mother tried to advise me.

"No," I said. "Where is Steven? I want to see him."

My family was evasive.

"Oh, he's somewhere else," they told me. "Sit down. We'll bring you up to date . . ."

"No," I cut them off angrily. "I want to see him now."

In fact, I'd learn later, his family had already seen him. His brother Thomas had been standing over the bed when Steven woke for the first time in Bellevue. "Steven, please don't die," Thomas had cried, and Steven had recognized him. With his right eye bandaged, a tube in his mouth, and his head immobile, the only part of his body he could move was his left eye. So Steven had winked.

I'm all right, he'd tried to say. Then he'd fallen asleep.

After a few minutes, the hospital relented, and I was allowed into the three-bed emergency ward, just off the trauma room. The area was tiny, and with the others pressing around me, felt claustrophobic. Then I saw Steven. I was shocked.

The man in the bed didn't look like my husband.

Whoa, I thought. *This is not happening. I'm going to wake up tomorrow morning, and this will all go away.*

Steven was swollen, blown up from the trauma. Now I know that's a typical trauma symptom, but I didn't then. He was a mess, swabbed in yellow Betadine. The respirator tube was in his mouth; they hadn't performed a tracheotomy yet. He couldn't communicate at all, but he was awake and saw me. He doesn't remember that today, but I knew he recognized me.

I still couldn't get a grip on what he'd experienced.

Tomorrow, I thought, *I'm going to come back and they're going to tell me this isn't as bad as it looks. Because there's just no way this is happening to us. We're having a baby in seven months. This is just not reality.*

I wasn't prepared for this reality—all of a sudden the life I'd led felt so sheltered, where the worst thing that might have happened to me was a dent in the car. Seeing my husband fighting for his life is not real. But it was.

I left his bedside. "There's nothing you can do," one

doctor told me. "You've got to go home and rest. Get some sleep. Come back in the morning."

A New York cop drove Julie and me to Malverne. Our apartment was just as Steven had left it that morning, and I walked through it slowly, looking at every little thing. What had he been doing before he left? What had he been thinking?

Dishes were piled in the sink. The bed was unmade, and he knew I hated unmade beds. He must have been in such a rush, I thought, and probably figured he'd clean that night. I wasn't coming home; he'd have had plenty of time.

I didn't want to touch a thing. Just to imagine what his morning had been like. I felt like crying. Not that I thought he wasn't coming back.

A few blocks away, my mother was calling my obstetrician from the house I grew up in. "Is Patti Ann in danger of losing the baby?" she'd asked.

"She's healthy," my doctor had assured her. "She's going to make it. If she's going to lose it, she's going to lose it. This is not going to bring on a miscarriage."

I didn't know what my mother knew. I wasn't that worried. A couple of weeks, I guessed. Steven's hurt, but in two weeks, he'll be home.

Finally, exhausted, Julie and I went to bed.

Tomorrow, I knew, things would be much better.

WITNESS:

Mayor Edward I. Koch

I was called by Brian Mulheren, who's assigned to first Deputy Commissioner Condon. Mulheren is on the scene of every accident or catastrophe—it can seem there are ten Brians in New York City—involving policemen or firemen, before anyone else. He makes the call to the police commissioner, and to me.

When Steven McDonald was shot, though, I was out of town and didn't get to Bellevue until later the next day, a Sunday as I remember. I came down from Gracie Mansion, my residence, and was immediately taken to the hospital where Steven's parents and in-laws, maybe twenty-five different relatives altogether, and a lot of them young, were waiting. They were obviously in shock, greatly distressed.

I'm always overwhelmed by the injuries and deaths of police officers. Not by death per se, mind you. I'm not afraid of death myself. I'm a fatalist. I take most deaths quite calmly, though sadly. With one exception. The deaths of my parents overwhelmed me, left me in tears at their unfairness. But otherwise, I take death quite calmly.

Not when it comes to police, though. Then and there, invariably I am brought to tears when I come into the room where they are injured, or dying, or dead. When I meet their families under those circumstances, I'm really overwhelmed with grief. We're faced with so many pathological personalities in the city. And every single day, cops confront an amazing variety of problems, problems that you'd have to be a priest, a lawyer, a social worker and a doctor all rolled into one to deal with. And, with great style, panache and a good sense of humor, they deal with every one.

So I really like cops, and they like me for a number of reasons. One, I made it clear that I know there are individual cops who are rogues, and who'll violate the law, but that I believe cops deserve a presumption that they've acted professionally. Cops have the authority to use force, deadly force, and when someone alleges brutality, that person has the burden of establishing that charge. Cops shouldn't have to be on the defensive. As Ben Ward once told me, "Charges of police brutality come when a cop tells you to do something, and you don't want to do it."

Cops are on the front line, and I stand up with them.

I've also shown my respect for cops by attending every single police funeral, unless I'm out of the country. Whenever I'm asked to speak—as I began to be a few years ago—I always do, and never use prepared remarks. In fact, whatever I say will have been created as I sit and listen to the family and the minister or the rabbi. I speak from the heart, and everybody knows it. Without trying to sound arrogant, this spontaneity probably makes for some of the best speeches heard in the church or the temple, because the speeches are not intended to be well-phrased and adroit. They're intended to say what is in my mind and my heart.

I was greeted by the McDonald family with extraordinary warmth, and filled in by my aides about the young cop upstairs. He was probably paralyzed, I was told, although the extent hadn't been confirmed. I was comforting the family, and being comforted. Then Monsignor John Kowsky, the police Catholic chaplain for Manhattan and the Bronx who usually attended crises like these until he died, said, "Why don't you come upstairs with me, Mayor?"

Steven's room was rather dark, but I could see his face was very discolored. One eye was injured, exactly how, I couldn't tell. We didn't say anything. He couldn't talk, I couldn't tell him his injuries weren't life-threatening, and his family had already been gathered. I went back downstairs, where Brian was waiting for me. "This is a very religious family," Brian whispered. "Very religious."

That was clear to me too, that the strength of their faith was carrying them through. I decided to call John J. O'Connor, the Cardinal. I'd never done that before—it had seemed ridiculous, given his job and the availability of other priests—but I'd never witnessed such faith either.

By chance, he was at the rectory, and came to the phone.

"Your Eminence," I said, "I'm at Bellevue hospital. This is an extraordinary case, and I wouldn't normally call you, but this family is so religious, and this boy is in such terrible condition, that I'm calling to suggest if you're free . . ."

Then I broke down, weeping. "Excuse me, your Eminence," I said, "while I take a moment . . ."

I got off the phone for a half minute. The Cardinal understood. "Take your time," he assured me when I picked up again. "I'll be right over."

Minutes later, he arrived. First he greeted the family, and they were so pleased to see him. Then he went upstairs. I didn't go with him.

I didn't want to intrude.

Two

Bellevue Hospital, July 16, 1986

By Sunday afternoon I'd been moved upstairs, to the intensive care unit on Bellevue's fifteenth floor. The doctors put me in a small cubicle, a tiny room with its own door, and a variety of machines and computers were monitoring my vital signs. The scene was chaotic, I guess, with my family, Patti Ann's family, the cops, the city officials, and everyone else who wanted to see me crowding in.

The chaos was lost on me, though. Ask me what someone said to me during those first few weeks, or when someone visited me, or how I reacted to a piece of news, and it's mostly a blur, with only brief moments of clarity. Even today, when I'm being put into bed, or I'm riding in the van, I'll close my eyes and see Bellevue: people hovering over me, talking, and I can't communicate. In my flashbacks, I don't understand what's wrong with my body. In them, I'm surrounded by people who, for the most part, I don't know. Nurses and doctors come and go. My throat aches from the tube forced down it. And I just want to close my eyes.

The doctors agreed I needed exploratory surgery on my neck to trace the bullet's path—a routine operation that looks for damage to the esophagus, the carotid artery, the vocal chords, and the oral pharynx—and a tracheostomy, in which a hole would be cut at the base of my throat, and a metal tube implanted to carry air from a mechanical respirator into my lungs. The tube the Bellevue doctors chose is called a cuff trache. It had a balloonlike device at its end, an inflated condom really, which prevents air from leaking back out the tube. The hospital, I understand, feared that my paralysis wouldn't let me retain enough air without it. That proved, later, to be untrue.

The cuff trache allowed the hospital to pull the air tube out of my mouth, which was positive. But there was a negative side effect, too. The air balloon was positioned so it pressed against my vocal chords, not permitting any air to pass over them. For the next several months, my helplessness was compounded.

Even with the tube out of my mouth, I couldn't speak above a whisper. To understand what I was saying, you either had to read my lips or put your ear next to my mouth.

Bellevue was a trauma hospital. From the cops' point of view, it was the best in the world. But it wasn't skilled in dealing with a chronic patient, which I would soon become. Everything was geared to stabilization, and immediate treatment. As long as there was the sense I was improving, the hospital could aggressively treat me. But once the improvement stopped, they seemed to have little idea what to do next. Or even why something should be done.

Less than twenty-four hours after the shooting, however, "improvement" seemed to be wishful thinking. The first deputy police commissioner, Richard Condon, had been told at Metropolitan by one surgeon, "If I had wanted to do the most damage to the human body, without affecting the mind, I'd go in with a scalpel right where that bullet lodged."

Condon said he expected that the doctor's diagnosis would be either too optimistic, or too pessimistic. In this case, he said later, it was right on the mark.

He had met my father and the rest of the family at Bellevue when I was brought in. When he learned my father was a retired police officer, he decided to talk to him first. As Condon remembered, "There was a young sergeant with me. I don't know his name. 'Look,' I told him. 'Find out exactly what Steven McDonald's condition is medically. The family may have questions, and I want to be able to answer them.' The sergeant got briefed and together we walked down the hall to the family room.

"'I guess you get used to doing this,' the sergeant said to me.

"'I don't know,' I said. 'I've never done it before.' Horrified, the sergeant exclaimed. 'Oh, no?'"

When he saw my family, Condon said, my father was blaming himself for everything that had happened.

"Look," the deputy commissioner said to him, "you're going to have to pull yourself together. You're going to have to handle this for the sake of the family."

Later that first night, my father remembered, he

stood next to my bed, waiting for my moments of consciousness and—when I came to—yelling at me, like a Knute Rockne or a Lou Holtz, "Don't go under! Don't go under!"

Malverne to Bellevue, July 16, 1986, 8:00 A.M.

At seven in the morning after Steven was shot, I went to mass with Julie and my mother in Malverne. I hadn't watched any television and read only the local paper, so I didn't have any sense that what happened to Steven was being reported. Although the New York papers were reporting the extent of his injuries, I hadn't seen those stories and I still expected he'd make a complete recovery. He'd looked bad at Bellevue Saturday night, yes, but no one had suggested to me he wouldn't be okay.

When we got back to the hospital on Sunday morning, the previous night's crowds had dispersed. I expected to go back to Steven's bedside right away, but a young doctor I didn't recognize took me aside and asked Julie and me to step into his tiny office.

He began by describing the few treatment options available to a patient in Steven's condition, a condition he seemed to believe I was familiar with. Casually, he used the word, "paralyzed."

"What are you talking about?" I asked, genuinely dumbfounded.

"Oh," he said, suddenly officious and distant, "didn't they tell you? Someone should have told you."

Quickly, coolly, formally he explained that one of

the bullets had crippled Steven, leaving him paralyzed from the neck down. The condition, he said, was in all probability permanent.

I couldn't breathe. He might as well have punched me in the stomach.

"No, no, you're wrong," I insisted. "There's got to be someone somewhere in this country or anywhere in the world who can correct this. You've got to find that person because Steven is not going to be paralyzed."

The doctor shook his head.

"I'm afraid," he said, "that we're the best."

"No," I said, my voice rising, "I want you to get the best."

The best doctors, he insisted, were the ones Steven had. I couldn't accept that. And I still couldn't catch my breath. The room seemed claustrophobic, a closet whose walls were going to crush me. "Julie," I gasped, "we have to leave. I have to get out of here."

There's got to be someone who can do more than this damn doctor, I thought. Someone more human, who wouldn't give news like I'd just heard in such an insensitive, uncaring way, as if this were just another everyday problem. Oh sorry, Mrs. McDonald, your tire's flat. Your roof's leaking. Your husband's paralyzed. This was the blackest nightmare a police officer's wife could have, worse perhaps even than death, and I'd heard it from a stranger, in passing. No tact, no consolation—just an institutional callousness, as if it had been taught to the doctor as part of his medical school training . . .

I was furious. And anguished.

And devastated.

* * *

I went upstairs to Steven's room, but I couldn't say anything. I stood there, my arms wrapped around my stomach where our baby was growing. I wanted Steven to hold me, to tell me everything would be all right. But he couldn't reach out to me. And he couldn't talk.

He looked at me and mouthed a sentence.

"I'm paralyzed," he tried to say.

I nodded my head to show I understood, but I couldn't speak either. All I could do was cry. My mother put her arms around me. She'd known Steven's legs were paralyzed, but not the rest. "Well, you never know," she told me. "Maybe it'll come back." I'd cling to that hope for a long time.

Soon his family began to arrive and I decided I had to leave, to go back to Long Island. I felt overwhelmed and needed to be by myself, away from the crowd, the press, and the attention. Another doctor gave me a mild muscle relaxer, and when I got back to the Malverne apartment, I managed to sleep for a couple of hours.

Early in the afternoon, the Nassau county police picked Julie and me up and drove us to the city limits, where we were transferred to a patrol car driven by a New York City highway patrol officer, Bob Dalia. Bob would become our regular driver, assigned by the department first to ferrying me back and forth in an unmarked NYPD sedan, then later to the van Steven now rides in.

The traffic was awful that Sunday, as it usually is heading into the city from Long Island at the end of a summer weekend. Over the police radio, we could hear one of the officers at Bellevue report, "The mayor and the cardinal are here . . ." The implication in the message was clear: get her here as quickly as possible.

I watched Dalia switch on the siren and lights.

The mayor and the police commissioner regularly go to hospitals when police officers are shot, I knew, but His Eminence John Cardinal O'Connor, the leader of the Catholic archdiocese of New York City, rarely—if ever—did. To me, it could mean only one thing.

Steven's dead, I thought. Why did I ever leave the hospital? What will I do now?

Bellevue, July 16, 1986, 5:00 P.M.

When Mayor Koch came to my bedside Sunday afternoon, the shooter was already under arrest, and the details of his background were being published in the dailies. Later, I'd piece together how it happened.

Eddie Wagner, the cop from the Twenty-third Precinct, brought Shavod Jones to the precinct detectives' unit. Two other boys, both fourteen, had also been picked up and delivered to the detectives. Wagner had become suspicious of Jones's story about being mugged for a gold chain, even more so when Jones began muttering nonsense in the back seat of the radio car as they drove.

Early Sunday morning, the detectives decided they'd heard enough from the other two boys to charge Jones. "Sitting with Jones that night," recalled Wagner, "I got the feeling he was unconcerned about what happened to Steven. At one point, he turned to me and said, 'I wish I'd run into you without your gun or shield.' "

The reporters working on the story found that Jones shouldn't have even been on the street. He'd been arrested and released on his own recognizance three months earlier, in April, after he'd pulled a knife on a couple of bike riders at 108th Street and Fifth Avenue in Harlem. A few weeks later, in May, he'd been indicted by a grand jury and pled guilty to the crime in state supreme court. A judge had deferred sentencing until July 3, and on that day—nine days before I was shot—she pushed it back again until July 18.

The July 3 sentencing, I learned, was postponed because a Legal Aid lawyer representing Jones had told the court that Jones was going to be reenrolled in the Cedar Knolls School, a residential treatment center for troubled youths in Hawthorne, New York, a Westchester County suburb less than an hour from Jones's grandmother's apartment in East Harlem, where he lived. That, however, wasn't true. Jones had been at Cedar Knolls in 1984 but had been expelled after he kept running away.

When Jones's grandmother, a social worker named Lenora Jones, tried to get him readmitted in June, the month before he shot me, the Jewish Board of Family and Children's Services, which runs the school, rejected him.

Jones, the press discovered, had a history of problems, both mental and legal. Jane Gross of the New York *Times* called him "a classic example of a severely troubled youngster who had slipped through the system, whose problems were recognized but remained unsolved and therefore spiralled." When he was ten, he'd been prosecuted for braining another kid with a mop handle, and had moved to Florida with his mother. A year-and-a-half later when he returned, the family court had dismissed the case, saying it had taken too long to prosecute. Then, in September 1985, he and a couple of buddies were arrested at 97th Street, next to the park, and charged with mugging a ninety-two-year-old woman and stealing her pocketbook. That case was dropped too, when the only witness who could identify Jones turned out to be a seven-year-old kid.

His mental problems had apparently driven his seventy-four-year-old grandmother to distraction. In 1983, he'd begun getting psychiatric treatment at Mount Sinai Hospital, where I'd worked before joining the department. In November 1985, the city's board of education, through one of its district committees of the handicapped, designated Jones as eligible for home instruction, meaning he didn't belong in a classroom. But no relative was available to "chaperone" the lessons, which was required.

Finally, at family court, Grandmother Jones had twice tried to get her grandson a PINS designation—"person in need of supervision." The first time came in November, but Lenora Jones neglected to bring Shavod with her, and the court asked her to return in a month. She hadn't. In May, she did come back and spoke to a probation officer who referred her to the Children's Aid Society. The society's solution had been to refer Jones back to Cedar Knolls, which had been futile.

On the morning of the day he shot me, the press reported, he'd told his buddies he had something new for their exploits—a handgun—which he'd said he was ready to use.

The press also reported that Jones's mother, Sharon Harris, had said how sorry she was about what had happened. "I've been praying for that policeman, his wife, their unborn baby," the *Post* quoted her. Her son, she said, had wanted to be a cop when he grew up. He'd also picked up a nickname. "He was a fat baby and had a big stomach and big fat cheeks. He was a cute baby. My sister said when he was three months old, he looked like a little Buddha doll."

Buddha, she said. The name just stuck.

When he read that, Eddie Wagner would say later, he had to laugh, comparing the mother's remorse with what he'd seen and heard Saturday night and Sunday. Baby Buddha, he'd say, was well known to the local cops. As a friend and boon companion to the dirtbag crack dealers on 112th Street and Eleventh Avenue.

Malverne to Bellevue, July 16, 1986, 5:00 P.M.

Bob Dalia got a radio message from Brian as he drove out of the Midtown Tunnel. Avoid the front door, Brian said, the press had gathered there. Go to the rear. Bob followed the order.

Inside, my parents, Julie and I were directed into a small room—a pharmacy, I guess, because there were jars of medicine around and prescriptions were being filled for patients—and were told to wait, that the mayor and the Cardinal both wanted to see me.

Steven was stable, I was told. There'd been no change.

Thank God, I thought. He's alive.

With the news, my spirits were lifted. Steven admired both, and had wanted to go to St. Patrick's Cathedral one Sunday, to the 10:15 A.M. Mass, celebrated by the Cardinal. We'd never made it.

The Cardinal came into the room, and I was struck by the kindness in his face. He was smaller than I'd expected, his hair slicked back and his glasses perched on his broad nose, and he carried himself with grace and assurance.

Someone introduced us. He touched my head gently, asking how long we'd been married.

"Eight months," I said, feeling anger at how little time we'd had.

"How many months are you pregnant?" the Cardinal wondered.

"Three," I said. We hadn't told any of our friends on Long Island, but Steven had apparently mentioned it to some of the officers in the Central Park Precinct. They, in turn, told the press.

"I will keep you in my prayers," the Cardinal assured me.

"It was important for Steven that you came," I said. "We'll survive this."

The Cardinal then took my mother aside. "I've been a priest for forty-five years," he told her, "and I've never met anyone like her." But if I'd known then what I know now about all the challenges before us, I wonder if I'd have found the strength.

His Eminence left and I went up to Steven's room. Any moment—and this feeling continued for the first few days—I expected the doctors to tell me they'd found a treatment for my husband and that he'd be out in a couple of weeks. I still wasn't looking at Steven as someone who would need a miracle to walk again.

"Wow!" I said. "Can you believe it? The Cardinal and the mayor were here! Isn't that something! They came to see *you!*"

Steven began mouthing words and I leaned closely to pick them up. "The Cardinal's saying Mass for me tomorrow," he said. Steven assumed it would be at St. Patrick's and wanted both our families to go. But during the summer, the Cardinal travels to the different parishes, and, in fact, the Mass was scheduled at an upstate church, not the soaring Gothic cathedral on Fifth Avenue in midtown Manhattan. I didn't know that, however. I came downstairs, and told the family and Brian, "Okay, everyone, we have to go to St. Patrick's at eight in the morning. The Cardinal's celebrating a Mass for Steven there and Steven wants us to go."

Brian knew I was wrong but was careful not to blurt that out and risk embarrassing me and hurting my feelings. Instead, he diplomatically suggested I let him make some calls to confirm everything. That was my first sense of the extent of Brian's connections. Before the evening was over, we got a call at home in Malverne, telling us that a private Mass would be said for us by the Cardinal in the chapel in his residence on Monday.

That Monday morning, the mayor, Brian, and Monsignor Kowsky joined our families at the residence on Madison Avenue, just a block from the Cathedral. The monsignor had been out of town for most of the weekend, but from that day on until six months later when he suffered a heart attack, he would say Mass in Steven's hospital room six nights a week. He became a valued friend.

The residence seemed as regal as Versailles. Not opulent, but quietly tasteful. The furnishings were all antique, and a portrait of the late Terence Cardinal Cooke dominated the living room, where we paused before going into the chapel. The housekeepers, whom I've gotten to know well, spoke in soft Irish brogues. After the rectory at Our Lady of Lourdes, the Cardinal's residence was astonishing.

Wow, I thought, so this is how they live. I didn't know whether I could touch anything. I didn't even feel comfortable sitting on one of the couches.

In the months ahead, when I'd return, I'd realize that the rest of the house was lower-key, and that the priests who lived there were unmaterialistic, no different than parish priests. The parts of the residence I'd seen that morning were where the politicians, the movers and the shakers, were greeted and entertained.

The chapel itself was smaller than I'd anticipated—eight short pews seating three, maybe four people in each one. The atmosphere was pleasant and comforting.

"We don't understand why this happened," Cardinal O'Connor said in his homily. "But we've got to keep believing in our faith. Otherwise, in any tragedy or illness, we succumb to a loss of that faith.

"God," the Cardinal said, looking at me, "is still with you."

The words remain with me, but then I felt trapped in a dream. Forty-eight hours earlier, I'd been having breakfast with my sister's family in Pennsylvania, talking about . . . who knew what? The baby, perhaps? Becoming a mother? Summer vacation plans? Now I was sitting in the Cardinal's private chapel and he was saying Mass for our families, as the mayor of New York City, leaning forward, chin resting on folded hands, nodded in solemn sympathy.

Can this really be happening? I asked myself.

At the end of the Mass, the Cardinal took me aside to tell me again how sorry he was and to offer his support and strength. He didn't have to do that, I thought. He didn't even have to say this Mass.

Steven's father met with the press later that day, as he would for the rest of the week. "It's a long road he has to walk . . ." he said that afternoon, then corrected himself, wincing, "travel." Fighting back tears, he talked about Shavod Jones.

"We have no room for anger," David McDonald said. "The first thought is my son, our son, Patti's husband. There's too much to be sorry for, and too much to be thankful for to be angry."

By Friday, July 18, I decided it was time for my voice to be heard. For a week, I hadn't spoken to any of the press. Steven's father had taken over—remember, Steven and I had been married only eight months—yet so much of the mail, the good wishes and condolences, had been directed to Steven and myself. I wanted people to know how appreciative we were of their support—and how much it meant to us as we began to realize the struggle ahead of us. That afternoon, I told Brian.

I was not expecting a press conference or anything like that. But we had a meeting scheduled with Dr. Joseph Ransohoff, Bellevue's chief of neurosurgery, that afternoon, and we'd never met with him before. Around the hospital he was known as "The Boss," and the other residents in neurosurgery, including Dr.

Michael Handler who was responsible for Steven, treated him with reverence. Ransohoff had a reputation for decisive action and he was going to tell us, for the first time officially, Steven's prognosis. By now, my hope was beginning to wane. Steven hadn't improved all week and none of the doctors had suggested there was much indication he would. But I still had faith that God would help Steven get better even if the doctors couldn't.

Steven's parents, Brian, and another officer, Sergeant Henry Frick, joined me in Dr. Ransohoff's office.

"I expected to tell you people that's it," the doctor said gruffly. "That there's nothing I can do, to forget it, there's no hope. But the tests we've performed show some sensation on the left side."

Dr. Ransohoff discussed the test results, which indicated what Craig Hospital in Denver would confirm nearly a year later, that Steven could feel, crudely, pressure on his left leg. And nowhere else below his neck.

"We're going to wait and see what happens," Dr. Ransohoff concluded. "Don't give up. There is some light. Steven has some sensation and, according to our x-rays, there shouldn't be anything. There is something happening."

This was something, we agreed, that the press could hear. They'd been hounding all of us and until now, none of us had had anything positive to say. Brian arranged for the reporters to meet us outside, near the entrance to the emergency room.

I'd never been to a press conference before, although I was, technically, a member of the media, an editorial assistant at *Parents* magazine, working with the director of photography. I was anxious. But the press was very nice. First, I read a written statement from the doctor, outlining Steven's diagnosis, then I just let them know how I felt. Steven's a fighter, I said, and he's going to make it.

"He told me, 'Patti, I'm alive and that's what matters,'" I told the reporters. "His spirit is remarkable. This diagnosis is the first ray of sunshine since last Saturday. I believe anything is possible. I believe in Steven."

I wanted to let everyone know that we were still hoping, that we hadn't given up.

"Do you still like New York?" one reporter asked.

"Steven loves the city," I said, "and loves being a police officer. We'd never think of leaving New York. We've lived here all our lives."

Bellevue, July 20, 1986

The day after Patti Ann spoke to the press, the doctors moved me from the intensive care ward on the fifteenth floor to the special neurosurgical ICU on the seventh floor. This was an open ward, maybe six or seven beds, with no private rooms, no doors, no walls.

For me, it meant no sleep. A couple of beds away, lay a lieutenant from the Fire Department. A day or two before I was moved, he'd been hit on the head with a two-by-four—it may have been an assault, I don't know—and it had scrambled him up pretty badly. All night long he'd scream or yell incoherently.

Even the drugs they were giving me wouldn't let me rest. The morphine, the Demerol, the painkillers . . .

They helped me avoid thinking about the way I was. And the way I had been. No more basketball. No more football. No more dancing until four in the morning. With the drugs, I'd escape. From the paralysis, from the people around me, from Patti Ann. It would be weeks before anyone could bring me back and focus me on the future.

Future? There was, I thought, no future.

Three

Rockville Centre, New York, 1957–75

Moving to Rockville Centre opened up new opportunities for me as a kid. There were organized sports, and after-school activities I'd never had. Thinking back, I'm left with good memories: scoring a winning run in a Little League championship game, making a pin in a wrestling match, hitting a running back so hard he fumbled. Football was the game I really loved, but the Southside coach and I just didn't get along. I felt that kids with less ability were playing ahead of me. But I thought I was just as good as they were, if not better. So senior year—instead of playing with my classmates—I joined the Long Island Tomahawks, a Senior Pop Warner League squad that played most of its games in New York City. For two years, I was a starting linebacker, a testimony, I guess, to my enthusiasm and willingness to hit anybody. Small-boned, I didn't carry a lot of weight, though at six-two I had good height.

The defensive coach of the Tomahawks, George Gregor, was impressed enough to invite a couple of college scouts to take a look. One, he said later, came from the Naval Academy. Navy! My dream was to play football for one of the service academies.

My grades just weren't there, though. I was never encouraged to apply.

That was a huge disappointment, but like many athletes, I had deeper fears than not getting into college. One of my darkest was that one day I would be paralyzed and not able to move. At night, in bed, I sometimes used to wonder about people who couldn't tell the difference between hot and cold.

That's my reality now.

I was born on March 1, 1957, the first son after my mother had borne two daughters. My father worked dawn through dusk at two jobs from my childhood until I got out of the four-year Navy hitch I enlisted for in 1975, so he could afford to raise eight children. And he wasn't alone, or unique. I knew plenty of men, friends of my father, who did the same. As a result, he sacrificed knowing his children. We never saw him.

To this day, I feel the effects of that. But it was the only way he could give his kids what he didn't have. My father's father had been a hassler for the New York City Sanitation Department, a driver whose horse, Tony, pulled the garbage wagons. The horse, my grandfather would say, had been named after Tom Mix's, the cowboy movie star of the early talkies. My father was a big strong man who wasn't afraid to take a swing at someone he was angry with, a common-enough attitude on the Queens and Brooklyn streets where he grew up. He joined the Merchant Marine during World War II, then became a paratrooper in occupied Japan. He'd made eighty jumps and become an instructor by the time he left the service and—like a lot of other guys of his era—became a cop.

My mom was left with the responsibility of bringing the family up practically by herself. There was no family support for her, either. Her mother lived in the Bronx, and her father died, much younger than he should have, from complications stemming from a bullet he'd taken in the lung during a shootout following a barroom robbery, as I described earlier.

My mother was the mother of a cop, the wife of a cop, and the daughter of a cop. True, there've been 175 years of New York policework in our family—my great-aunt had been one of the first New York City policewomen, starting the job in 1925—but my grandfather and I, I believe, were the only family members ever shot.

After he was shot, Grandfather had a good career as a detective: Mayor Fiorello LaGuardia personally congratulated him when his investigation broke up a robbery ring in the Bronx. He collared auto thieves, rapists, punks, and colorful types like a barge captain who was bartering with inmates on the Hart's Island reformatory for discarded aluminum and copper and a wacko who was painting all the yellow fire hydrants in the Bronx red. He also led an investigation searching for, according to the *Daily News* at the time, a "maniac" wanted for strangling an eight-year-old boy in the Bronx's old Starlight Park but as far as I know, he never made that collar.

I still remember his funeral. He'd been retired ten

years, but because he was a medal winner, he received an honor guard. Grandmother was crying, her friends were weeping, there were even tears in the officers' eyes.

And the American flag was draped over his casket.

My mother and father had their first child in 1953—they eventually had seven more—the year after they married and two years after my father joined the force.

A couple of times as a kid, I'd get to ride in Dad's radio car, basking in the aura of his uniform. In a child's eyes—at least this child's eyes—a cop was bigger than life, someone important. And when that cop was your father, it became even more special. Kids read about policemen and firemen in grade school; they're in so many of the books. And because my father was a sergeant, a boss of other cops, he received special treatment, treatment that was extended to me when I was with him.

Summers, until Dad bought a plot of land in Pennsylvania and put a house trailer on it, we'd vacation at the police camp upstate in Tannersville, a huge hotel the Patrolmen's Benevolent Association had bought. The place would be filled with cop families, and ours was one of the largest. It was quite a mix—from the lowest cops on the beat to lieutenants, captains, even chiefs. My parents would hang out with other Irish-Americans and their families, shooting the breeze about the job, and what it was like to be married to a cop. Those were good times, maybe the best Mom and Dad had together.

Dad loved the job—"It's the only job," he'd say—

but the department was changing. The fiscal crisis of 1975 had brought massive layoffs, and the military confederacy was being eliminated.

"It's the changing of the guard," he'd say.

At that time my father's second job was as director of security for Leonard's of Great Neck, a huge catering and banquet hall facility that specialized in bar mitzvahs, weddings and anniversaries. He worked there often, including Saturdays and Sundays. He'd come home, change into a tuxedo, and rush out the door to make sure his floormen were where they were supposed to be, and give directions to people who couldn't find the bathrooms. If there was a problem, my father and his men were to get it under control. In a less sophisticated environment, you'd call him a bouncer.

Even without the second job, our family would have been under strain. All families on the job shared this experience; the McDonalds weren't unique. The biggest problem was the shifts: 8:00 A.M. to 4:00 P.M., 4:00 P.M. to midnight, midnight to 8:00 A.M. You go around the clock, and it eats away at a marriage. In some precincts, you handle twenty, thirty jobs a night. They can be domestic disputes, a man with a gun, a fire in a building, an accident—people's lives can be hanging in the balance, and you've got to pick them up, all the while following the rules and regulations. Meanwhile, back home, the kids can be sick, and you're fighting with your wife over the hours.

Throughout my childhood, Mom was a regular churchgoer. Dad wasn't—he sometimes worked on weekends—though I can remember him going with her when I was young. Mom would speak about being Catholic in Ireland—her grandparents came from

Galway—and how you were exploited and discriminated against. And, she'd tell me, these acts continued when they got to America. Mom also participated in the block rosary, where once a week the women would come to a different house to pray. Occasionally, it'd be in our living room, and I can recall two neighbors who'd always say it in Italian. When we lived in Queens, we felt closely connected to the church and our parish priest, but when we moved to Rockville Centre, where the bishop lived, things were different. The St. Agnes congregation—and the church itself—are huge there, and people would come for a while, then disappear. I don't remember seeing the parish priest much.

Out of fear of everybody, both here on earth and above, I was at church every Sunday and to Confraternity of Christian Doctrine classes twice a week. Up until junior high school, that is. Then, I stopped going to CCD, and by high school, on Sundays, I'd go into the back of the church, grab a copy of the bulletin that noted who was saying the Mass, then head to the pizza parlor.

"Who said the Mass?" Mom would ask when I got home. "What was the gospel about?"

"Aw, ma, I don't know," I'd say. "Some guy in a robe."

I'd give her the old blah, blah, blah, and either she'd believe me, or she wouldn't.

Later, when I joined the Navy, religion became important again. I missed my mother dearly then, and got involved in the church in boot camp to try to fill the emptiness. I wasn't a lapsed Catholic in the truest sense, and I wasn't a C-and-E Catholic either, someone who only went to church on Christmas and

Easter. But I'd only show up at Mass when I felt like it, or when it was convenient.

Patti Ann always went to church. She was a fixture in her congregation. She showed me again the importance of church, and the Mass, and what it had to offer. Until I was shot, though, and I thought I was dying, I didn't fully accept this. Patti says that, in the hospital at some point, I talked about seeing a "white light," but I don't remember. Dennis Brennan, another injured cop and a member of the department's Self-Support Group (the fraternal organization representing disabled NYPD officers), told me when he'd been shot, and thought he was gone, all the things that people would do for his children flashed before his eyes: throwing a ball with his son, walking down the aisle for his daughter's wedding . . .

The same way I'd seen Patti Ann, I thought, as I lay in the mud in Central Park.

In the early fall of 1988, I spoke to a religious instruction class at a school near Malverne, trying to articulate these thoughts. "All these stories of the gospel," I said, "the saints, Jesus and Mary, all the players in God's grand plan for this earth . . . all the emotions, all the feelings when they were here, I chose to disregard. Like other people, I felt I'd go back when it was convenient. I should have done more of what I'm trying to do now."

Letters would come to Bellevue, and they come to our home in Malverne today, from people thanking me for what I've done for them. Tens, sometimes hundreds, sometimes thousands each month. Until now, I'd always thought giving help meant taking action. Physical action. But I can't do anything physically. For many months while I was in Bellevue, I couldn't even move my head from side to side, or forwards and backwards. Yet people seem to feel I can give them hope, even inspiration. All I can do, though, is tell my story. And keep fighting to live.

Malverne, 1962–84

Steven's grandparents were born in the United States, but mine—on my mother's side—were born in Ireland. My mother is a Boston Kennedy but not related to the president's family. Her father worked in a Boston public housing project and still lives in Mission Hill, a gritty neighborhood of working-class families. Like most Irish families in Boston, my mother's parents knew and worked for politicians. Her father campaigned for state reps and state senators with names like O'Connor, Kerry and Hennigan, and carried signs and handed out leaflets for a handsome young candidate for Congress named John Fitzgerald Kennedy. One of the girls Mom used to babysit, Maura Hennigan, is now a Boston city councillor.

My father John's parents were born here, after my great-grandparents emigrated from County Cork. My grandfather Norris was a New York City fireman, as were two uncles, one of whom rose to deputy chief, but his profession was unusual in our family. Most Norris and Kennedy family members were, for the most part, teachers and salesmen. My father's parents settled in Brooklyn and then moved to Springfield Gardens, a Queens neighborhood that is frequently considered part of Long Island. Both my mother and father went to parochial schools, and my father then attended Loyola College in Baltimore, studying English. "I wanted to do something in the verbal area," he once told me. "I would write for newspapers as a kid, and I remember the thrill of seeing my byline published over a high school sports story."

Mom and Dad met in Boston, where he was doing graduate work at Boston University. She was still in high school, "working for the telephone" as she puts it, on weekends and during the summer, and would sometimes go with her girlfriends to a roller-skating rink in Allston, a Boston neighborhood not far from the Boston University campus. My father, who was now studying English literature and radio and television broadcasting, had started to organize parties at the rink—probably the same way so-called "private" parties are run at dance clubs—to bring in new patrons. Anyway, Mom began to go to some of his parties, and they noticed each other.

I have no idea if it was love at first sight. But my father must have cut a dashing figure with his athletic physique, sonorous baritone voice—I think he thought a lot about a radio career for himself—and winning Irish good looks. My mother was quick-witted and sharp, with the same white-blond hair I've got, and a terrific vivaciousness.

By the time Mom had graduated, Dad had moved back to New York and was teaching at Lynbrook High School, where he's the chairman of the English department today. (He never did have that broadcasting career, but he was elected to the Malverne board of trustees, a village council that governs the community.) In February 1957, they were married.

For two years, my parents lived in an apartment in

Lynbrook. Then, in 1959, they moved to the large white colonial on the corner lot in Malverne. Our Wonder Years began.

I was the third oldest of six, with a brother, John, and a sister, Julie, ahead of me. John's five years older, Julie four, and Dierdre, Billy and Katie are one, two and five years younger respectively. While my father worked, moonlighting when he had to, my mother was always home. But there was never any real tension in the house; my father was mild-mannered, and you really had to get him going to get him angry.

All the kids were pretty close, sometimes too close, and we all liked living at home. There wasn't any competition between us—we were different enough to avoid that—and I used to look up to Julie a lot. She was pretty and popular, and even though she dated Kenny McGuire, now her husband, straight through high school, other guys would seek her out. She seemed to have everything together, and when she left home at the end of my freshman year in high school, I felt a major loss.

We were a Catholic household, and I went to parochial schools, first to the Our Lady of Lourdes parish in Malverne, then to Sacred Heart Academy in Hempstead. Julie, Katie and I were the most regular churchgoers, although for a while I got into sneaking out of Sunday services, grabbing a church bulletin on the way so I knew who'd said the Mass. My father instilled the importance of faith, and respect for the church in all of us. "While you're living in this house," he'd say, "you go to church."

At Sacred Heart, I was an average student, more interested in extracurricular activities than in classwork. I swam, played volleyball, hung out with friends. My sophomore year, I was elected class captain for Sports Night, the biggest schoolwide event of the year. I worked hard on that project. I'd leave home at 6:30 in the morning, and return at 8:00 at night, organizing teams, writing speeches, planning displays. None of my sisters had ever been picked for the honor and I jumped into it with everything I had.

Once I graduated from the academy, though, I began to feel adrift. Fashion merchandising, I'd decided, would be my field—I'd worked at Macy's department store during vacations and holidays, and had loved it—and the Fashion Institute of Technology in Manhattan seemed the logical choice for college. FIT was part of the state college system so it'd be fairly inexpensive, and it was tied closely to the city's garment district and fashion industry. FIT students could find work without much trouble.

My father wasn't as certain. The local community college also had a fashion merchandising program, he pointed out. "Why don't you go to Nassau," he said, "and see if you feel comfortable with the program. Then we'll look into FIT." I agreed.

Nassau Community College was a difficult time. I became an introvert, I gained weight, and began having anxiety attacks—though I didn't recognize them as such—thinking, "Am I going crazy? What's going on?" Even my friends from high school who'd gone to a college near home such as St. John's University seemed to avoid me, more concerned with their campus cliques than their former buddies. I felt abandoned.

That spring, I had my tonsils removed—not an easy

operation for an adult. I lost weight—not being able to swallow makes that pretty easy to accomplish—and accepted some invitations. Life was looking sweeter going into the summer when a girlfriend and I were in an auto accident. I broke my foot and was still in a cast and receiving therapy when the fall semester began. So I skipped it and worked full-time at Macy's. I'd been there long enough to choose my hours and I didn't plan on returning to Nassau. The semester there proved one thing to me: FIT, and the city's fashion industry, was where I wanted to be.

That summer, I learned how disruptive and devastating a catastrophic injury can be to a family. In July, on a winding country road in Pennsylvania, a motorcycle carrying two college students spun out of control and smashed into a tree. The driver died. And the passenger in the back, a twenty-year-old boy named Billy Mackel, appeared to be dead too. He wasn't, though. He was, however, in a coma from which few thought he'd emerge.

Billy grew up in Massapequa, a community a few miles from Malverne. His sister, Lynndel, went to Sacred Heart with me, and Billy's mother and my mother had both been presidents of the school's parents' association. We knew them pretty well and four months after Billy's accident, when his mother and father brought him back to New York from the Scranton hospital, I volunteered for the therapy team his parents were setting up.

While they were in Scranton, Billy's mother and father, and Lynndel, had been by his side twenty-four hours a day. But when summer was over, Mr. Mackel, a teacher in Rockville Centre, had to go back to work. Lynndel had taken a leave of absence from the temp agency she worked for, but she and her mother couldn't handle the therapy by themselves. Coma victims, I'd learn, needed a stimulation program lasting twelve hours a day, every day, to break out of their unconsciousness. The program—called "patterning"—included both range-of-motion exercises (moving the head, arms, legs, even toes) and stimulation of the senses, particularly sound and smell.

The Mackels first had Billy admitted to the South Nassau Communities Hospital, where they were taught how to do the patterning themselves and where the program was begun for Billy. Two weeks later he came home and for the next year we worked with him, giving him things to smell like lemons, cinnamon, even crushed cigarettes, then playing tapes with familiar sounds—dogs barking, doors slamming, phones ringing—sounds that would remind him of home, of life.

There were lots of volunteers—Billy was popular, a great, good-looking guy who'd just finished his freshman year at Villanova University—and I felt a special bond with him: we shared the same birthday, March 15, 1962. I had an hour a week with him, Wednesdays, from 4:00 P.M. to 5:00 P.M. Soon we realized the patterning was working. In late fall, Billy opened his eyes and for the first time in four months recognized his family and asked for something to eat. A bowl of Cheerios, I recall.

I encouraged Billy and his nurses to call me at home whenever he wanted to talk and I tried to explain to my mom about his condition. "Don't hang up on him," I warned her. "He's just learning to talk again on the phone. It will sound like a crank caller or a missed connection. It takes him a while to get, 'Hello,' out."

Occasionally, his nurse would call on Wednesday and say he didn't want visitors. But I'd go anyway. I had to be strong, even when he said no. Otherwise, he'd never get better.

I continued to see Billy through January, also stopping by on weekends with Deirdre, even spending New Year's Eve with him. Eventually, he moved into a rehabilitation institute in White Plains, just north of New York City, and after that back to Pennsylvania where his father moved the family after taking early retirement. After I'd met Steven, I introduced him to Billy and they became close too. Lynndel's wedding was a few months before ours and at the reception, Billy asked Steven—out of everyone present—to help him to the bathroom. "Why he chose me," Steven remembered, "instead of someone from his family, I'm not sure, but I remember thinking how difficult, what a burden to carry through life."

I can also remember Steven hanging up after a call from Billy, and turning to me, saying, "I don't know if I could be as strong and determined as Billy."

Of the four daughters she's had, my mother says, I'm the one who could handle a tragedy like my husband's injury the best. "God doesn't send you anything," she told me, "that he doesn't give you the strength to bear up under." Then she points to Billy's injury as evidence.

Well, maybe.

But I never thought I'd be in the same situation as Billy's family. I saw how their lives changed. I never thought mine could change as much. A newspaper columnist once suggested the same premise as my mother, that I'd served an "apprenticeship" in caring.

"I know it's helped me a lot," I told him. "They became such a part of my life and I just felt so good every time I left there, because I saw what an improvement Billy made. And it was all the combination of the person himself, his determination, and then the support and the love."

I knew Steven had the support and the love, I told the writer. That gave me hope.

My classes at the Fashion Institute began shortly after the New Year in 1983. After my broken foot, working with Billy, and selling at Macy's, I was ready to return to school. It was interesting in the evenings, when the classrooms would be filled with people like myself, who'd already started working. They'd share their experiences on Fashion Avenue, what it was like to be an entry-level go-fer for the top designer showrooms. They had a realistic attitude about what was out there.

That spring, I met Steven. I'd seen him in Rockville Centre, a good-looking, athletic guy who looked familiar. It turned out I knew one of his sisters, Clare, and she'd been telling me—for months—that I had to meet her brother. She was right. I knew, after I met him, he was the one.

Steven was working at a hospital in Philadelphia, managing the housekeeping department. He'd come home on weekends and hang out at a local pub my girlfriends and I would go to. It was a weekend night in April, and I saw Steven standing there, and decided to talk to him. Who knows what I said? But we exchanged addresses and phone numbers and started seeing each other every weekend he came home. Miniature golf, movies, the beach—a classic middle-class, suburban courtship.

Before the summer was over, every other guy I'd gone out with seemed an infatuation by comparison. I'd never pursued a man, or called if I hadn't heard from him, but during those first few months—if we'd argue, if he didn't phone—I'd pick up the telephone.

"Listen," I'd tell him in Philadelphia, "we've got to discuss this. What's the story?"

The Navy and Afterwards, 1975–79

I didn't expect to become a police officer. College was out of the question though, once I realized I had no chance for either a football scholarship or an appointment to a service academy; I wasn't interested and didn't feel I was going to get what I should from the experience.

At the same time, I couldn't see staying at home. My dad and I were knocking heads too much. Through high school, I'd developed a patriotic fervor. That, and thoughts of my grandfather's service in the Fighting 69th, and my father's as a paratrooper, ran through my mind. I'd play Kate Smith's version of "God Bless America" over and over. One of the few, one of the brave. That was me. So naturally, I decided to join the Marines.

My two brothers-in-law, Bobby Kelly and Timmy Gallagher, told me I was nuts. Bobby had served in the Navy's hospital corps, and Timmy as a member of the Army's military police. One evening, they got me alone in the corner of our living room, and said, "You're not going to do this. You don't want this."

"If you really want to be with the Marines," Timmy told me, "consider what Bobby did, because then you won't have to wear their uniforms, or get their haircuts, or run through their boot camp. It's no damn fun."

I listened to Bobby and Timmy carefully, and decided they were right. That summer, while the rest of the family was vacationing, I enlisted in the hospital corps. After I'd signed up—I said I'd start in December, this was 1975—I drove with some friends to the family trailer in Pennsylvania. When my father heard, his face dropped. He looked surprised, hurt by the fact I'd make a decision like that without first consulting him.

Right after Christmas, I left for Navy boot camp in Orlando, Florida. At eighteen, I'd never really been away from home and the family or in such a regimented environment. My dad had been tough, but, I realized now, not *that* tough. From Orlando, I moved to San Diego, California for hospital corps school; then in June, I was shipped to field medicine school in Camp Lejeune, North Carolina. There we trained with the Marines, and I had my first experience handling a gun—there hadn't been any at home, nor at Navy boot camp—as well as learning how to pack a backpack, and treat a wound. A month and a half later, I was ordered to Parris Island.

No one had told me I had to pay my own way. No one had told me, in fact, that I needed to save money at all. I didn't have a dollar, and I was scared. I had to be at Parris Island the next day, and had no idea what to do. Finally a buddy suggested the emergency relief office, where I was advanced the cost of a bus ticket. The bus pulled into Beaufort Naval Hospital in the middle of the night, and I was starved. No one had told me I wouldn't be able to find anything to eat.

At Parris Island, I was promoted to the petty officer in charge of the psychiatric ward. In the emergency room, where I had duties, I'd see young Marines—boys who'd bought into the Marine promise to "make a man out of you" as a cure-all for their personal problems, and who'd then realized the problems wouldn't go away—suffering from overdoses and other, more bizarre attempts to quit the service. Some would drink Wisk, the laundry detergent. Others would swallow bottles of antibiotics. "I'm trying to kill myself," they'd say, and we'd pump their stomach, or make them drink ipecac. Then we'd babysit them until a psychologist could fit them onto his schedule.

I enjoyed the corps, especially the medical side of the work—suturing, applying casts, diagnosing complaints. In November 1978, I was transferred to the Brooklyn Navy Yard, giving me the best of both worlds. I was close to family and friends, and working with experienced personnel, not recruits. I felt I was growing, maturing. Perhaps this would be the life for me, I thought. I'd enroll in nursing school, and rejoin the Navy as an officer in the corps.

Reality struck again, when my hitch ended in 1979. No nursing school would take me because of my high school transcript. I went on unemployment long enough to get one check, then took a job in the housekeeping department at Mount Sinai Hospital, a prestigious Manhattan institution on the fringe of Spanish Harlem. I was a supervisor trainee, meaning I had to clean toilets, walls, floors, whatever. Within a year, I was promoted to manager and ran a crew of three supervisors and forty-five employees, all older than I. For the most part I was negotiating and meeting with administrators and department heads who'd gone to top graduate schools. And I was holding my own, filing quarterly reports, writing personnel evaluations, earning good money. In 1982, my salary was $25,000, and I'd just turned twenty-four.

I also had my first brush with the violence that racism breeds, an encounter that scared me not only because a black man hated me for being white, but also for my ugly reaction to his bitterness. It was a Sunday morning at Mount Sinai, a tough time to get the cleaning crew to work, since they'd usually been partying the night before. This day, we were short-staffed to boot, and I was walking the halls, changing assignments so everything would be finished when the shift ended.

My reputation was as an easygoing boss, I thought. The crew was mixed: men, women, old, young, black, white and Hispanic. Some didn't speak English well, others weren't in good physical condition. But everyone there needed the job because they had someone to support: mother, father, husband, wife, children. They didn't want to give me trouble either, and we had a live-and-let-live relationship.

Except, I discovered, with Charlie, (not his real name) a black man, older than I, and smaller. His usual assignment was to mop floors, but—since I was short of help—I asked him to bag garbage.

"I'll do it with you," I said.

Charlie shook his head, negatively.

"C'mon," I said, "I'd consider it a special favor."

Uh-uh, Charlie's head shook. Then he screamed, "I don't really give a shit."

"Hey," I said, gesturing with my hands, "I've always been square with you."

He pushed my hand away, and threw his mop on the floor. "I ought to kill your lily-white ass," he said. I was shocked. Where was he coming from with that remark? I tried to laugh it off, but he came at me.

As Charlie swung, I grabbed him in a bear hug. He kept flailing away. Finally, he slowed, and I thought he was spent. I loosened my grip, and he suddenly pulled free to hit me in the jaw. Staggering back, I saw him come again. I swung my right arm, and my fist hit his nose. I could hear the crack as he fell to the floor in a ball.

I couldn't believe what I'd done.

"Honky bastard," muttered Charlie, picking himself up, and skulking away. Even though I was defending myself. I felt ashamed. Not only was the guy smaller, I thought, he was working for me. You're not supposed to give your employees nosebleeds. Maybe I *was* a honky bastard. Maybe for his whole life, in one way or another, white guys like me were tagging Charlie on the nose.

Shaking, I looked at my fist. It was red and swollen. I wanted to go into a dark closet and hide. My supervisor was in the cafeteria drinking coffee. He listened while I told him what happened. "I don't like what I've done," I kept repeating.

A situation had spun out of control because a black man had looked at a white man, and felt hatred. And, in one horrible moment, I'd been pulled into that hatred.

"I've got to go home," I said.

In the fall of 1982, I decided to go to college, and joined my brother Owen at the New Paltz campus of the State University of New York. But I didn't even last the semester. In December, the New York City Police Department announced it would hold a civil service examination for officer candidates. Even though I planned to go back into hospital housekeeping I signed up to take the test. I'm not sure why except time seemed to be running out. I'd been in the service and enjoyed the military structure. I wanted to be working in New York, in a career where I could be of service. And I couldn't get over the feeling that a police officer's job was special. All the police functions and events I'd been to in my life had left an indelible impression.

I went to Philadelphia in February to work for a friend who had set up a new institutional housekeeping company. He had landed a prestigious contract with several affiliated hospitals there. I'd run the entire operation for him, getting in on the ground floor of the company as well.

Patti Ann came into my life in April, and we'd see each other on weekends. By July, I'd decided to come back to New York. Patti Ann was one reason, to be sure, but I'd grown homesick for the city too. I loved walking the streets of the East Side, the West Side, even Times Square. Later, when I was a cop, on foot post in Central Park, I'd stand back and gaze up at the skyline, the lights on the horizon, the gleaming towers and apartment buildings. The most beautiful place in the world, I'd think.

The hospital cleaning business was turning political, too. In Philadelphia, I was making $28,000 and, on the surface, the possibilities seemed limitless. But when the health-care economy experienced a downturn—through insurance cutbacks, or whatever—the first place to cut was in housekeeping. At unionized hospitals, the older workers were protected, even though they'd be expected to do the jobs of two or three people. They weren't going to be moving any quicker than they had before the layoffs, and I knew their manager would become the scapegoat. I didn't want to be a scapegoat.

So I came back to New York, worked for nine months at the Beekman Hospital, and vacationed in England. Patti Ann would complain that I never wrote. Not once. But had I realized how special she was, how much I would come to depend on her in the years ahead, I would have written every day, every hour.

. Four

Malverne, 1984

Steven never told me he was going to become a police officer, not when we were first going out. His father had retired from the force eight years earlier, and when I'd go to Rockville Centre, to his home, I didn't feel a part of that culture. What I did know of the life of a police officer and his family didn't sound great. One girl in high school whose father was a cop had a terrible home life, it seemed to me, and she was the only cop's child I knew well. My other friends' fathers worked in white-collar jobs—on Wall Street, or in teaching. But no one worked as a cop. I wasn't brought up with it at all.

No, there was one other—the daughter of a police chief who worked with me at Macy's. "I'm never going to marry a cop," she told me time and again. The stress, the strain, she'd say, were too much to bear. Nevertheless, in the summer of 1988, that's exactly what she did.

Not only did Steven never tell me his ambition was to be a cop, I don't think it was his plan when we first met. At least, not consciously. But by the time I'd fallen in love with him, he'd decided that was what he wanted. When he told me, I couldn't respond, "Oh, this is great! I'm so happy." I wasn't happy at all. I wasn't sure I wanted to get married to a man who would be a police officer.

In fact, Steven didn't tell me until the New York Police Academy called him and told him he'd been accepted. "By the way . . ." he'd begun.

By the way?

It was June 1984. "By the way," he said, glancing at me as I settled into the front seat. "I got a phone call today. I'm going to be starting at the Police Academy in a month."

"A month?" I gasped. We'd been going out over a year. I loved Steven, I knew that. Some day we'd be married, I suspected that. But did I want to become a policeman's wife? I'd heard the stories of guys who didn't come home, who drank till all hours in cops' bars, who spent years working midnight to 8:00 A.M. shifts . . . was that something I wanted to try to handle?

We hadn't had any serious discussions about my feelings, any at all. I looked at him closely. He really wants this, I thought.

"I'm nervous about this, Steven," I said. "I'm even a little scared."

We drove quietly to my parents' house. By the time we pulled to the curb in front, I'd decided to let things happen. Just go with the flow, I told myself.

New York Police Academy, 1984

On July 20, 1984, I reported to the academy, which was located in a modern gray low-rise on East 20th Street, just off Third Avenue. I was relaxed about what I'd face. Unlike many of the recruits, I'd served in the military, and knew the five-and-a-half months ahead would be easier than anything I'd seen in boot camp. All of us filled out registration cards, with our pictures on them. On the backs, we described why we'd joined the force and, so the instructors could get a sense of our personalities, I guess, we listed our favorite books, movies and plays.

"Book—Leon Uris' *Trinity,"* I wrote. "Movie—*Quiet Man, Christmas Carol.* Play—*Philadelphia Story."*

As to why I wanted to be a cop: "Traditionally policemen have been in a position to help people in many ways, for many reasons, which has led to a high profile. It is a job where I can make a mark and a difference in society. A job I will be proud to be connected with."

We were a good-sized class, 1,856 when we all gathered that first morning in the auditorium. Because of our numbers, we were divided into two shifts—the academy couldn't handle more than one thousand recruits at one time—and then subdivided into companies of thirty-five each. At twenty-seven, I was older than a lot of the guys and I decided I'd compete to become the company sergeant, or coordinator. One of the instructors, Sean Doran, tried to talk me out of it.

"It's a lot of responsibility," he said, "and you don't get much credit. The other cadets can consider you a boss. And an ass." There was the myth of the company sergeant, too, other cadets would say. They were like second lieutenants in battle: the company sergeant was always the first guy shot. In fact, I wasn't the first shot. I was the second. The first was John Reilly, shot by a sniper, in the Bronx, less than six months after graduation.

I stuck with it, and was one of five guys nominated by the floor instructors. My age, military experience, and other life experiences may have been what tipped the decision in my favor.

The academy had, and still does have, a quasi-military atmosphere. Recruits stand at attention every time an outsider steps into a classroom, and salute superiors in the hallways. We were required to carry STAR cards in our shirt pockets—STAR stood for Student Training Activity Reports—and if an instructor or an officer in the Integrity Unit saw that we were out of uniform, or late to muster, or in the hallway when we were scheduled to be in class, he'd make a mark on the card. Five of those, and you'd be on disciplinary probation. Getting sent into the hall was being made into shark bait, we'd say; the Integrity Unit officers were the sharks. I can't remember it ever happening to me, though my social science teacher, Jim Hines, who has visited me since my accident, says he once nailed me for an incomplete homework assignment.

There was a less macho attitude inside the academy than there'd been in the early seventies, when you'd have to fight your way through those first few months to prove how tough you were. We weren't even allowed to spar with each other in physical education classes, and I realized later that for some recruits, both men and women, it was possible never to have hit someone, or been struck, before it came time to step onto the street for your first patrol.

The days were divided into blocks of time for each course—police science, social science, law, and physical education. A lot of the classroom work focussed on role-playing. Two recruits would be sent into a hallway, while the rest of the class watched a confrontation between a shopkeeper and a thief, each played by a recruit. The shopkeeper would have his gun drawn and aimed at the thief whose gun would be lying on the instructor's desk. Both men would be circling warily, eyeing each other and the guns, and screaming, "Motherfucker! Fuck you! Don't shoot me! I oughta kill you!" at the top of their lungs. The pair of recruits in the hall then entered the room, guns drawn, and tried to take control of the situation by disarming and handcuffing both men without any shots being fired, or anyone hurt.

No matter how badly a recruit screwed up, he'd never get "shot" by either the shopkeeper or the thief. I occasionally wondered why. Jim Hines told me. "We never shoot a recruit in role-playing," he said. "What would they learn? Just that they got shot."

Personal safety was hugely important. "Your safety is number one," I remember one instructor telling us. "It's all that should be on your mind. Leave your other thoughts in your lockers." Another officer told us, "You have to be personal and selfish about it." Now, as part of their training, cadets watch a videotape of the ABC "20/20" story about Patti Ann and me that aired in December 1987. And Sean Doran and I are developing a presentation that I could deliver to each academy class personally.

The courses we took in 1984 cover the same material they do now—everything from traffic checks, determining license suspensions and reading traffic meters to making arrests and disarming perps. Our pistol training was on a range in the Bronx, and a couple of days before we graduated—Badge and Shield Day, it's called—we'd be given our guns to take home. Until then, you simply turned them in at the end of practice.

For many trainees, that's the moment of truth. They'd take their guns home, go into their bedrooms, and admire, touch, fondle, cock and flash the weapon, sometimes in front of a mirror. Some guys would even stick the barrel into their mouths—playing with the gun, they'd say—to prove they were tougher than it. I never felt that way, maybe because I'd trained with a gun in the Navy, maybe because my father had never made a show of his gun when we grew up.

I just put mine away. And for the two years I was a cop, I only pulled it out of its holster once. That was the time I saw a bunch of kid bike thieves pull a gun in Central Park, a month before I was shot.

On December 18, 1984, 1,755 of us graduated. We'd lost 101, for different reasons. Some couldn't handle the academics, some weren't fit, and some weren't ready to deal with the stress and the danger. One fellow made the saddest choice. A month after classes began, he stepped in front of a Long Island Railroad locomotive. Our class, tinged with tragedy from the outset, gathered in Madison Square Garden for the graduation ceremony. My family and Patti Ann's both came, meeting each other for the first time.

There were some mixed emotions, I guess. To this day, I haven't seen one photograph of me in uniform prior to being shot.

Not one. Not even from graduation.

Now I was one of twenty-seven thousand uniformed officers. The Blue Wall. Which was still mostly white and male. Of the total, three thousand were black, three thousand were Hispanic, and three thousand were women.

My first six months as a police officer were termed field training, and each academy grad would be paired with a field training officer, usually a detective with many years on the job. This education was critical—a lot of the guys came from suburban counties like Nassau, or Rockland, or Westchester. They didn't know what to expect on the street, where you had to think twice as fast, and be inventive and creative, just to stay on top.

I was assigned to Detective Bobby Reid. Reid, who's since moved into the organized crime division at Internal Affairs, was an ex-Marine who'd served in Vietnam. As far as I was concerned, he showed me everything a cop should be.

Detective Reid was in his early forties, a sharp-looking man about five-nine, slender, a head of trimmed black hair flecked with gray, an equally grayish mustache, who wore military creases in his uniform. He'd been on the job fifteen years and had a lot of respect for himself, and his uniform. He was smart—ten steps in front of everyone else.

During field training, I was assigned to Neighborhood Stabilization Units—both regular foot and radio car patrols—in five different precincts: the sixth, seventh, ninth, tenth and thirteenth, all in Manhattan, and encompassing West Greenwich Village, East Greenwich Village, the Lower West Side, the East Side near Bellevue and the Academy, and the gritty area by the Williamsburg Bridge. The seventh precinct was a particularly tough assignment—a predominantly black and Hispanic neighborhood, with lots of drugs, and violence, near Chinatown. And the ninth wasn't much different.

Bobby Reid and I would take car tours together—the most productive time I'd spend with him—and I'd use as much of the eight hours as possible to listen, and to pick his brain. In the academy, it had been book knowledge. But on the street, you had to learn common sense. Bobby was there for my first collar.

I was on a foot post in the Village, on West 8th Street. Our patrol supervisor, a desk officer, pulled up in a radio car, and told me to get in. We sped a few blocks to Crazy Eddie's, a discount electronics supermarket at Sixth Avenue and West 8th. The store security guards were holding a kid there who'd been caught using a forged credit card. I took a good look at the kid, listened to what security had to say, and felt a wave of sympathy: he seemed similar in background to me—white, Catholic, Irish, from out on Long Island. He'd come into the city to do something stupid, I thought. Maybe I'll be able to do something so they'll go easy on him in court.

The supervisor gave me the arrest, and I took him into the precinct house and handcuffed him to a chair while I figured out what to do next. I'd never processed an arrest before, and the guys in the house aren't that willing to help a rookie—it's a sink-or-swim mentality once you're out on the streets, unless you're working with a partner—so the Neighborhood Stabilization Unit was called to give me support. The NSU had to be called anyway; it was supposed to know my whereabouts at all times. Within minutes, Bobby arrived to help with the fingerprinting and the paperwork. He brought a bunch of other rookies with him. It would be on-the-job training for everyone.

"Get the evidence," he told me.

I'd been given the forged credit card at the store and had left it on a table near the chair I'd handcuffed the guy to. Now it was gone. As I crawled on the floor, looking for it, I could feel everyone's eyes on me. Oh Jeez, I thought, I've messed up major. I was sweating, and felt like crying. I'm twenty-eight, these other rooks are twenty-one, twenty-two, and expected me to be more responsible, more knowledgeable. And here I am, I thought, looking like a jerk.

Bobby was watching the handcuffed kid closely. "I want you to come with me," he said to the suspect, and told me to unlock the cuffs. We took him into a back room, where the kid began to talk tough. But not as tough as Bobby.

"What'd you do with it?" Bobby kept demanding.

Eventually, under intense questioning the kid broke. He had a drug trial coming up. This would make matters worse. He also had a brother who was a cop stationed in Brooklyn; he knew enough about felonies to understand that, without evidence, there wasn't a case. We went back to the chair the kid had been sitting in. The material in the armrest was cut, and he'd managed to work the card into it without anyone noticing.

"Don't trust anybody," Bobby reminded me. "That's number one."

It wasn't long after that I responded to my first 1013—a radio code meaning "officer needs assistance"—the highest priority call you can make. When a 1013 is broadcast, everyone in listening range tries to answer; traffic can come to a halt as radio cars careen down streets in the wrong direction and chaos ensues. A 1013 can mean a cop's life is on the line, and your only thought is to get there before anything bad can happen.

I'd been assigned to a drug post at Union Square Park, a kind of DMZ at 14th Street between the East and West Villages, a long city block from lower Fifth Avenue. Dealers and users had become a presence in the park, and our post's responsibility was to push people along. We'd issue summonses for minor infractions just to make sure these guys got the message. In the evenings we'd also keep our eyes on the area dance bars, especially just outside the entrances.

This night I was working a 4:00 P.M. to midnight shift, and at 10:00 P.M. found myself standing at the upper end of the park, near a dance club named The Underground. The portable radio in my back pocket began squawking as the dispatcher shouted "1013 going down." Two cops were chasing a guy over rooftops. "Heading towards 17th and Fifth," she continued.

I was already on 17th Street. I'm right *there,* I realized.

"Central," I called into my radio. "I'll respond to the 1013 at 17th and Fifth."

"All right," she said.

The pursuing cops were broadcasting the progress of the chase, and I listened as I ran to that corner. A radio car came flying by me, and stopped just long enough for a Neighborhood Stabilization Unit sergeant to stick his head out the window and yell, "Stay right here. Don't move. We're trying to box the guy in."

So I stood, by myself, in the dark. All the other cops were down the block, or rushing into apartment buildings to get to the roofs, where the chase was.

Suddenly, a black man stepped out of a doorway a few feet to my right. Casually, he pulled out a cigarette and lit it.

I walked over to him.

"Excuse me, sir," I said. "We have a situation here. I just need to ask you for some identification. What are you doing here?"

At first, he gave me what I took to be a song-and-dance. Then he started bitching. "Hey, just 'cause I'm black," he said, "is that what you stoppin' me for? What're you botherin' me for?"

"It'll just take a minute or two," I said. "I've just got to call, and if everything's okay, I'll let you go. Just bear with me."

I was being nice, because I didn't suspect him of anything. Well, I did suspect, not because he was a black man walking down the street, but because he fit the description I'd heard from the dispatcher. I wanted to check it a second time, and if it didn't match, I'd let him go. With my right hand, I raised the radio to my mouth. My left hung in the air, near his shoulder.

"Central, can you give me a description of the perpetrator?"

"Unit that was in pursuit," she said, "can you give me the description?"

"Five foot eight, male, black, dark jacket, tan shirt, no hat . . ."

"Central," I continued, "can you give me a description of the footgear the perp was wearing?"

"White!" the cop exclaimed. "White sneakers!"

With that, I grabbed the perp's arm, and he bolted. As he dragged me down the sidewalk, I shouted into the radio, "Central, 1013! 1013!"

"Give me the location," she said. "Give me the location."

I couldn't. The guy may have been five-eight, but he was built like a brick barn. I didn't want to lose him, because I figured he'd leave me in the dust in a footrace. So I kept yelling "1013, 1013," as I tried to get a foot in front to trip him. Finally, I tripped both of us. We spun to the pavement, and he began pulling at everything I had on me: gunbelt, night stick, handcuffs. The struggle, scary as it was, took on a dreamlike quality. Time seemed to stand still.

Then sirens broke my reverie. Several radio cars pulled up, and other cops spilled out, grabbing the guy and cuffing him. One told me he'd stolen $8,000 worth of jewelry. A terrific arrest, I thought. I was wrong.

"Give up the collar," an FTO—not Bobby Reid—told me. "Let the guys who started the chase have him."

In the end, though, I got named in the commendation. That was some consolation. In the New York City Police Department, your work on a job is only recognized if you're mentioned in the write-up. Otherwise, officially, you weren't even there.

I knew I'd been there. I was proud of it. I was proud of another thing, too. No one—not myself, not the perp, not another officer or bystander—had been hurt.

Malverne, 1985

When we were dating, Steven didn't have his license, so I'd do all the driving, in a beat-up yellow Volkswagen Beetle my parents let me use. I'd never heard of that before—the boy allowing the girl to drive. Never. So there had to be something special about him. We'd usually end up at my house for dinner, and he and my father would watch TV and talk about police work, sports, movies, whatever. One night shortly after we were married, Steven talked about a gang of bike thieves he'd arrested, and how one of them had carried a gun. He'd seen where they lived, Steven said, in the forbidding tenements near Central Park's north end. Many of those forced to live there were victims, good people whom the system had failed, Steven said. My parents had been present at the time. My father listened quietly, but my mother was dismayed. Steven's awfully idealistic, she said to me later, to have such sympathy for a teen with a gun.

"Does he have enough street smarts?" she wondered.

"Of course," I told her.

We'd often go to movies, which Steven loves. Since I've known him, about five years now, he's probably watched *The Quiet Man,* the John Ford film starring John Wayne and Maureen O'Hara, more than one hundred times. That's the one where Wayne plays an Irish-American fighter who accidentally kills a man in the ring, swears off boxing, then moves to Ireland to try and start a new life. He falls in love with Maureen, whose character is his neighbor's sister, is on the verge of losing her because he won't stand up to her brother, eventually fights him, gets married, and lives happily ever after.

If it's not *The Quiet Man,* it's *Prince of the City,* or *It's a Wonderful Life,* or . . . well, you get the idea. Films were a big part of Steven's life and we spent many dates in front of flickering screens.

We were sitting in a movie theater, watching *The Razor's Edge,* when Steven proposed. We hadn't discussed getting engaged before then. The movie was about a man who realizes too late that he's lost the woman he really loves, and Steven must have felt specially touched by it. He turned to me, took my hand, and said, "Let's get married."

It had been about a year-and-a-half since we'd first met and I was caught pleasantly offguard. The relationship still seemed new.

Why now, I asked.

"I felt like asking," Steven said. "It feels like the right thing to do."

I said yes.

Our engagement lasted a year and we found an apartment in the center of Malverne, the same one-bedroom walkup we were living in when Steven was shot. It was modest but near my parents house, where I lived until our wedding. Steven did some of the decorating—he hung a *Razor's Edge* poster over the bed—and he and I continued our commutes to the city, me to the Fashion Institute, and he to whichever precinct house he was working out of that month.

I wasn't interested in moving in with him before we were married. I didn't even want to leave home. My mother never kept my sisters, brothers and me from doing what we wanted to do, and perhaps it would have been fun to live by myself for a while. But I never did. Living together with Steven, though, would have been immoral. And kind of stupid. I've got a friend, a good friend, who's been living with a guy for two years. She wants to get married; he doesn't. I'd hate to have put myself in that situation.

With me, if you love me, if you want to be with me, you marry me. We set the date for November 9, 1985.

As the year began, I graduated from FIT, and went to work at the Norma Kamali showroom on Fashion Avenue. The job was as a go-fer, classic entry-level, getting coffee, answering phones, things like that, but at least I was in the business, and not selling perfumes in a department store. Then, that August, I moved to *Parents* magazine. A friend's aunt was the magazine's photography and fashion editor and was looking for an assistant. I interviewed, got the offer, and made the move.

Three months after I started at the magazine, we were married. The wedding was a special moment—one of those perfect afternoons and evenings where everyone looks like they've stepped out of a storybook, the jokes are all hilarious, and the singing and dancing infectious. Steven took me into my parents' parlor and had the photographer pose us just as John Wayne and Maureen O'Hara had posed for their wedding portrait in *The Quiet Man*—Steven seated, back ramrod straight in his morning coat, me standing next to him, hand on wingback chair, my gown and veil spilling to the sides.

The wedding ceremony was at Our Lady of Lourdes, where I'd received all the sacraments—my baptism, my first Holy Communion, my Confirmation. My cousin, Father Seamus O'Boyle, flew in from England to say the Mass. Then the party, two hundred of us, drove to the Rockville Centre Country Club for the reception. Finally we wound up at my parents' for more revelry.

Standing at the altar, listening to Seamus, all I could think of was how wonderful everything was going to be. The usual problems a cop's family faces—the hours, the stress—those were going to be for others. Not ours. Steven wasn't going to be the normal cop. I wasn't going to be the normal police wife. We were going to be a regular, happy couple, I thought.

I glanced at Steven. He was crying.

Later, I asked him why.

"I was so taken aback," he told me. "You took my breath away." He also said, as he watched me come down the aisle, that another priest poked him in the ribs, and whispered, "She'd look good even in overalls."

I felt like a princess, in a fairy tale that could only have a happy ending.

"Steven," said Father O'Boyle, "do you take Patricia for your lawful wife according to the rite of our Holy Mother, the Church?"

"I do," Steven said.

"Patricia," said the Father, "do you take Steven for your lawful husband according to the rite of our Holy Mother, the Church?"

"I do," I said.

Steven gave me his right hand. For better or for worse. For richer or for poorer. In sickness or in health. Until death do us part. He was mine. I was his. The possibilities seemed endless. It would be a wonderful life.

So I thought.

Five

Central Park, 1985–86

When my field training was finished, I was assigned to the Central Park Precinct. Within the department, such an assignment got mixed reviews. Some guys laughed, calling the precinct "Squirrel Patrol"; for others, though, it can be R-and-R, a chance to escape from the stress of Harlem or the South Bronx.

Some people say that Central Park is New York City's finest architectural achievement, the landscape's crown jewel. I won't argue. I was always in awe of its beauty—especially at night, when the lights of the towers along Central Park South and West would twinkle above the treetops. The guy who designed it, Olmsted, never intended parkgoers to be able to see the city—in 1856, when construction began, the city had barely reached the park's southern end and buildings were no taller than five or six stories—but I loved the contrast. Olmsted also wanted the park kept pastoral—no parking lots, no rinks, no playgrounds.

He even objected to the construction of the Metropolitan Museum of Art on the park's eastern boundary near East 82nd Street, but later gave in.

What Olmsted fundamentally wanted, though, he got: a gathering place for every race and class in the city, a true democracy. On hot summer afternoons the crowds would swell into the tens of thousands and, jammed around Bethesda Fountain, you could feel as if you were in a subway crowd—boom boxes blaring, Spanish mothers screaming for their niños, punks selling dope, yuppies jogging, teens making out.

Needless to say, making arrests while in uniform wasn't easy in Central Park, particularly if you were assigned to street narcotics, like I was. At the precinct house, an old brick stable, we'd joke it was like the Revolutionary War. The bad guys were the colonists, and they got to hide behind the trees and wear anything they wanted. We were the British and had to stand in the open, in straight lines, and wear bright red uniforms. Like lots of dark humor, there was an underlying truth.

In winter, when the park was more or less deserted, and I was standing out on a foot post, freezing my butt off, I'd sometimes wonder if I'd made the right choice of profession. But in spring, fall, and especially summer, there was plenty of crime to keep you busy, and an interesting cross-section of New Yorkers to come into contact with.

The year I came into the park, 1985, seemed a relatively safe one for New York City cops. No one had been killed. But the statistic was deceiving. One hundred and thirty-two officers had been shot at, twenty-one more than 1984, and forty had returned fire. Only seven had been wounded, however, down from sixteen in 1984, when three officers were killed.

Until Shavod Jones got me, I had never been shot at either. But I'd faced a knife one afternoon in a bizarre confrontation, one the department regulations said I should have avoided.

I was stationed at a drug post on Columbus Circle, an ugly, noisy, chaotic traffic rotary bounded by the park on one corner, a massive gray brick exhibition hall called the Coliseum on another, and the headquarters of the city's Department of Cultural Affairs, a white marble structure, on still another. I'd made enough collars while on foot patrol to receive a lateral promotion into street narcotics, a special precinct detail.

The Columbus Circle post, on the southern edge of the park, is at 59th Street and Broadway, and 59th Street is the boundary separating the Central Park Precinct from the Midtown North Precinct. As a standard rule of procedure, you're never supposed to leave a drug post, no matter how many passersby come up to you and complain, "You know, you're standing here, and down the block they're dealing." The problem is, because it's department policy, the dealers and their steerers—the guys who direct the buyers to the drugs—have figured that out. If you're standing on your post, they'll go across the street, and down the block. And if you're a cop, you can either live with that, or decide it's garbage.

One day, I said it was garbage. I'm going to go where they are, I decided, and either move them on or hang around until their clients got the message they weren't going to be open for business as long as I was standing there.

I went down the block, and everybody moved. But now I was out of my precinct. I made a right on 57th Street, heading towards Eighth Avenue. My plan was to walk uptown on Eighth, and return to my post. If I saw any dealers or steerers, I figured, I'd demand identification and take their names. Give them a hard time. This was nothing unusual or heroic; everybody I worked with did it.

At 57th Street and Eighth Avenue, a young black girl approached me, crying. "Officer, officer," she sobbed, "this man came up and stole my chain. He ran off into that restaurant."

Oh no, I thought. I really shouldn't be here. But what was I going to say to her. Wait here, I'll call a cop? Which, in fact, I couldn't do because my radio wouldn't work in that zone. A different dispatcher than the one I was connected to controlled the area. My frequency wouldn't reach her.

I went across the street, although I had no idea whether the girl was lying, or whether any crime had been committed, or what the story was. What did he look like, I asked the girl.

"It was a black man," she said.

The restaurant was on an upscale block, near the Hard Rock Cafe, and served a yuppie clientele. Inside, there was only one black, in the back and to the left. I was reasonably certain that had to be the guy. He was holding the menu up around his eyes, peering over it at me. The girl, meanwhile, was following me and she spotted him too.

"That's him," she shouted. "He's got it."

"What?" he said innocently.

"Please stand up, sir," I asked politely.

"What?" he demanded, more assertively.

"Just stand up, sir," I repeated. "I want to ask you a couple of questions."

While I was speaking, the girl leaned over the divider separating his table from the others. She grabbed the bottom of his jacket, and lifted. "There's my necklace!" she yelled.

The guy jumped up. At six-two, and over two hundred pounds, he caught me by surprise and bowled me over. I hadn't felt threatened—the girl never suggested he was carrying a weapon—and I hadn't pulled my service revolver. I just wanted to question him. Now he was getting away.

Just before he got out the door, a waiter—a small Greek guy—threw a cross-body block, knocking the guy into a countertop. I ran to him, and we began wrestling, knocking over tables and chairs. Then he grabbed a knife off one of the tables, probably a butter knife, but in the heat of the moment, it looked like a butcher's knife to me. I jumped on his back, wrapping my arms around him in a bear hug.

"Call the cops, somebody," I began screaming. "Call the cops." Then I tried to focus on the knife-waver.

"Calm down," I said. "Put your arms behind your back."

None of my orders was registering on his face. He seemed completely out of it. All sorts of horrible scenarios ran through my mind. What if he gets free? What if he holds the knife to the girl's throat? What if . . . ?

After what seemed like an eternity, another cop burst through the door, grabbed an arm, and helped me put the cuffs on.

I was so pumped up, I wanted to smack the guy. But

I caught myself. Oh Jesus, I thought, don't lose it here, in front of a bunch of letter writers. Don't put your own head in a noose. Then I realized the diners were thanking me. They were *applauding.*

I took the guy to the North, the Midtown North precinct house, to process the arrest. The desk officer wasn't happy to see me—he knew I wasn't supposed to be in that precinct—but Central Park never called me on it later, to my relief. As the booking proceeded, the arrestee made one of the three phone calls he's allowed. To my surprise, he called me over and handed me the receiver.

It was his mother.

"Do anything you can to help my son," she pleaded. "He's got a wife and a child, and he's been looking for work, but no luck. He's a good boy."

She sobbed.

"He's a good boy."

What could I do? I tried to figure out if there was a job I could steer him towards. He was crying, too. "Hey," I tried to comfort him, "I'll be with you through the whole process." Eventually, though, I lost track of him. Would he find someone else in the system to help him? I'd never know.

On April 8, 1986, I got my new assignment.

Anti-crime.

The anti-crime units were in operation all over the city, with guys in plainclothes trying to anticipate crime and stop the criminals before a citizen was mugged, assaulted, robbed, or worse. In high-crime precincts, the anti-crime units would be creative in their disguises to catch their prey, a risky role that took a lot of courage, patience and make-up artistry. In Central Park, we simply tried to blend in with the crowds.

Anti-crime was seen as kind of a promotion—you're in street clothes, or, in department slang, as I said previously, "out of the bag"—and I was ecstatic when I heard the precinct captain wanted me to go there. I hadn't had nearly as many arrests as some other uniformed guys in the precinct, but I was always active on arrests, on time to work, and in proper uniform. Sometimes, that's what the bosses are looking for.

The crimes didn't change dramatically, though. I was still writing tickets for illegal lane changes, commercial vehicles in the park, running red lights, and driving with expired plates. But I was also moving through the park in my own clothes, blending in as best I could—not easy as you moved north, into Harlem's end of the park—and watching for suspicious characters.

On April 10, Sergeant Peter King and myself nabbed a couple of guys throwing kung fu stars into tree stumps near 103rd Street and West Drive. This part of the park was known as Donkey Hill—where the Irish set up shanties in the mid-1800s—and was a rise, surrounded by oaks and maples. This was my first anti-crime patrol, and I felt anxious. Stepping out of the woods, my shield in front of me, I ordered the men to come towards me.

They took a long look, then took off. I followed.

"Steve, get back in the car!" yelled the sergeant. He wanted me with him in the police car, but I was afraid I'd lose them outside the park on the street.

"I'm gonna make the collar!" I shouted, and kept going. It was only a misdemeanor, I knew, but at least I'd be on the books. A full-fledged member of the unit.

I hauled ass under a stone bridge, and ran up a hill onto the 102nd Street cross-drive. My chest heaving, worn out, I scanned the drive. Nothing. I now knew that making a collar in the park wasn't going to be easy or routine, regardless of how I dressed.

Sergeant King and the rest of the unit pulled up. They were laughing. "Nice running, Stevie," the sergeant said. "But, like I told you, there *is* an easier way to do this."

We drove outside, and at 103rd Street and Fifth Avenue, spotted our men jumping the park's stone wall.

I pulled my gun, holding it down to the side, and hailed them.

"Police! Against that wall!"

They were terrified.

"O.K., O.K., O.K.," they begged. "Please don't hurt us."

I searched them for the kung fu stars, but they had none. Sergeant King arrived and said he hadn't seen any left on Donkey Hill, either. Furious I'd gone on a wild goose chase, I took their names, and let them go.

A week later, I did get on the books. I arrested a twenty-seven-year-old man riding a stolen moped; he had a seven-inch-long butcher's knife tucked into his belt. Then, on May 2, we picked up seven young black and Hispanic boys, a gang we'd been tracking who, as we'd watched stole a bike right in front of our noses. One of them had pulled a pistol from his slick leather jacket and forced a preppy-looking kid off his bicycle.

I was stunned. I couldn't believe we'd accomplished such good police work.

Five of the kids froze when we stepped from the bushes, and the other two ran down West 72nd Street, hoping to lose us in the West Side traffic. The sergeant and Tom Culhane cuffed the kids who'd stopped, and I jumped into the car Carlson was driving to try and catch the other two. They'd gotten two blocks, to Columbus Avenue, when we caught up. After a foot chase, we got both.

Because they were juveniles and they hadn't been in a lot of previous trouble, the boys were "recoged"—released without bail on their promise to return to court when their cases came up—to their parents. Somehow, I forgot to give the paperwork to one family and decided to deliver it at the end of my shift. The boy's name was Paul, I recall. He was fourteen.

The department doesn't encourage social work on the part of officers any more, but I thought I might see if there was anything I could do for the boy, and if I could learn why he'd done what he'd done.

The apartment, in a tenement on 103rd Street just off Madison Avenue, was small and dark, and smelled of rotten food. It was 11:30 at night, maybe midnight, and all the children—five, I counted—were awake. The boy's mother and father both looked like walking corpses, as ashen, unkempt and blankfaced as the characters in *Night of the Living Dead.* They were overwhelmed.

Your boy's in a jam, I told them, I'd like to help if I could. If he wanted to get into a basketball league, or to sign up with a volunteer program to do work around the park, something constructive, I'd be glad to help, I said. I'd seen lots of cops do this before, on their own time, for people they'd arrested. It seemed appropriate, especially with children.

The parents' English was poor, and one of the kids acted as an interpreter. Paul stood to one side, looking confused. The man and woman nodded their heads, as if they understood. I handed them a card with my phone number on it. Everybody nodded again, and the boy's father closed the door as I left.

In the hall, through the thin walls, I could hear them laughing. No one ever called.

I went downtown to Central Booking and called Patti Ann, telling her what I'd seen.

"After that," I said shakily, "how could anyone blame these kids for the lives they lead."

May passed into June, and then July. The Mets were making a run for their division title, and Patti Ann told me she was pregnant. The first of six, I hoped, although she wanted to stop at four, then think about it. Life should have been sweet, but we were having bitter arguments.

My hours weren't in sync with Patti's. I had to work overtime to make sure I had enough money for the doctor bills we expected with the baby, and for the apartment we wanted in Manhattan. We were on the waiting list at Stuyvesant Town, a middle-class, rent-controlled development of towers surrounded by lawns, playgrounds and walks rather than streets. Stuyvesant Town was on the East Side, by the East River, no more than a block or two from the Police Academy, and featured security, front doors that locked, elevators, intercoms, parquet floors, and rents of less than $500 a month for a one-bedroom apartment. For young cops and their wives, getting an apartment there was to be admitted into paradise, which was why there was a seven-to-ten-year waiting list. I'd been on the waiting list quite a while, too, but we were moving up quickly.

Money was going to be tight, though. Patti Ann's salary at *Parents* didn't amount to much, enough for her personal needs, and my medical benefits only reimbursed us for 80 percent of the pregnancy and delivery. By selling our car, and not needing our monthly commuter rail passes, I figured we could squeeze by. It was worth it, I thought, to be living in Manhattan, to walk the streets of the greatest city in the world, to see movies and plays and ride our bikes through Central Park.

The last check I collected in July, the day I was shot, totalled $810 in take-home pay for two weeks' work. Of that, $200 was overtime, which I was working as much as I could, putting in eleven- and twelve-hour days. If I started at 8:00 in the morning, I'd be up at 4:30 in order to get to the station house on time. On the 4:00 P.M. to midnight shifts, I'd get home after 1:00 A.M. Often, Patti Ann would be asleep when I got home, and would leave at 6:00 A.M., before I woke. The tension was building, the isolation between her, her family and me growing, but there was nothing to do. We'd threaten each other with divorce, then I'd storm out. After fifteen or twenty minutes, walking through town and out to the vegetable farm on Ocean Avenue, I'd return. We'd make peace for the evening; the next day, or the day after, the battle would begin again.

Looking back, I can see these were the problems any

police marriage faced. But I'd been so sure I could avoid them, that the stereotype wouldn't fit me.

Other police departments, in other cities, allow their officers to take paid details outside jobs in uniform—say, a night club owner hires you to watch his door, or a construction company pays you to steer traffic around a work site. When I was in Colorado, I met a Denver captain whose nickname was The Broker; he's the one you went to to get these jobs. In New York City, there's none of that—things hadn't changed since my father was on the force. People would sue you if there were any hassles. Then they'd sue the department. The lawyers would be in a feeding frenzy. Instead, you've got to find a second job, if you're not making enough collars to pick up the overtime that the paperwork, the trips to Central Booking and the District Attorney's office, and the court appearances generate.

Still, I couldn't have been *too* worried, I think now as I look over my black leather memo book for those first twelve days of July. I'd made no arrests through July 11, 1986.

And as Sergeant King and I climbed into radio motor patrol 681, clocked the mileage at 40,547 and the fuel tank as half-full, and checked the back seat for any guns or contraband, I had no particular reason to believe we'd arrest anyone that day, either.

Twenty-five minutes later, I met Shavod Jones.

Malverne, 1986

When I thought I was pregnant, I asked Steven to come to the obstetrician with me. To tell the truth, I wasn't completely confident this was the right time. We'd only been married five months, and as newlyweds we'd fantasized an almost carefree life, with long romantic walks under balmy, starlit skies. I also knew our incomes were modest, and I wondered how we were going to make ends meet.

We wanted to live in Manhattan, yes, to enjoy it as a couple. After we'd saved some money, I thought, *then* we'd raise a family. I called my mother, saying I was nervous, even scared.

"Patti, there's a reason," she reassured me, with that Boston Irish pluck she's always had. "It'll work out. There's no greater blessing than a child."

At the doctor's office, Steven held my hand. When the examination was finished, and the doctor had assured me my suspicions were correct, I began crying.

"Why are you upset?" Steven demanded, almost brusquely.

"I don't know why I'm crying," I sobbed, and I didn't know. I guess it was just being pregnant.

"I'm going to be with you," he then said, softly. "I'm going to be sure I'm there every time you visit the doctor."

I looked at him, his face beaming, and knew he was telling the truth. His father hadn't been there for his mother, since he worked two jobs. And my father hadn't been there for mine. But this was going to be different.

He's going to be with me, I thought.

This is *great!*

How was I to know he'd be with me in a hospital bed, arms at his side, unable to hold me, unable to feel this child. How was I to know we'd be together, and so unalterably apart.

Six

Bellevue's Seventh Floor, August 1986

By the end of my first week in Bellevue, I'd been moved out of neurological intensive care and into a private room on the seventh floor—the neurology department. In the rooms around me patients were clinging to life by their fingernails. Lights shone day and night, and you could become psychotic trying to figure out what time it was.

My body was no longer my own—it was out of my control, punctured by needles and tubes, tied into computer monitors. A large plastic tube pumped air into my chest from an oversized respirator next to my bed. Another tube led into my stomach, where some blenderized food concoction would be fed into me. Intravenous lines sent glucose and medicines into my arms. A small tube inserted in my penis, a Foley catheter, removed my urine.

I felt none of it. My entire field of sensation extended from the top of my forehead to just below my jaw, and back on either side to my ears. There was nothing else, not even enough strength in my neck muscles to lift my head and hold it straight. Instead, it lolled to one side or the other, until someone thought to straighten it out. Drifting, I'd find myself on the football field, leading the Tomahawks' defense. Or on a Carolina beach, watching the dolphins play in the calm inlet. Or with Patti Ann, at the movies. Dreaming. This was all a dream. Soon I'd wake. Rockabye baby. High on the treetops. Don't fall don't fall don't fall. Mommy, where are you. Help.

Fevers wracked my body, which now had no internal temperature controls. Patti Ann, my family, friends would come and go, but I was only dimly aware. The right eye was still swollen from one of the bullet wounds, and there seemed to be more strangers than friends around every time I swam back into consciousness.

One of the first I began to recognize was Monsignor John Kowsky—a stranger who became a friend. With a broad face, a high forehead topped with a crown of white hair, horn-rimmed glasses, and a long-stemmed pipe forever in the corner of his mouth, the monsignor looked like an oversized Irish elf, a giant leprechaun. Soon, I came to think of him as my angel.

Not all cops—even police chaplains—are willing to spend long hours at hospitals, caring for the injured. It's too much like looking in the mirror, remembering your own mortality. But the monsignor—like Brian Mulheren, his good friend—had embraced that responsibility. He had a heart problem complicated by diabetes and looked thin, ten years older than the sixty-four he was when we met. Even so, he'd make it to every job. Any cop died, he'd be there. And if they didn't die, he'd also be there. He was the only chaplain who always, always showed up. Some of the officers told stories about him taking his own police action when they were late getting to the scene. Like the night the monsignor was walking his dog in Battery Park and discovered a distraught citizen about to take a suicide leap into the harbor. The monsignor had his radio with him and called for assistance. By the time the RMP arrived, he introduced the jumper to the officers, whom he also knew, suggest they call for an ambulance, and promised the citizen, "I'll be by to see you tomorrow. God bless!"

As Cardinal O'Connor left my hospital room that first Sunday, the monsignor assured His Eminence he'd say Mass for me, for Patti Ann, and for the family whenever we wanted. "I'll come every day," he offered. And he did, sometimes twice a day. He'd always arrive just after our dinner, around 5:30, and would greet me the same way. "Hello, my Steven," he'd say, caressing my forehead with the sign of the cross.

Listening to him, I imagined he was Clarence the Angel to my despairing Jimmy Stewart in *It's a Wonderful Life.* That's the story where Stewart is filled with doubts, and an apprentice guardian angel named Clarence is sent from heaven to earth to help him out. The monsignor lived his life as if he were Clarence and would constantly reassure Patti Ann and me that things would improve, that there was a reason to keep on going. He'd touch me, even though I couldn't feel his hand, and rub my arm. He'd talk about his combat experience—twenty-eight years in the Army, being the ranking chaplain in Vietnam, surviving an attack in which the helicopter he was flying in was shot down—and listen. He was a good listener, I'd been told even before I met him. Other cops said, if your life was a mess, if you didn't know where to turn, he was there to sit with you, nonjudgmentally, without hitting you with religious rhetoric.

Whenever important visitors would arrive to see me, and they were coming constantly, the monsignor would disappear. When they'd leave, the monsignor would be back at my side. He'd go out of his way to keep out of the spotlight. He had a sense of humor about it, too. If the Cardinal was on his way, the monsignor would whisper, "The big guy's coming."

The masses would start after Patti Ann's parents, Mr. and Mrs. Norris, and my family could get there. The room was too small to hold any more. The monsignor would spread his field kit with its chalice and host on a table next to the bed. Reading the gospel, he'd sound like James Cagney.

"You know, Steven and Patti Ann," he'd say, pausing in his reading, "right heah . . ." And with that New York accent, gesturing with his hands, talking out of the side of his mouth, he'd try to tell us what the players in the Gospels were doing and what it meant to us. A wonderful performance.

Then the monsignor would go downstairs to the small family room and celebrate a second time for whoever else was waiting to see me. Afterwards, he'd help me pass the time with his stories. When I grew more alert, and stronger, I found I couldn't watch that much television. I was trying to understand what was going on with me—not being able to move, not being able to feel, Patti pregnant, little family fires flaring that had to be put out—and he'd tell about the helicopter falling out of the sky, smoke and fire all around, or his Lithuanian father and Irish mother, or his hunting trips with Paul Ragonnese, a hero emergency services cop, and it'd be better than a movie. He'd sing Irish ballads to me in a fine tenor.

"You're going to get your miracle," he'd say as he left, and Patti and I would believe him. Or he'd listen to my mother, as she told him, "God has a reason for saving Steven's life. God's going to give everything back to him, and to us."

"I believe too," he'd say. "I can sense His presence."

The monsignor was frail, but I didn't expect him to die. In March 1987, he suffered a heart attack. We'd only have Mass twice a week from then on. And even before the heart attack, he'd hint he didn't think he had much time left. Talking about stalking deer—he wasn't in it for the killing, he'd say, just the chance to chew the fat with the boys—he once told me, "I'm not lucky, and with my heart and diabetes, I'm not going to get any more chances to get lucky." Even so, he couldn't resist whatever sweets there were in the room, and there was always something—cake, cookies, candy. Brian tried to keep an eye on the monsignor, to discourage him, but every time Brian stepped out, Monsignor would sneak a bite. "Is Brian coming?" he'd ask furtively, hiding what he hadn't swallowed.

Bellevue, August 1986

Through the summer, I'd drive in from Malverne every day with Bob Dalia. Steven was being given VIP status and allowed virtually unlimited visitation, but not many could understand what he was trying to say.

I had a small stool I'd stand on, next to the bed, so I could lean forward, my ear next to his lips, to pick up the words. Then I'd pass them along.

There was always someone who wanted to hear—his family, the press, the cops who guarded the doorway to his room and who were also stationed at the end of the hallway, and the dozens of friends and celebrities who wandered in and out—the governor's wife, Matilda Cuomo, or Mayor Koch, or police officials, or the Mets' pitcher, Ron Darling. Steven would always try to respond to their kindness. When Ron Darling offered, "I'll pray for you," Steven smiled.

"I'll pray for you," Steven whispered, "that the wind is blowing in on Monday."

Darling lost the game, and Steven seemed disappointed.

The visitors would ask how Steven was progressing, and I'd tell them the same thing. "You have to keep a positive attitude," I'd say, "no matter what. I really believe in miracles. Who's to say they're not happening all over the place, all the time.

"I'm not saying we never get down about this. Sometimes we get upset, and we cry. But we really believe."

I did. And I do.

As my pregnancy progressed, my stamina shrank. I wanted to be with Steven every night, to pray with him and for him at Mass, and after—just before I left—to pray again, saying seven Hail Marys, seven Our Fathers, and seven Glory Be's. But late nights were getting too difficult and I'd leave before he was ready to go to sleep. Afterwards, I'd call to say goodnight. We'd worked out a system to communicate, he spitting into a phone held by either a nurse or one of the cops watching him, and me interpreting. One spit meant "Yes"; two spits, "No."

The conversations were simple.

"How are you doing?" I'd say. "Are you okay?"

"Pssp."

"Who's there? Brian? The monsignor? The nurse?"

"Pssp. Pssp."

"Are you tired?"

"Pssp."

"Do you want me to hang up?"

"Pssp. Pssp."

Then I'd tell him I loved him, and sing. "You are my sunshine, my only sunshine." We'd say the Our Father a final time, and I'd hang up.

The family and I were following Shavod Jones's progress through the courts with only the most peripheral attention. On August 5, 1986, he was arraigned in Criminal Court, and pleaded not guilty. His lawyer, Peter Zeiler, told the judge that Jones was despondent and concerned for Steven. The papers said that although Jones would be tried as an adult, he couldn't receive an adult's sentence if he was convicted. Normally, attempted murder resulted in an eight-and-a-half to twenty-five-year prison term. But Jones could only get a maximum of three-and-a-half to ten years under New York state law because he was fifteen when the shooting occurred. And Steven, I was beginning to fear, had gotten a life sentence.

I concentrated on the baby. If it was a girl, we decided to name her Caitlin. If a boy, we'd call him Conor Patrick, after the hero in Leon Uris's novel *Trinity*. The name Conor confused a number of people, who assumed I'd named him after the Cardinal, who was now trying to see us at least once a week, and who was a tower of strength for me. Every time I saw him at the hospital, the first thing he'd ask me was, "How do you feel? How's the baby?"

I'd give Steven an update every day. "I heard his heartbeat for the first time," I'd say. Or, "I felt him kick today." I brought a cassette tape of the baby's heartbeat, and played it. I'd try to stretch over him to let his cheek feel the baby, but even when I stood on a stool and bent over him, I couldn't get my belly closer than six inches from his face. I wouldn't let Steven see my disappointment though. To do that would create one more reason for him to give up.

Bellevue's Seventh Floor, August 1986

I was a neurological patient for a couple of months, as the hospital continued to assess my injuries, fight my fevers, and maintain my bowels. It was, as one of my doctors said, "a rough course." I barely made it through a bout of sepsis, blood poisoning from bacteria created by the bullet wound in the neck. The bullet had penetrated my larynx, the back of my throat, and had caused an infection from contamination. That had been compounded by an abscess in my neck, and by pneumonia. And, of course, I was drugged.

The x-rays and CAT scan pictures showed that the .22-caliber bullet had shattered into three fragments that had lodged in the spinal canal around the spinal cord. Their placement was high on the spinal column, between the second and third vertebra—the bones in the back that protect the canal and cord from bruising —below the brain stem. The cord was partially severed. Below the C-2 vertebra, my nervous system was out of operation. I was a quadriplegic, with no control or feeling in my arms and legs. I could not breathe on my own, nor urinate, nor defecate. I couldn't feel hot, or cold. My autonomic nervous system, which normally controlled my blood pressure and my body temperature, had also been derailed. Later, I'd find out I'd be susceptible to light-headedness, and fainting, when I was elevated too quickly; I'd be vulnerable to hypothermia and hyperthermia, getting either too hot or too cold; and there'd be spasticity in my arms and legs, a reflex action generated by the healthy spinal cord, located below my injury, that was no longer regulated by the brain. In the first months, though, the family took everything as a positive sign. The bullet was still in there, they said, so maybe removing it would heal the spinal cord. The spasticity was movement, they argued, so eventually it could be controlled.

You have to have hope, they told me.

I'd been moved into a private room on the seventh floor, and Patti Ann and my family and hers were going to great pains to keep it homey and stimulating. There was one window, looking out towards the East River and the Waterside apartment houses along the shore. But the window was ten feet from the bed, and trying to look in that direction took all the strength I had. It seemed too far away to be worth the effort. Outside the room, in the hall, a name card was posted, listing my religion. Hebrew, it read. Mayor Koch laughed when I pointed it out to him. "I told them not to change it," I added. He grew teary-eyed.

The yellow door and the tan-and-white walls were obscured by hundreds of pictures, letters, drawings, get-well cards—one had even come from the drug dealers in Central Park. A giant teddy bear sat in one corner. Murals covered the walls not already decorated with photos. President Reagan wrote, as did Attorney General Edwin Meese. "Nancy and I were sorry to learn of the injuries you suffered in the line of duty," the president's letter said. "We understand that your Dad and one of your grandfathers were police officers, too. It's clear that you share their spirit and that you have what it takes to meet this challenge, and then some. Steve, I am sure that with your heritage, your proven determination, and with the good Lord's help, you will pull through.

"For now," the letter ended, "remember that many people love you and care about you. Please count us among them. May the love and concern of those around you be a source of strength, and may God bless and keep you and Patti Ann. I look forward to news of your progress."

Private duty nurses had been hired, and one—Nina Justiniano—and I would watch the soaps together, and films on the VCR. I'd go through phases—horror movies, *The Quiet Man,* cop films.

Mostly, though, I just wanted to close my eyes.

Looking back now, what I remember most vividly are the drugs—the morphine, the painkillers, the demerol. I was asking for them into October, seeking the oblivion that would deflect the reality of my injury. And they worked. When I consider my bowel program now—the one, or two, or three hours every other day that it takes for a nurse and me to coax out the . . . what? feces? shit? . . . is there any way to broach this politely enough to disguise how revolting this dependency can be?—I'm amazed that I don't even remember doing it those first months. Of course, I must have, along with the catheter and the IVs, and every other day a resident or a nurse rushing in because another vein collapsed, and they'd have to start a new IV, and give me more shots. At two in the morning, if I'd been lucky enough to fall asleep, I'd be woken for x-rays. Then I'd struggle back into oblivion, always on my back, always staring at the ceiling. I'd never slept on my back before I was shot, always on my stomach, or side. But from the night after I was shot, until the night after I arrived in Colorado nine months later, Bellevue never laid me in any other position.

The drugs shielded me from everything, even the people who were caring. I can't remember when Monsignor Kowsky first began saying Mass, or when Brian Mulheren first began regularly visiting. I didn't want to deal with it. My mind was undamaged, and that seemed to me to be the problem. Even when I didn't have pain, I'd say, "I need another shot."

I just didn't want to see the white walls and the fluorescent lights, and the nurses I didn't know. All of a sudden, Patti Ann wasn't a regular part of my life—she had to go home every afternoon, and again every night—and it was just me and the cops assigned to my room, most of them from Central Park, like Kevin Flanagan, who took my slot in anti-crime, and Dennis Breen, who became our fill-in van driver. Most of them guys I'd known for a year, maybe less.

"You were such a nice guy," Kevin would say. "You tried to make things better for every guy in the precinct."

It hurt when he said that. Because it reminded me how, finally, I'd had everything I wanted—a great job, steady hours and days. I hadn't been an English redcoat any more. I'd been part of a unit giving everything it had, to set ourselves up to be ripped off or hit upon by potential perps.

By the early fall, I'd begun to recognize Monsignor Kowsky, Brian Mulheren, and the others, to sort out who was who in the constant ebb and flow of visitors to the small room. Patti Ann, my nurse Nina, and my mother were pressing me to stop relying on the drugs. They urged me to help them resurrect me.

One afternoon, a lawyer named Peter Johnson, another friend of Brian's who'd been visiting off and on through the summer, took it upon himself to try and talk me out of my despair. I didn't really know Johnson; like other visitors, he'd come into the room, say a few words, maybe stay for Mass, and leave. Since I couldn't respond, except with a whisper or two, there wasn't much give and take. A visitor could swiftly grow uncomfortable, and feel he or she was an imposition. Soon after, they'd bid a slightly embarrassed good-bye, and leave. Peter, like so many of the others, was a familiar face. Nothing more.

Physically, Peter Johnson seemed about my age, with a friendly smile and eyes that missed nothing. His dark hair was mussed, and though he had a baby face, he wore the formal black-and-blue suits of a much older man. Later, Brian told me his father was a famous Wall Street lawyer, his brother Chris a highly decorated detective, and that Peter himself was Mario Cuomo's lawyer. Before practicing law, Brian said, Peter had worked in television, and as a speechwriter and press aide for the governor. In 1984, when Cuomo captivated the country with his keynote address at the Democratic convention, he'd been reading some of Peter Johnson's lines. Or so I was told. Not so, Peter told me, when I asked. At least, that's what Peter says.

"I heard you were down," Peter said, speaking sympathetically. "I heard you wanted to give up. You really don't know me, but we have something in common. When I was eighteen, I had cancer. Hodgkin's disease. The people around me thought I was going to die. I knew better.

"You've come through the hardest part," Peter continued. "You understand that even when it looks the most hopeless, it's not."

I tried to nod that, yes, I understood, but I wasn't sure I did. Did we have more in common than I thought?

"I'll pray for you," I mouthed, as he left.

Finally, it clicked.

I knew I wasn't going to die. I'd gotten to the point where I could tell myself, "Jeez, this is the way it is for now. I can't kid myself. It's not going to go away."

I began to handle the isolation, and the separation from Patti Ann, better. I missed her and the life I'd had before, but I had to try to cope. And it was so hard. I could tell myself to adjust to and accept these circumstances, but every night I was still left alone with a nurse I'd only known a short time, and the cops who were my friends, but not people I knew well. Everybody that I loved—Patti, my parents, brothers, sisters, aunts, uncles and cousins—were miles away. I couldn't talk, or move. The food was terrible, and I was frightened to eat it. I couldn't feel it go down my throat, and never knew if I was choking or not.

It was your basic worst-case scenario.

Bellevue, September 1986

No one who stood by Steven in those early days had to be there.

Brian's duty had been completed, essentially, after the first week-and-a-half, once it had been established that Steven's injuries were in the line-of-duty and that the medical costs would be paid through the Patrolmen's Benevolent Association's workers' compensation. Monsignor Kowsky didn't have to offer to say Mass every day; to have said he'd be there on Sundays would have been sufficient. The cops guarding Steven's door—Dennis Breen, Steve Fuchs, Dave Martelli, Brian DeLaurentis and the others could have been out collaring people, but they chose to be at Bellevue.

The hospital, meanwhile, was giving Steven almost all the medication he asked for. Steven was straight his whole life. I didn't want him to become an addict now. One early fall day, I don't remember exactly when, I found him wiped out, semiconscious.

"What did you give him?" I demanded.

"It's not so high a dosage," said the doctor.

"Well, why is he so out of it?" I said. "It's five o'clock in the afternoon and he's zonked out. He's been sleeping the whole day."

I began sobbing, and Steven's mother joined me.

When he finally awoke, and was alert enough to recognize us, we confronted him.

"What do you want to do?" I said, my voice rising. "Are you going to lay here in a daze forever? Is this what you want to do? Never mind walking out of here paralyzed. Do you want to walk out of here being a drug addict, too? Do we have to do that, too?

"Steven," I said, softly, "I love you. You've got to stop, for me and for the baby."

Behind me, his mother wept. Steven said he'd try.

Seven

Bellevue's Seventh Floor, September 1986

Brian Mulheren was looking for a white knight, a doctor who could step in and turn my case around.

Mulheren was tired of threatening the Bellevue staff that he'd have their sheepskins shredded if they didn't pay closer attention to me. But, once I'd been stabilized, Bellevue's expertise no longer applied. At least, not on the neurosurgical floor, where I lay. So Brian searched for a physician who could plot the next step in my care. And in September, he found the white knight he'd been seeking. Dr. Gregory Fried began taking an interest in my case.

Greg Fried had just been promoted to deputy chief surgeon in the Police Department, freeing him from the office duties he'd had as a district surgeon. The district surgeons—there are twenty-eight of them, assigned to sixteen zip code-defined districts—are responsible for confirming that cops who are on sick leave, or assigned to desk jobs because of injuries, are in fact still sick or injured. It's a part-time job, two-and-a-half hours of office work a week, plus another two-and-a-half that might include hospital visits. Most of the doctors who accepted the appointment were part-timers, too. The money—$50,000 a year—was good, and the demands minimal. I'd never even met my district surgeon.

Greg Fried was unique. Like Monsignor Kowsky, like Brian, he was on call all the time because he wanted to be not because he had to be. If a cop was shot, he'd go to the hospital. If a cop or a member of a cop's family needed advice or a consultation, Dr. Fried would be available. As a district surgeon, though, he'd had no jurisdiction over me. As deputy chief, he could do pretty much anything he wanted. Brian encouraged him to want me.

Dr. Fried was intense. He was short, slight, with a shock of black hair and enough energy for both of us. When he first looked at me, he must have winced.

"Your medical condition was lousy," he'd say later. "You were staring at the ceiling, unable to communicate. You had round the clock nursing, but you might as well have been on a funeral bier, covered by a shroud. You looked like Sleeping Beauty, or Snow White, lying still in the forest, surrounded by the Seven Dwarfs."

There's no comprehensive plan for me, Dr. Fried told Brian. There's a doctor for his arm, a doctor for his bladder, a doctor for his eye, Dr. Fried continued. Steven's mute, and he's overdriven. A normal human being breathes twelve to fifteen times a minute, each time inhaling between six hundred and seven hundred cubic centimeters of air, Dr. Fried explained. My respirator was programmed for twenty-two breaths a minute, each one calibrated for fifteen hundred centimeters of air.

I was a prep, Dr. Fried concluded. A neurological thing that no one had bothered to bring back to physiology. A lump. A warehoused lump.

I was still on my back, Dr. Fried observed, after two months. "Any patient who's long-term becomes uninteresting to the staff," Dr. Fried told me. "They don't visit as much. They want acute-care cases where they can resuscitate someone, fix them up. Long-term, you become a habit, a chair in the building."

There'd been no rehabilitation for me, he saw. I hadn't even sat up in a wheelchair. I was too dependent on the respirator. The Foley catheter, to remove my urine, had been implanted and never taken out. Complications were developing, and soon I would have contracted urinary sepsis, which would have destroyed my kidneys. My hands had curled up, and my toes pointed down.

Whatever depression I felt, Dr. Fried told Brian, would be resolved soon enough in these circumstances. In three more months, he said, I could be dead.

Bellevue's Sixth Floor, September 1986

Dr. Joseph Ransohoff, Bellevue's chief of neurosurgery, wasn't happy. He wanted Steven out of Bellevue, and transferred to Goldwater Memorial. No way, I said.

Goldwater's patients had respiratory problems, and some were on ventilators, I knew, but their breathing troubles came from illnesses, like polio, not spinal cord injuries. I hadn't seen Goldwater, but others had. It was a depressing place, they said. Steven wouldn't get the rehabilitation he needed. He'd be no better off than he was at Bellevue.

"Young lady," Dr. Ransohoff growled, "you don't understand. This is the best alternative. The sooner he gets into a situation with a wheelchair, with other ventilator-dependent patients, the better off he'll be." Bellevue had spinal cord patients in rehab, we both knew, but none on ventilators.

"I'm pregnant," I reminded him. "As I understand it, Steven can be here for as long as he wants. We want to stay here until the baby is born, and then we'll make a move."

A few days later, Steven was transferred to the sixth floor, where the Barnard Baruch Center for Rehabilitation was based. His room was good-sized, normally holding three beds, and we moved all the memorabilia—the jerseys, the baseball gloves, the footballs, the family pictures and get-well cards—into it. The nurses began to make sure Steven dressed each day, and sat up in a wheelchair. Nina would take food Steven's mother brought from home—chicken, ham, mashed potatoes—grind them up, and pump them into his feeding tube. He was off the drugs, and we fought to keep his spirits up.

Parents magazine gave me a maternity leave. But I was barely aware of my pregnancy, driving out to Mercy Hospital in Rockville Centre for regular checkups, but otherwise focused on Steven. If he hadn't been hurt, I'm sure I would have behaved like any other first-time pregnant wife, asking for breakfast in bed, massages, whatever. But every emotion, every need I had was directed towards Steven. One of the three doctors I was seeing—Tormey, or Devrhes, or Glynn—would say I looked fine. Then I'd head back to Manhattan.

In September I moved into a two-bedroom apartment eight or nine blocks from Bellevue. I was close enough to go see Steven in the morning, when he woke, and return in the afternoon, for Mass. No matter how comfortable Stuyvesant Town was, though, I could never relax. One afternoon I'd come to the apartment for lunch, with my youngest sister, Katie. I wanted to call Steven's room—why, I don't remember—and before the phone rang by his bed, a nurse picked it up. She sounded hysterical; all I could make out was, "Stat, stat, he's not breathing properly." By the time I rushed back, the situation was under control. A new nurse had pushed the wrong button on the respirator. The incident gave me severe fright and I always feared a recurrence.

Most days, I'd spend five or six hours at Steven's bedside, talking to him, greeting visitors, answering the phone. Then, after Mass, we'd eat. Not Steven, though. He couldn't feel the food in his esophagus and was frightened of choking. Nor could he tell when he was full, or satiated. It took months to get him to chew food, and he never ate what Bellevue had to offer. Instead, we'd buy hamburgers from Melon's, or steaks from the Water Cafe or Irish stew from the Green Derby Restaurant, and milkshakes from McDonald's.

By the time I'd get home, it'd be ten or eleven at

night and I'd been noshing all day—on the sweets in the room, the cases of soda I'd bring in for the cops, the cakes and cookies the Malverne Bakery would send. I gained twenty pounds; so did everyone else.

Please let this baby be nine pounds, I'd think at bedtime, looking in the mirror. Or twelve.

There's a phrase the police department uses, "to reach out," which means to get in touch, to contact, no matter where the individual is. Brian Mulheren's reach was as long as any I could imagine—from restaurateurs to politicians to priests to the press—but on September 24, 1986, it astonished me.

At 7:30 in the morning, as the sun filtered through the partially closed blinds in Steven's room, I picked up the receiver to the telephone. Next to the bed, a black speaker box sat on a table. Around Steven stood his brother Owen, and his mother and father.

"Hello, Patti," an unmistakable voice said, filling the space with its western, fatherly twang.

"Hello, Mr. President," I responded, looking at Steven. His eyes were bright, and he was smiling. From hundreds of miles away, aboard *Air Force One,* President Ronald Reagan continued.

"Patti," the president said, "I just wanted to tell you both how much his heroism impressed not only New Yorkers, but the entire country. His heroism in the line of duty is to be commended. I know the saying, 'I love New York,' but I know New Yorkers love Steven McDonald and you can add forty-nine other states to your list of supporters."

"Thank you, Mr. President," I said. I tried to imagine him, sitting in his jet, high above us. He seemed a faraway image, one I couldn't focus on. I pressed the receiver closer to my ear, as if I could eliminate the static, the echo, the distance. A tear came to Steven's eye.

"Patti," the president continued, "I know you are expecting your first child soon, and when that child is a little older, and can understand, he'll be proud of his father's heroism to protect the people of New York. Nancy and I send our best wishes.

"Patti, our thoughts and prayers for Steven's speedy recovery, and I think from all over the country, are with you. God bless you both."

I felt overwhelmed. Steven's mother and father were wiping tears away. I also felt tongue-tied.

"Thank you, Mr. President," I managed, "for taking the time to call."

Then he was gone.

Once Steven began eating, we focused on weaning him from the respirator. The respirator he was on was supplemented by an oxygen feed programmed to give him more oxygen-laden air than he'd breathe on his own. The hospital's plan was to reprogram the feed, gradually bringing the oxygen level to that in the room, at the same time reducing the number of breaths per minute. At that point, they figured, Steven would have the trache tube pulled out, and would use his neck muscles to swallow and hold air, which would be identical to what he'd been getting on the machine. The reduced oxygen left him depressed, though, and sapped his strength.

We didn't know it in the fall, but it seemed the oxygen had become another drug, a substitute high for the morphine and Valium. There was an "assist" button on the respirator, and when no nurse was around, Steven would have one of the cops watching him press it, giving him a pure hit. Like the drugs, it was more of the anything-Steven-wants-Steven-gets syndrome.

"No, Steve, we'll get in trouble," Dennis Breen would tell him. And after they'd been caught a couple of times, another officer, Dave Martelli would worry, "They're gonna take my shield away."

The guys were smart enough to realize they weren't helping. Steven would even ask them to press on his chest, imagining that would aid his lungs to take in more than the machine was giving him. So when Steven would ask them to press the button, they'd fake it. It was all psychological.

"Yeah, thanks," Steven would whisper. "That felt good."

Another aspect of Steven's physiology, of any quadriplegic's physiology, hadn't been explained properly to us. His blood pressure. Any spinal cord injury makes one susceptible to postural hypotension, particularly if the injury's as high on the spine as Steven's is. Postural hypotension is a condition that results in a decrease in blood pressure when you sit or stand. When that happens, you get light-headed, and may faint. The nervous system, I learned, no longer automatically pumps the blood to the head and brain. Instead, it pools in the pelvic area. When you've been on your back for a long time, as Steven had been, sitting up will be an invitation to blacking out.

We were taught that lesson in late October, the day the Mets held their World Series victory parade. The

Boy Scouts, like a lot of other organizations, wanted to give Steven an award. They'd originally scheduled the day earlier in the year, but we'd had to cancel. Now we were on again—Steven's first meeting with the press since he'd been shot, the first time he'd leave the room.

We'd tried to give the media as positive a picture of Steven's hospital stay, and recovery, as we could. We owed that, I felt, to the New Yorkers who'd written us, given donations to the Steven McDonald Fund, and shared their support and their prayers. Steven was being portrayed as a hero, and that was giving all of us strength. Having him face-to-face with the reporters, even just to accept a plaque, would be another step forward.

It didn't work that way.

I was just outside, in the hall, with Mike Koleniak, an ex-cop who'd just started reporting for the New York *Post.* This was his first assignment—he'd been offered a choice of the Mets parade or the award, and he'd picked Steven—and he'd gotten to the hospital early. How's Steven doing? he'd asked me, and I was bringing him up to date.

Steven was inside, with his nurse, Nina Justiniano, and his father. As they sat him in the chair, he fainted. Steven's father rushed out and ran down the hallway, yelling, "Get a doctor! Where's a doctor!" I couldn't figure out what had happened.

"Don't go in there," Mr. McDonald yelled back at me, as I started towards the door.

I ignored him and walked in.

"Steven, stop it! Stop it!" I said. "Steven, what's wrong?"

Steven was unconscious. His lips were blue. He looked like he was suffocating. Outside, Steven's father had triggered a wave of shouting and screaming. Other reporters left the sixth floor lounge, where the cameras, lights and microphones had been arranged and the presentation was to happen, curious about the commotion. As they did, a handful of doctors rushed into the room.

"It's all right," one of them assured me. "A sudden change in blood pressure. We'll recline him. He'll be fine."

Mike Koleniak tried to comfort me, asking if there was anything he could do. It isn't always like this, I told him. But Steven never made it to the press conference. Instead, I accepted the award.

At the conference, a reporter asked me what had happened.

"What happened?" I said. "Well, we have our good days, and our bad days, and this was one of the bad ones. You've got to accept it. Steven can't be here today, but that doesn't mean he won't be here some time in the future."

And the press did accept it. Steven's good days would come later.

Bellevue's Sixth Floor, November 1986

There were so many things I was frightened by.

The vent, with its unrelenting *whoosh, whoop.* The paralysis. The lack of feeling except for the ever-present pins and needles sensation. The dependency.

But changing the cuff trache was the worst.

After a while, its balloon would start to leak and I'd lose the air it was pumping into me.

"Okay, Steven," a nurse would say, "it's time to change the cuff."

"No," I'd spit in the code Patti and I were using on the phone. *"Pssp, pssp. Pssp, pssp."*

"Yes," they'd insist, and soon the ear, nose and throat residents, just out of medical school, would arrive in their white coats and operating room greens.

I still had some feeling in my neck, and no one was going to risk giving me anaesthesia. The yanking was the most painful experience I've undergone, and their jamming a new tube back in wasn't much better. They thought the entire procedure had to happen quickly, in a matter of seconds, before the tracheostomy closed down.

A frightening, violent minute would pass. My eyes wide, unblinking, in horror; pain on the faces of the doctors and nurses as they rushed to complete the change; blood flying up from my neck.

Afterward, one of the nurses, Nina or Jeannette Francis, would try to calm me. Monsignor Kowsky would tell a joke. His young assistant, Robert Tucker would touch my arm reassuringly.

I appreciated their efforts. But there seemed no end to the pain and discomfort. It was maddening, trying to understand what a future of not being able to go to the bathroom, to shave, to cut fingernails, to brush teeth, held. My face broke out in pimples, and Nina and Jeannette stopped letting visitors touch my face. The itching was intolerable. When they left, I'd get someone to scratch. And, at night, McElroy James, a male nurse, would massage my temple and cheeks. I'd let him go forever. It was so good to feel something like I used to feel.

The weaning was bad, too. A resident would reprogram the vent, and I'd strain for air myself, my eyes like saucers. Choking, panicking, I could never get enough. I was strangling. Maybe a hypnotist would help, Dr. Fried suggested. "We need you to breathe for twenty minutes," he'd say, "in case the respirator fails." So a psychologist, Dr. DeBetts, spent hours trying to put me in a trance, playing tapes of the ocean washing against the shoreline, of surf lapping gently on the sand.

It didn't work. Okay, come on, relax, I'd tell myself. I couldn't. I might as well have told myself not to think of a big white bear.

November 9, 1986, our first wedding anniversary, and my feelings of loss were as strong as ever—of not being able to hold Patti Ann, to kiss and caress our baby when it came, to walk outside and feel the sun on my face and the wind in my hair. The anniversary Mass was painful.

Monsignor Kowsky couldn't make it. Once a week, he'd counsel officers and their families in the suburbs, and this may have been one of those days. Instead, Father Mychal Judge would say our anniversary Mass.

Father Mike, as I'd call him, was a Franciscan. He had a craggy, handsomely worn face, a mop of silver hair, and a street-smart perspective on the world. He lived in the order's Manhattan residence, a rough corner on the West Side, on 31st Street, where the priests operated a daily soup line and distributed free clothing. The Fire Department chaplain, Father Julian Deacon, also lived there and in early September had asked Father Mike to substitute for the monsignor one evening. When Father Mike read the gospel, I was astonished. The inflections in his voice made it come alive. It was as dramatic and moving as any I'd ever heard. I'd never felt that close to our God.

At the end of that first visit, Father Mike gave me a prayer that helped me begin to understand my feelings towards Shavod Jones. "Lord," Father Mike prayed, "make me an instrument of your peace. Where there is hatred, let me sow love. Where there is injury, pardon. Where there is doubt, faith. Where there is despair, hope. Where there is darkness, light. Where there is sadness, joy."

What is that? I'd mouthed.

"The prayer of Saint Francis," he said.

On his second visit, when I'd sunk into one of my deepest depressions, he'd talked about his own emotional struggles with the bottle. There was a statue of the Blessed Mother, Mary, in front of the church on 31st Street, he said, a statue he prayed to every day. He knew Patti Ann prayed to the Blessed Mother, too, he said. "I'll pray for you, every time I pray to her," he told me. "I'll pray to her as a mother, and the care she had for children."

So I was pleased that Father Mike would be saying the Mass. Maybe there'd be less pain. Father Mike was caught by surprise, however. Somehow, neither the monsignor nor Father Julian had told him the significance of the date. He improvised, speaking about the sanctity of marriage, the happiness a child brings, but when he gave the eight blessings, everybody began crying. "I started praying to myself," he said later, " 'Oh Lord, this isn't supposed to be teary. Please help me, Lord.' "

He noticed the sports memorabilia, especially the Notre Dame University pennant, and was inspired. Divinely, I guess.

"When Irish eyes are smiling," he started to sing, "the whole world smiles with you . . ."

Everybody began to laugh.

"When Irish eyes are smiling . . ." he continued.

"Thank you, God," Father Mike said to himself. "You're a great God. I'll never sin again."

Later that night, the Cardinal visited to give us his blessing. And afterwards, Patti Ann sat with me. "It's going to be okay," she told me. "The next anniversary, we'll be at home. We're lucky to be together, to have something to celebrate."

The pep talk worked. I can't give up, I thought. I can't throw in the towel, and say this is the way I'm going to be forever. Because I can't be this way forever.

Eight

Bellevue's Sixth Floor, Christmas 1986

Thanksgiving I'd spent in the Bellevue cafeteria, my first trip off the sixth floor. Two other cops with spinal cord injuries joined us, and three of the officers Bronx gunman Larry Davis was accused of shooting. There wasn't a lot of laughter. "What do I want for Christmas?" Mary Buckley responded to the Macy's Department Store Santa. "Five front teeth." She'd taken a bullet in the mouth.

And now it was Christmas. The memories of my family gathered in Rockville Centre haunted me—my mother's turkey, the white onions, the stuffing she made from scratch based on a recipe her grandmother brought from Ireland. Here I was in a hospital, one I hadn't left since the summer.

Patti Ann and Brian thought I could get to Midnight Mass at St. Patrick's, and I liked the idea. But the arrangements terrified me. The medical emergency rescue van was going to take me there. The emergency services unit's cops, the department's crisis specialists, were going to escort me. But the emergency medical technicians responsible for me seemed overwhelmed by the journey's complications. If all this is involved in getting me to church, I wondered, how can I ever have a life?

In fact, I almost lost it two days earlier. Greg Fried, on a routine but unplanned visit to the sixth floor just before he left town for the holiday, found me sitting in a wheelchair in the hallway by myself. "You were blue-black," he told me later, "the color of a dark blue suit. About to have a cardiac arrest."

Dr. Fried grabbed an ambu-bag, a respirator you squeeze with your hands, and pumped oxygen into my lungs. He then ordered blood tests, the results of which indicated to him that in weaning me from the respirator by reducing the volume of air I'd get each minute, the carbon dioxide in my blood had been raised to dangerously high levels.

"You would have died in a couple of hours," Dr. Fried said.

Not surprisingly, the doctors were reluctant to allow me to leave the hospital two nights later. The weather was foul, too, on Christmas Eve—gusting rain, and a chill that was driving the homeless off the streets. My Uncle Frank and Aunt Jackie, my mother and father and Patti Ann's—sixteen from our families in all—were planning to join the Cardinal on the altar. I ached to go, just to feel a part of life outside. But I could see, as afternoon extended into evening, everyone was growing hesitant. Around dinnertime, Brian called Dr. Fried at Kutsher's, the Catskills resort where he was spending the holiday.

"I don't think he should go," Dr. Fried advised. "Wait until next year."

Patti Ann and Brian came to tell me, but I wasn't shocked, just disappointed. Patti Ann was upset, though, that we'd been left hanging until the last minute. While Patti Ann tried to reach Monsignor Kowsky to ask him if he'd say Mass in the room, Brian sent the rest of the family to the cathedral. At midnight, we turned the television on.

Under St. Patrick's soaring neo-Gothic columns, the Cardinal spoke about us.

"My top religious news story of 1986," he said, "is in Bellevue Hospital this very moment, Police Officer Steven McDonald has been lying in a hospital bed now, for more than five months, with his bride of thirteen months constantly at his side, always encouraging him, always praying with him.

"What makes this news? Many police officers have been shot. It's almost as if all of the world's suffering can be summed up and placed in that hospital bed with Steven McDonald. Not for one single instant has their simple childlike faith faltered. Time after time, their doctors have told them that humanly, there is no hope; medically, there can be no progress. Time after time, Steven and Patti Ann have insisted that a miracle will take place. To me, this is the miracle. This is the meaning of Christmas. That's faith. That's a simple faith. That's a childlike faith.

"Theologians, medical doctors, scientists, historians, scripture scholars may all know better, but Steven and Patti Ann will live every day in hope. They will accept what they see as the permissive will of God, when so many understandably would be shaking their fist at God, threatening God, hating God. They have accepted what God has permitted to happen, with no bitterness, no rancor towards the assailant, no resentment, no cries of revenge. Now how can you do that without faith? It's as remarkable as any faith I have ever seen."

The room was quiet, except for the flickering television. Monsignor Kowsky, his field Mass kit open on the table next to the bed, listened intently. Patti's hands were clasped together. Behind the TV, against the wall, a Christmas card the size of a stop sign rested. A few weeks earlier, Dick Fay and Arthur Crames, partners at the Bear, Stearns brokerage house, had dropped by, as they often did. Fay tried to cheer me out of a depression by betting, in my name, every horse in every race one afternoon at an off-track betting shop. The losses were his, Fay said, and the winnings mine. When he figured out the payoff would be $306, Crames said he'd double it.

"See, Steven," said Fay, "we beat the system." He asked me what we should do with the money.

"Give it to the homeless," I'd mouthed to Patti.

The money had been sent to Father Mike, at the St. Francis of Assisi Friary. He'd bought underwear, socks, gloves and hats—clothing that's never donated, he'd said. "We clothed fifty men with the OTB bets," Father Mike told us. And, a few hours earlier, he'd carried the huge Christmas greeting into the room.

"Merry Christmas," it read. "Thanks from all the homeless at St. Francis. We love you."

On the screen over my head, Cardinal O'Connor brought his midnight homily to a close.

"That faith," the Cardinal said, his voice echoing slightly off the cathedral pillars, "radiated from them as the glory of the angels that radiated on that first Christmas morning."

Patti's praying for a miracle, I knew. But maybe the miracle, I thought, is that we've tapped into the love and faith of so many others.

On television, the choir began singing. The numbness was everywhere, as it had been. As, I still feared, it would be.

Bellevue to Mercy Hospital, January 1987

As my delivery date approached, the nurses told me to stop coming to see Steven. The baby was due the twenty-first. Too much stress, Nina Justiniano said, too exhausting. Save your strength for the delivery.

It'd be hard for Steven, but he'd gotten a boost the week earlier, a jolt of encouragement from an actress he'd always idolized. The phone had rung late Thursday afternoon, and a Spanish-sounding woman had said she was Maureen O'Hara's secretary. Right, I thought. That *The Quiet Man* was his favorite film had been in all the papers; this is a hoax, I was convinced. In August, a messenger had brought an autographed picture from Miss O'Hara, but we'd heard nothing since. I was guarded.

"Miss O'Hara would like to come up and visit Mr. McDonald," she said, asking what floor he was on, and how to get to the room.

On Sunday, the day she was to come, I went to the hallway, and asked one of the cops to watch the lobby. "Make sure no one comes up," I said, "who's not supposed to. If it's Maureen O'Hara, make sure it's Maureen O'Hara."

A few minutes later, she walked in the room.

Entered the room, I should say. A presence, wrapped in mink, her hair a glowing red, a fabulous gold pendant like a miniature sun around her neck. Steven's jaw dropped, in awe. He was tongue-tied in disbelief.

A Pan Am flight attendant had told her about us, she said in a lilting brogue. Then she began to tell about her life, her struggle with cancer, the need to keep fighting. She stayed for Mass, and after, for still another showing of *The Quiet Man.* On the screen, she slapped John Wayne. On Steven's bed, she laughed, "I hit him so hard," she said, "my arm hurt for a week."

The Cardinal arrived, the mayor called. "One of these days," the Cardinal said to her, as Steven watched with the biggest smile I'd seen in months, "you should be grand marshal of the St. Patrick's Day parade."

"It's my lifelong dream," she assured the Cardinal. "And I want to do it with Steve. He deserves the honor."

When she left that evening, she assured us she'd be back. And she has been, many, many times. Her friendship has been a gift we treasure.

On January 21, I went to Mercy to see Dr. James Tormey, the ob-gyn Chief at the hospital. I wasn't dilated. "Come back next week," he said. "We'll start stress tests then."

"What do you mean, stress tests?" I asked, all of a sudden nervous. There's nothing to be worried about, he assured me.

The stress test—and the suggestion that something else in my life could go wrong—was like a December plunge in the Atlantic. I'd been so wrapped up in Steven, I'd forgotten how important the baby was. I was carrying a part of Steven, a part of us, and I'd pushed that reality aside. Now it hit me: in a very short time, I'd be a mother.

Within a day or two, I was convinced I'd have the baby on the twenty-ninth. I was staying at my mother's and told her my conviction. Sure enough, the contractions began that morning—far apart, but I could feel them—and I knew I was in labor. I wasn't in a good mood though; I was lonely and feeling sorry for myself. My unhappiness spilled over the night of the twenty-eighth, when I began arguing with my mother over what I should take with me to the hospital. Soon it escalated, me telling her she'd never understood what I was going through.

I was miserable when I went to bed that night. I missed seeing Steven. But there was too much risk I'd get stuck in the city, and have the baby in Bellevue. Many of our friends, and some of the cops, thought that would be best for Steven. What about me? I'd argued. I loved Steven too. This child is being born for both of us, I'd said, why should I take unnecessary chances by not having my own doctor around?

The weather was lousy—it had been all week—and I called Joanie Muldoon, my Lamaze partner. She said she'd meet me at Mercy. Remember the breathing stages, I told myself, remember when to push. Then I called Steven.

"I'm in labor, darling," I said. "I'm going to the hospital and I'm going to have our baby." I tried not to let my fear and my sadness—that he couldn't be there with me—come through in my voice.

The drive took ten minutes, and we pulled into the parking lot at 7:00 A.M. I wondered if Dr. William Devhres would be working that morning. I hoped so.

He'd been the first to examine me, before Steven was hurt. And I'd always felt close to him.

"No problem," my mother was saying. "Don't worry about it. It's going to be okay. I'll be with you." Yeah, I thought, that's easy for you to say. You've gone through this six times. I was in pain, and still upset about our argument the night before.

Joanie Muldoon was waiting. Low-key, laid back, an old family friend and neighbor, Joanie was the perfect partner, if I couldn't have Steven. I got into a hospital gown, was examined and admitted. I still wasn't very dilated and could have gone home for a while. But Joanie and my mother were there, and Brian had been told too. It made sense to stay put.

To my relief, Dr. Devhres came on duty. "I'm so glad it's you," I said. He smiled.

Throughout the morning and early afternoon, a fetal monitor recorded the baby's heartbeat. By 3:00 P.M., I was fully dilated—ten centimeters. The contractions were sharp and painful, and I groaned and sweated with every one. "She's ready," I heard the doctor say. Then, a few minutes later, someone said, "We're losing the heartbeat . . ."

I couldn't believe it. Fetal distress. How, after all I'd gone through, could *this* be happening? The monitor picked up the beat again, then lost it a second time.

Dr. Devhres, Joanie and the nurses moved more quickly now. An oxygen mask was slapped on my face. Stat calls filled the room. Outside, on the slick ice of the parking lot, a pediatrician fell and nearly got knocked out rushing in to help. A nurse put a mask over my face. "Dear God," I prayed, "let everything be okay. It's in your hands." No panic. Just a calmness. Another nurse picked up a syringe, and I felt a prick on my arm. The anaesthesia started to take effect. Then I was out.

Two hours later, I woke in the recovery room. Now I was anxious. Was my child all right? How serious had the complications been?

"Do I have a baby?" I asked Dr. Devhres.

"You have a baby boy," he answered. Is he telling me the truth? I wondered for an instant. Or trying to spare me still more pain? No, looking at his face, I was certain my baby, my boy was well. We were a family now. Conor Patrick. Thank God.

I began crying for joy, the first happy tears I'd shed in half a year. "I want to see my mother," I sobbed. If I couldn't have Steven there, I wanted to share this moment with someone—with her. In a few seconds, she was by my side.

"I'm so sorry," I wept, "about how I acted towards you last night. I love you."

She smiled at me and I knew all was forgiven. We hugged.

Conor's umbilical cord had wrapped around his arm and neck, they told me. Not life-threatening, but there was no way to know that until they opened me up. Joanie had kept her cool and hadn't run into the waiting room to tell everyone about the cesarean. I was so grateful for her sensitivity and support—and I knew exactly why I'd wanted her there at my side at my baby's birth.

The sea of well-wishers and media had followed me to Mercy, Dr. Devhres said. There was a score of reporters just outside the door. Unbelievable. This most private moment of my life was turning into a public spectacle. Later, I'd learn that at least one radio station was giving its listeners periodic updates all morning. I still had not adjusted to the fact that I was a public figure, and people I didn't know were interested in those details.

Did I want to meet the press? asked the doctor.

No, I said, I was exhausted and I hurt. "I'm not seeing anybody."

"Okay," he said, unconcerned. "I just had to tell you. My job was to give you the message. I'm not recommending you speak to anybody."

I was taken to a private room and my wheelchair passed the nursery. Inside, I could see the beautiful face of our baby, wrapped in blankets, innocent. A wave of sorrow swept through me. Steven, why couldn't you be here?

Visitors began to fill the room, Malverne friends for whom Mercy was the local hospital. New Yorkers and others were being stopped at the front door and told I wasn't seeing anyone; the locals knew you could sneak into the maternity ward through the emergency room. My brother Billy found the nursery, and—with a camera loaned him by a New York *Post* photographer—snapped away. One of his shots ran on the front page the next day.

From all my friends, I was hearing the same message: what a beautiful baby, they said, he looks just like Steven.

By the tenth visit, the novelty of that news had worn off, and in fact I'd gotten a bit irritated by it. When Father Leavey, my parish priest, walked in, I sensed from his exuberant manner that he was about to say pretty much the same thing.

"Don't say it, Father," I told him. "I don't want to hear it."

"What?" he responded, astonished. "What?"

"I don't want to hear one more time how much he looks like Steven. You simply can't believe what I've just been through, how much I ache right now. Doesn't he have my anything? Ears? Eyes? Fingers? Anything?"

But it was true. When the nurse brought Conor in for his first feeding, I examined every inch of him. He looked like a little leprechaun. Just like Steven. A miracle.

Bellevue's Sixth Floor, January 1987

When Patti Ann's due date arrived and she stopped visiting, the isolation we'd suffered at the beginning of our marriage returned. It had been bad not to be able to touch, to feel the baby inside. Now I didn't even have her.

Before I was hurt, I'd imagined I'd be the kind of expectant father Robin Williams was in that scene from *The World According to Garp,* where he traces a smiling face on his pregnant wife's belly, recalling the warm sanctuary of the womb. But I couldn't touch Patti's stomach, caress her belly, feel the baby. We were supposed to have had shared moments: the two of us, lying side by side in the middle of the night, she waking and nudging me, saying the baby had kicked, and taking my hand and gently resting it where the tiny foot had thrust. The best I could manage was my cheek against her dress, as she strained to lean across the side rail of my bed.

And there was no privacy. Even if Patti and I were

in the room alone, nurses and cops hovered on the other side of the door. The coming birth, and the media attention, only made it worse.

Patti Ann called the morning of January 29, then left for the hospital. My emotions were so mixed. Let the baby be fine, I thought. Then, am I the father a child should have? What can I give a baby? How can I be a companion, an influence?

I wanted to be at Mercy Hospital. The Cardinal was going. Patti's brothers and sisters would be there. Our friends. Not me. My connection would be via a video fax machine, hooked to a camera outside the delivery room. I'd be watching tiny black-and-white stills on a nine-inch monitor. This wasn't right.

At 3:56 P.M., the call came from the hospital. A few minutes later, the fuzzy pictures. I could barely make them out. A son. Who did he look like? Me? Patti Ann? It didn't matter. Thank God, he was healthy. But there was a problem, I was told. Patti had had a cesarean. She'd be in the hospital for a week, anyway. The baby would stay with her.

Another roller coaster. I couldn't hide my disappointment—a week seemed to me like forever.

"How's Steven doing?" a reporter asked my father.

"He's savoring the delights of fatherhood," Dad said. "His eyes were about the size of twenty-dollar gold pieces and about the same brightness."

In truth, though, I was filled with uncertainty.

And the press had another piece of news. Five hours before Conor came into the world, Shavod Jones, whose trial had ended in early December, two weeks after it had begun, was sentenced. For shooting me, he got three-and-a-half-to-ten years. For the bike theft he'd pleaded guilty to before he shot me, another three-and-a-half-to-ten sentence.

When Judge Preminger had asked Shavod Jones if he'd had anything to say, Jones said, "I'm not the person they say I am. They don't know who I am. Nobody really knows me."

Seven hours after Conor Patrick's birth, Dr. Fried hustled into the room, a videotape in hand.

"Got a present for you, kid," he said. "Nice baby. You do good work."

When Fried realized the fax monitor wasn't showing much, he'd called Patti Ann and asked her if he could bring his video camera to Mercy. Fine, she'd told him. For forty minutes, he'd stood in the nursery, capturing Conor's first gurgles and cries. Now I was seeing them.

"What do you think?" Dr. Fried asked.

"Overcome," I mouthed.

By the next day, the press had descended. The attention was exhausting—reporters, video technicians, photographers all trying to gauge my reactions to the tape. They asked, How was Patti Ann? Where did the name Conor come from? Wasn't the baby beautiful? The questions came too fast, and there were too many people. I was still trying to sort out my feelings about being a father. I wasn't there to give information. I was just trying to deal with what was going on. Collecting facts wasn't part of what it was all about.

"Son A Joy To Behold," headlined the article in the *Daily News,* but all I'd seen was a videotape. I wanted some peace and quiet. And I wanted to see my son. Not just his pictures.

A week passed, and I still hadn't seen Conor. Patti

Ann called daily, but she was hurting from the operation. She also reminded me that the church discouraged mothers from taking children out of the home before baptism. Then, on Saturday morning, the nurses wouldn't let me go back to sleep—the way I usually did—after they woke me first thing in the morning. Instead, they lifted me out of bed and put me in a wheelchair facing the window, my back to the door. They moved away, and all I could see was the window, the apartment buildings shrouded in the gray dawn, and the river beyond.

I must have dozed, because the next thing I knew, something was tickling my ear. I turned as quickly and as far as my neck muscles would let me. Our baby. Conor. I was stunned. His eyes closed, wrapped in swaddling, hands in tight fists, legs jerking . . . it was as if I could move my own arms and legs again. He looked just like me. He was me. A blessing. Patti Ann kept him close to my face, smiling at my wonder.

"Steven, I'm so happy to be with you," Patti told me, as I stared. "Being away was too hard. Everything's okay now, I'm going to be here always. You've got this beautiful baby, this baby we prayed for. We can thank God for this." She'd talked to the Cardinal, she said, and he'd encouraged her to bring Conor in.

She kissed me, and I kissed her. "Wow," I mouthed. Conor kicked and gurgled.

What's next? I wondered. All our plans had been geared to the baby. My waiting was over. Bellevue had been a safe cocoon, but I wasn't getting any better. And that gave me as much fear as Conor offered hope. I had lived long enough to know Conor. Would I live long enough for Conor to know me?

WITNESS:

Bob Dalia

When I first drove Patti Ann, I'd been a cop since the summer of 1968 and with Highway for five years. It was Sunday, the day after Steven had been shot, and I was out on patrol. They'd sent another car to pick her and her sister up at the Nassau County line, but that guy had responded to an accident call on the way. When the radio said someone else would have to get her, I responded.

At Bellevue, a Sergeant Johnson from employee relations was trying to coordinate the arrangements for Patti Ann. He knew me, and asked if I could stick around, and drive her home. No problem, I said. I got back to my own house at ten that night, and began the first of what would be nine months of sixteen-hour days. By the time Steven went to Craig, we'd put twenty-two thousand miles on the department's car.

Normally, the department would assign a driver from Steven's precinct. That was Sergeant Johnson's plan. But when he told Patti Ann, she said she didn't know any of the guys from Central Park. "Can the Highway guy drive me?" she asked. Johnson took it to me. Here's the deal, he said. There'll be no overtime, but we'll give you time back for the extra hours you put in. Okay, I said. To be honest, I figured the job would last a week. No one expected Steven to live. No one.

At Bellevue, I'd wait in the family room, telling stories, trying to keep people's spirits up, making coffee and food runs. It was tough on my wife, Mary, because it was seven days a week. But she never complained. It's part of your job, she told me when I tried to apologize for the hours, it's what a cop is supposed to do.

The worst time I had was when we brought the baby to Bellevue—the first time he would see his son in the flesh. Patti and I had become friends, and the night before she delivered Conor, I'd taken her to the doctor's. "Take her shopping," Dr. Martin told me. "Walk her around." So we drove to Roosevelt Field, and spent three hours wandering through the mall. She didn't buy much, as I remember, but by the time we got home to her mother's, it was 9:30 P.M. and she'd gone into labor. Two weeks later, I was taking her and Conor to see Steven. Patti's doctor told her not to do any lifting, and as we walked down the hallway towards Steven's room, I was carrying the baby. I can't walk into his room with his son in my arms, I thought. I just didn't want him to see that I could hold his kid, when he couldn't. "Patti," I said, "take him. No matter what the doctor said. This isn't right." And I handed Conor to her.

I tried to keep Patti cool, when I drove her. I told her everything I knew about union benefits—which was a lot, after nearly twenty years on the job—and how to collect them. I'd try to keep a conversation, a dialogue going, to take her mind off what was going on in that hospital room.

When Steven returned from Craig, I drove the van. Going to the Father of the Year awards, in the summer of 1988, was a highlight. He was as hyped up as I'd seen him, excited to be meeting Judge Sessions, the head of the FBI, Kris Kristofferson and Willie Randolph. And when Kristofferson invited them to the Bottom Line the next night, he got even higher. Coming out of the nightclub, though, the chair broke. The chair was always breaking down. Most quads use their chairs for six or eight hours a day. Steven uses his for twelve. So it gets twice as much wear and tear. This night, it wouldn't recline. And when the back won't go down, you can't get him into the van. He can sit up straight once he's inside, but the rear door's too low to go in with the chair back vertical.

That night, I had to use our radio to call for an emergency services unit to come and fix it. Which six of them did, after spending an hour taking the mechanism apart and putting it back together.

I got more tense a month or two later, when we were driving home on the Cross Island Parkway, and Steven says from the back, "Bob, we got a problem." It wouldn't recline again, and I thought, how are we going to get *out* of the van. Steven was nervous, too. Again, I picked up the radio. I said "1085—meet me at intersection of the Cross Island and Southern State parkways." A Highway car responded, and they followed us all the way to Malverne. Fortunately, they're big guys, weightlifters, and we heaved Steven and the chair—four hundred, five hundred pounds—up on an angle, and carried him out the side door and down our portable ramp. That was as hairy a move as we ever made. But Highway's been good to Steven. Like the rest of the department, they've been there whenever they're needed.

Nine

Bellevue's Sixth Floor, February 1987

As the weather turned more foul in New York City, fewer visitors would come. Patti brought the baby only once, laying him next to my left side. One test the Bellevue doctors had run showed some crude sensation there, but even when Conor lay on my leg, I wasn't certain I could feel him.

I wanted to find improvement, but it was hard. Conor's birth had been one more sign that life was moving on, but I wasn't progressing at all. The therapists would move my arms and legs each day, keeping the joints flexible, but I didn't get anything back. My mother would spread holy water on my body, and pray. There were days, though, when I'd ask Dennis Breen to pull the blanket up over my face, and leave it there. In that darkness, I could escape.

It's that nobody has had much experience with a patient like you, Greg Fried would try to explain. He told me of a meeting he'd had with a Chinese doctor, one familiar with the treatment of spinal cord injuries in that country. Through a translator, Dr. Fried had asked how many high quadriplegics—those with injuries to the spine as high up as mine—China was treating.

"None," the doctor told him.

None! A country with nearly a billion people, and not one high quad had survived. That's why no one gives you much hope, Dr. Fried would say, but there's nothing to lose. He was going to push me.

On the sixth floor, maybe thirty feet from my door, was the gymnasium, a long room overlooking Manhattan's East Side as it extended uptown. On mats and benches, other patients would work on rehabilitation exercises—paraplegics lifting weights, quads who had use of their necks and shoulders. I didn't like to visit the gym; everybody there, it seemed, had more to work with than I did. But Dr. Fried insisted. One afternoon, he placed my chair in front of a full-length mirror. My room had no mirrors, and for six months I had not looked at myself. The papers had run pictures, and my family or the cops would show them to me, but I had not seen my own reflection since I'd been shot.

"Take a look at your head," he said. "You can hold it up now. Six months ago, you couldn't."

I stared. Watching me was a young man in a sweat suit, his brown hair falling in bangs over his forehead. The young man in the mirror, his face straining with effort, nodded slightly. Dr. Fried was right. Sitting in a chair with my head erect, I'd gotten a piece of myself back. Not a lot, but it was a start.

On February 3, 1987, St. Blaise's Day in the church's calendar of the saints, Monsignor Kowsky touched the throats of Dr. Fried, Brian and myself with holy candles, blessing them. Saint Blaise had been beheaded in 1317, and among the miracles attributed to him was one where he'd cured a boy choking on a fishbone; now he's venerated as patron saint of throat diseases. The monsignor finished and put away the chalice and host.

"Steven," said Dr. Fried, "Monsignor just blessed your throat. Will you trust me to let down the balloon on your cuff?"

Oh no, I thought. I'll suffocate. The balloon in the trache kept the air in my lungs long enough for the oxygen to get into the bloodstream. The only time it had been deflated was to change it—and I wasn't ready to volunteer for the pain of pulling it out and replacing it.

"I'll show you that you can talk," Dr. Fried said. "Trust me, I'm not going to let you die."

Talk? I was willing to try almost anything to talk again, to find my own voice and be understood. Even some of my closest friends had feared I'd suffered brain damage, because I'd been able to say so little, and had so many times just given up trying.

Dr. Fried turned up the respirator to give me more air. With one hand, he gently held the valve on my trache tube, a plastic cylinder halfway between the respirator and the opening in my throat. With the other hand, he pressed a button on the valve. There was a slight hiss of pressure being released; inside my larynx, the balloon that had been pressing against my vocal cords sagged and flattened. For the first time in seven months, air could pass over the cords. The entire procedure had taken seconds and had been painless.

"Now talk," he said.

"Hello," I offered. My voice sounded mechanical, like a robot's. It could be heard though. The two or three seconds Dr. Fried spent deflating the balloon had given a gift I hadn't had during the past six months: the ability to communicate.

"How do you feel?" the monsignor asked. He'd known me since July; we'd never conversed.

"I'm okay," I said. Brian picked up the phone, dialed Patti's number, and held the receiver to my mouth.

"Hi, Patti," I said, in this foggy croak. "I love you."

"Steven?" she said. "Steven? Is that really you?"

An hour later, Cardinal O'Connor came by. Dr. Fried stepped into the corridor. "Your Eminence," the doctor said, "we've got a surprise for you." He gestured towards the door. The Cardinal walked in, looking around hesitantly.

"Hello, Cardinal," I said.

Tears came to his eyes. Like the monsignor, Brian, and Dr. Fried, he'd never heard my voice.

"It's a miracle," Cardinal O'Connor said.

Malverne, February–March 1987

When Steven called, I couldn't believe it! The voice was strained and deep, nothing like it used to be, when he'd call me at work with the greeting, "Yo, what's up?"

Even after I realized it was Steven, my joy was mixed with worry. He'd made progress, after we'd prayed so long for something. The doctors had never suggested he'd get that far, and now he was talking to me. How much more could we hope for? I didn't want to get overconfident, because each step forward reminded me how far there was to go, and whatever happiness I could feel was tinged with that nostalgia, that regret.

I'd been reluctant to ask the Cardinal to christen Conor, because I didn't want him to feel I was imposing. Through the pregnancy, I'd gone to the 10:15 A.M. Mass at St. Patrick's, which he always celebrated, and joined him for coffee after, at the residence. He'd take me aside and ask me how I was doing. I'd tell him about my faith, my marriage, and he'd sort out my confusion with me. We were close, but I worried he'd think I was asking because he was the Cardinal, and not simply the priest I now knew so well.

"You really should ask," Steven told me. "You should find out if he wants to do it."

Finally, I asked.

"I've been waiting," the Cardinal said with a smile. "I was afraid you weren't going to ask me."

"I didn't know," I said.

"What?" he responded. "Are you kidding? It's an honor."

"No," I said, "it's an honor for us."

Bellevue, March 1, 1987

Shavod Jones and why he would shoot me had never been entirely out of my mind as I lay on Six South, looking at the ceiling. I was puzzled, but I found I

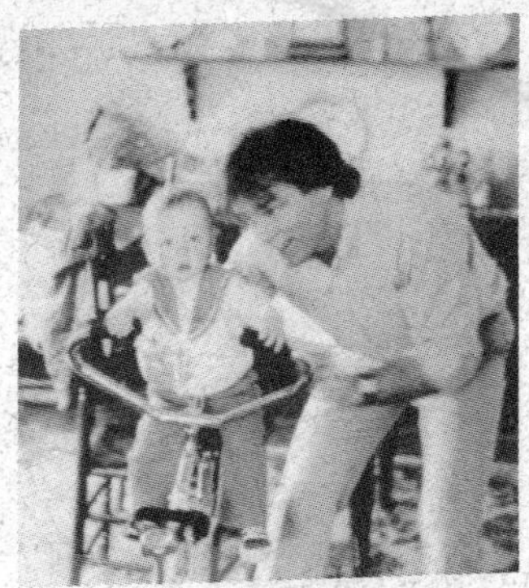

In happier times: Steven, with a nephew, had always wanted to be a father. "Six children," he once told a reporter.

Wedding Day, 1985: the bride cuts the cake.

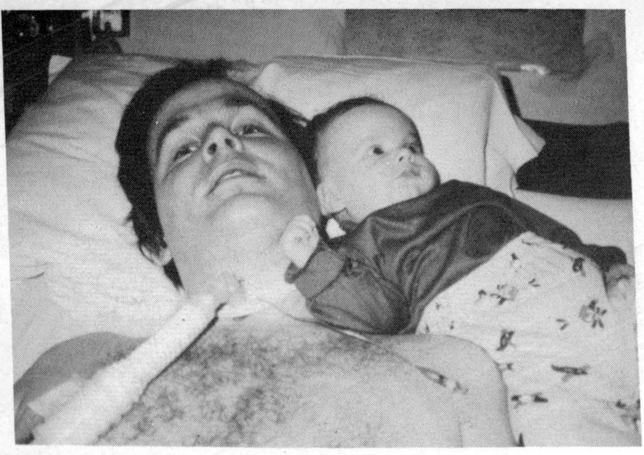

Steven at Bellevue Hospital: Patti would lay Conor next to him, so Steven could smell and feel—with his face—his newborn son.

Conor's baptism: Steven's brother Thomas stands between the proud parents, the Cardinal says the Mass, and Maureen O'Hara fights tears.

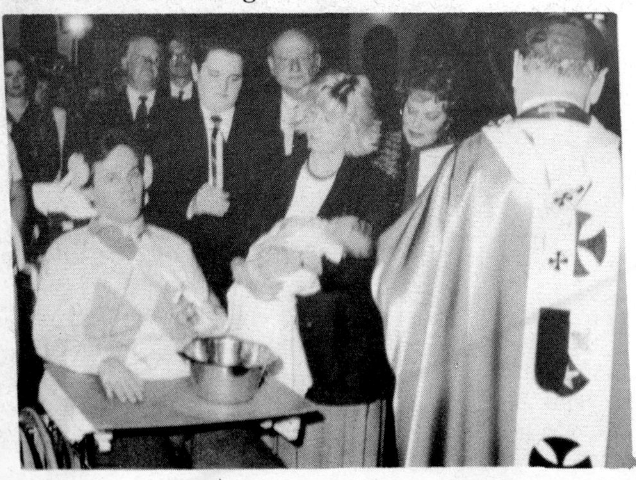

Leaving Bellevue: the three cops who'd be Steven's van drivers when he returned—(from left) Dave Martelli, Steven Fuchs, and Bob Dalia—arrive to help Steven pack up for the trip from New York to Colorado.

(*Photo credit: Michael Schwartz,* New York Post)

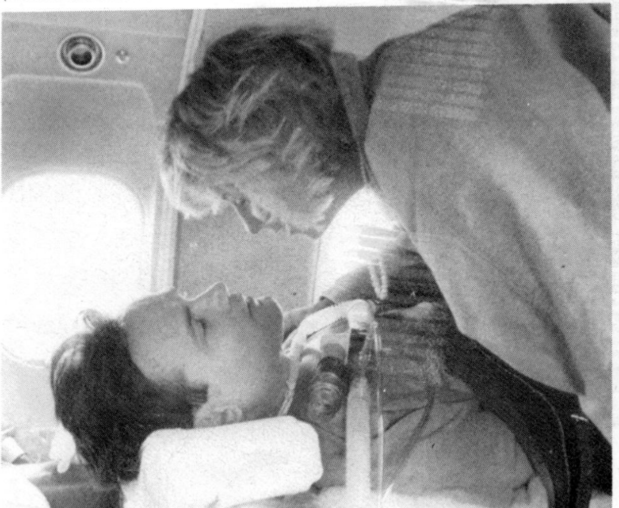

Leaving for Craig Hospital: in the New York police helicopter, Patti Ann offers words of encouragement to Steven as they begin what one newspaper called the "Journey of Hope."

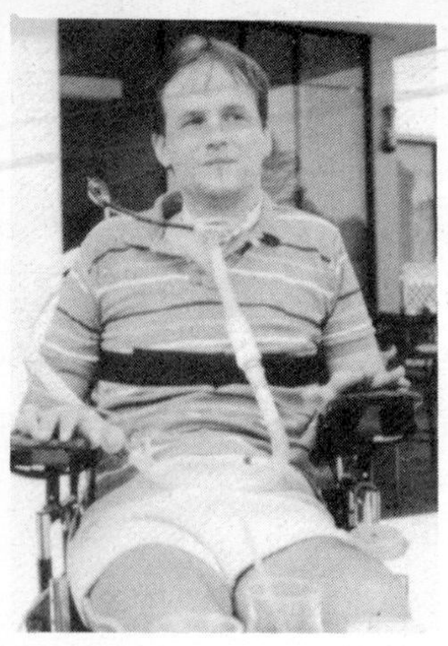

At Craig Hospital, where Steven was able to go outdoors for the first time in nine months.

At Craig Hospital, in Englewood, Colorado. Patti Ann scratches Steven's brow, while physical therapist Sharon Blackburn looks on.

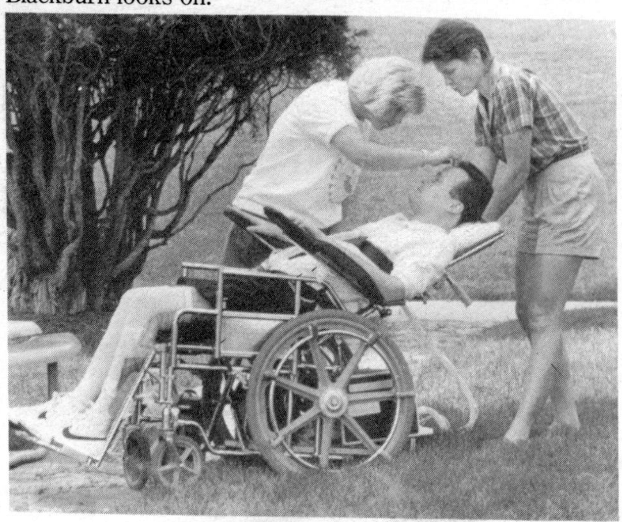

(*Photo credit: David Handshuh,* New York Post)

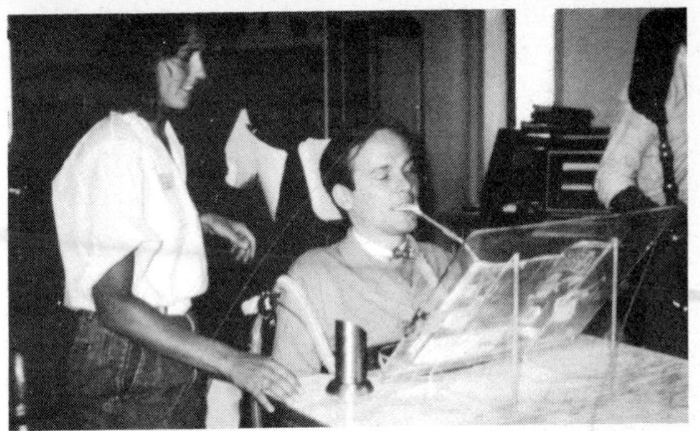

At Craig, with occupational therapist Gail Gelinsky, reading *Sports Illustrated,* using a mouthstick to turn pages.

At Craig, where Steven stood in a specially designed stall and realized his full 6′2″ height for the first time since he'd been shot.

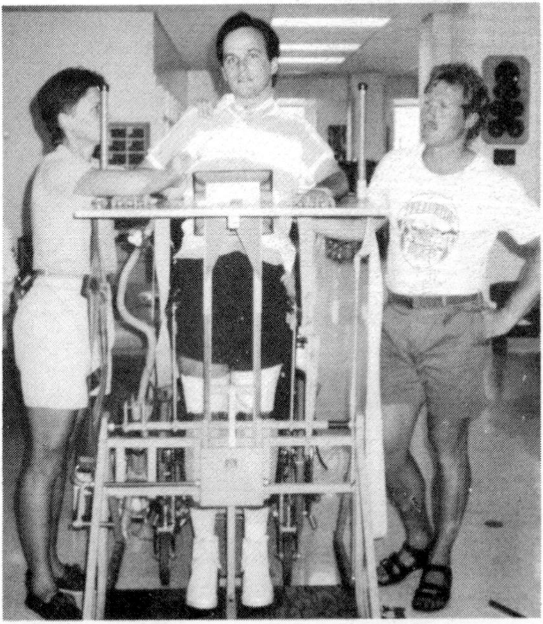

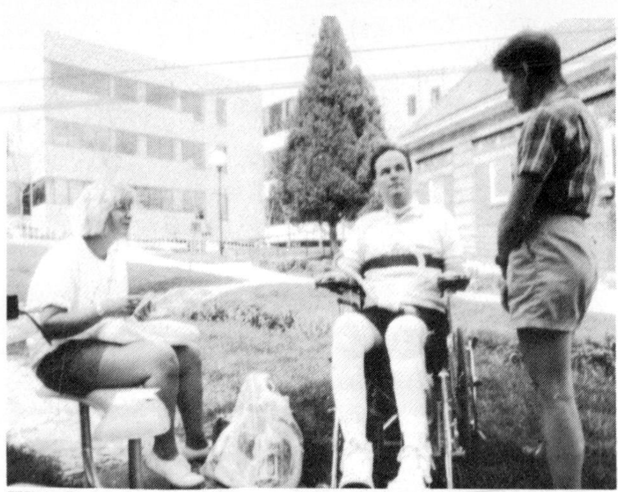

With Patti Ann and Sharon Blackburn at Craig Hospital: Steven wanted to feel the sun on his face. "Steven," Sharon would remind him, "we've got to do some work!"

The McDonald Christmas card, 1987, photographed at Craig Hospital. Steven has had his trache tube removed for the picture, and is struggling for those few moments to breathe on his own.

Steven in Colorado with New York cops Dave Martelli and Steve Fuchs, and friends.

At the Notre Dame–Air Force game, with cheerleaders and, behind Steven, Steve Karafiol (left) and Bob Arnzen, the project supervisors in the reconstruction of the Malverne home.

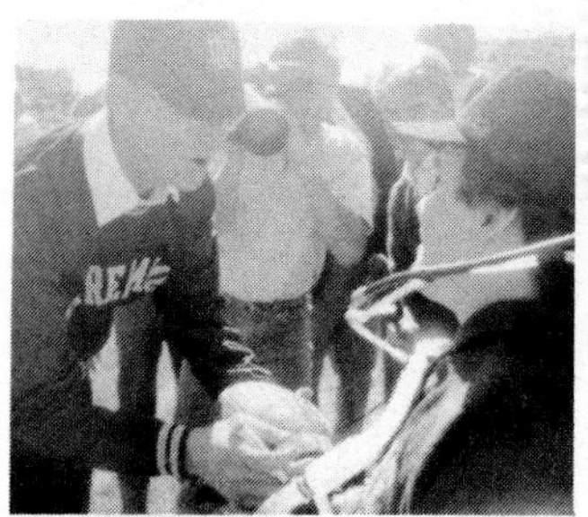

Steven meets Notre Dame football coach Lou Holtz at the 1987 Notre Dame–Air Force Academy game, and later Holtz gives him the game ball.

In Colorado, with Denver's Archbishop.

A banner hung at the Javits Center benefit for Steven in May 1987, which raised tens of thousands of dollars.

November 1987 homecoming: the Emerald Society pipers march ahead of Steven's van as it makes its way down Michel Court.

November 1987: Steven comes home from Colorado to a new house, and a crowd of well-wishers.

Steven with the cops who brought him from the 1987 Midnight Mass to the Cardinal's residence. Included are officers from Emergency Services, Neighborhood Stabilization, and the Midtown North precinct.

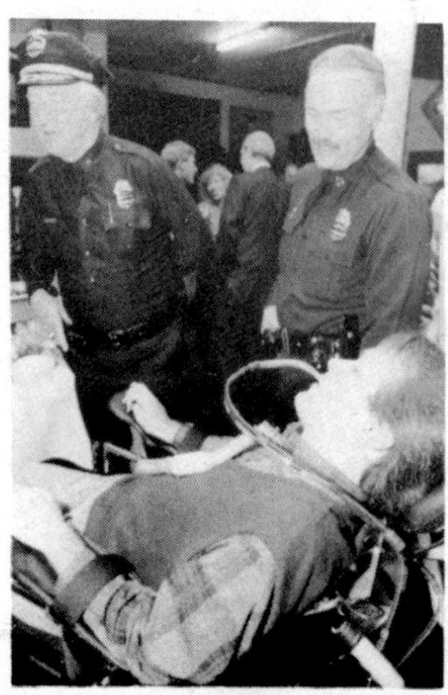

November 1987 homecoming: at the Malverne firehouse, Steven celebrated with the workers who'd remade his house, and the officers who'd stood beside him through fifteen long months.

With Barbara Walters, in December 1987, after the taping of "20/20" in their home in Malverne.

At Cardinal O'Connor's residence, following the 1987 Midnight Mass at St. Patrick's Cathedral.

With mayor Koch at New York City's Inner Circle benefit, 1988.

Steven and Patti Ann in front of the Malverne home, receiving the Nassau County Man of the Year award.

(*Photo credit: Miller photography*)

Field Day at St. Mary's Hospital of Long Island, where Steven has been a regular visitor.

Steven with children living at St. Mary's Hospital, including (at right) Bobby Mohammed.

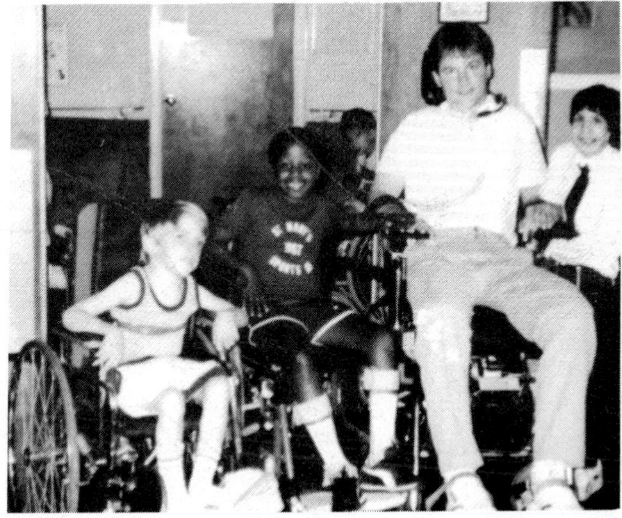

Patti Ann's bedroom in a peasant home in Medjugorje, Yugoslavia, on her October 1988 pilgrimage.

(Photo credit: Arturo Mari)

Patti Ann and Father Mychal Judge at the Vatican, meeting Pope John Paul II. Patti is showing the Pope a photo of the family and Steven's wedding ring, and asking for his blessing.

(*Photo credit: Joan Vitale Strong*)

Steven and son Conor with New York mayor Ed Koch and John Cardinal O'Connor at Gracie Mansion, the mayor's residence, for Conor's first birthday.

Conor and Steven, happy at home in Malverne.

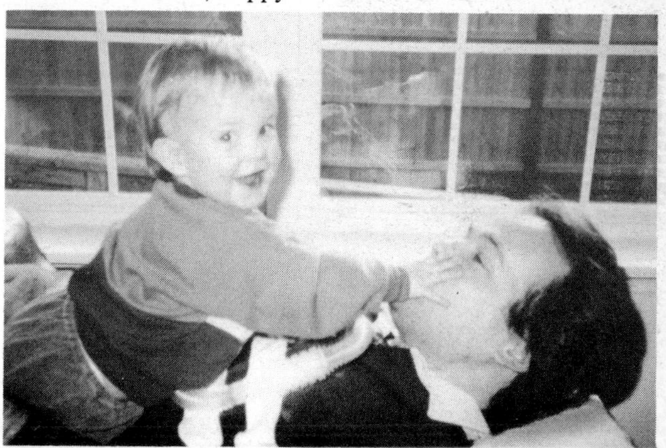

Steven, Patti Ann and Conor at home, summer 1988.

couldn't hate him, only the circumstances that had brought him to Central Park that afternoon, a handgun tucked into his pants.

I was a badge to that kid, a uniform representing the government. I was the system that let landlords charge rent for squalid apartments in broken-down tenements; I was the city agency that fixed up poor neighborhoods and drove the residents out, through gentrification, regardless of whether they were law-abiding solid citizens, or pushers and criminals; I was the Irish cop who showed up at a domestic dispute and left without doing anything, because no law had been broken.

To Shavod Jones, I was the scapegoat, the enemy. He didn't see me as a person, as a man with loved ones, as a husband and father-to-be. He'd bought into the cop myths of his community: the police are racist, they'll turn violent, so arm yourself against them. No, I couldn't blame Jones. Society—his family, the social agencies responsible for him, the people who'd made it impossible for his parents to be together—had failed way before Shavod Jones met Steven McDonald in Central Park. That's who I blamed.

On the night before the baptism, Peter Johnson, the trial lawyer and former aide to Governor Cuomo, came to my room. For two months, Peter had been discussing the possibility of a public statement. I'd agreed to it, and until the weather Christmas Eve kept me at Bellevue, we'd expected to release one at the Midnight Mass, with Patti Ann delivering it from the altar. Peter and I had more or less agreed to a message of thanks, acknowledging the prayers, letters and expressions of love Patti and I had received from all over the country. Conor's birth, and the promise of our new family, made me want to go further. Early on, Peter and I had discussed saying something positive about Shavod Jones to the media.

Now I wanted to help him turn his life around. I wanted to meet Shavod Jones, face to face. I wanted him to know me, and I wanted to know him.

Peter understood.

"I want to forgive him," I mouthed.

"Yes," Peter nodded. "That would be good. And inspirational. This city could use it."

I didn't know about that. I only knew it came from my heart.

The next morning, Peter read me a draft. Those were my sentiments, I nodded. Yes.

Brian had the rough copy typed, and fifteen minutes before we left the room for the chapel downstairs, we gave it to Patti Ann, for even though I could now talk, I could only carry on limited, quiet conversations and would not be able to project to a crowd.

Malverne to Bellevue, March 1, 1987

I woke early, dressed the baby in his white baptismal gown, packed Steven's clothes and left for Bellevue. I wanted Steven to look good; many people, including much of the press, would be seeing him out of bed and sitting in a chair for the first time. It was also his thirtieth birthday.

The Chapel of Our Lady Helper of the Sick was jammed with family and reporters, and we made space for Steven at the foot of the small altar. The mayor and Maureen O'Hara joined us as witnesses, fourteen other priests crowded on the altar, and the Cardinal led us slowly through the ritual, stopping to explain to the media the significance of it all. I couldn't believe the love and support in this church. Steven's brother Thomas and my sister Julie, the godparents, stood behind me as the Cardinal gently poured water from a golden cup over Conor's head, the brightness of the mini-cams' lights reflected in His Eminence's crimson satin robe. Steven and I, the Cardinal told the audience, "will be the first teachers of their child in matters of faith.

"I baptize you in the name of the Father, the Son, and the Holy Ghost," said the Cardinal. Conor cried, and Steven smiled. I took Steven's hand, and with it, traced the Cross on the baby's forehead. Our son had beome a sharer in Christ's life. As the fellow cops and family members came forward to take Communion from the Cardinal, they paused to kiss Steven's forehead, or touch his cheek.

Next to the Catholic chapel was the Protestant one, a larger space where Brian arranged for Steven's statement to be read to the press. While most of our guests went upstairs to the cafeteria where we were hosting a reception, Steven and I joined the media in the adjoining room. There were some good friends among them—Mike Santangelo, Mike Koleniak, Rich Lamb, Tim Schell, John Roland—but the number of press people surprised me. There were dozens, from every paper, radio and TV station across the country.

I unfolded the sheets of paper Brian and Peter had given me and glanced at Steven. Under his hand, the baptismal program rested on a plywood table. He looked uncomfortable. The dry air in the chapels clogged his trache with mucus, and he was having trouble getting air. Sitting was tiring, too; he'd never been in a chair this long.

Focus on the words, I thought, before you begin to cry.

"The past eight months have not been easy for Steven and me," I read. "There have been many dark and difficult days when we believed that the cloud that had fallen over us would never lift."

Don't look out at that sea of cameras, I told myself. Look at Dad, at Steven. Concentrate and you'll get through this. Just like everything else.

"But there have also been many sunny and happy days," I continued, "in which Steven and I have been warmed not only by the love we have for each other but by the kindness and affection of thousands of New Yorkers, of every race and religion who have shared their prayers and support."

The chapel was silent, but for the clicking of cameras, the whirr of tape recorders, and the *whoop-whoosh* of Steven's respirator.

"On this happiest day of our life together," I read, my voice beginning to crack with emotion, "Steven has asked me to let you know what he is thinking. So I read this letter from Steven to the people of New York City.

"I became a police officer to help the people of New York in any small way I could. My father and my grandfather before me had the same dream. When I was growing up I was so proud of them. When I first wore the badge of a police officer I was so proud too, and hoped that I would be able to live up to its tradition of courage and compassion. I hope that I have. There is no group of men and women who care about this city as much as the men and women of the New York City Police Department."

Again, I looked towards Steven. He managed a small smile. Next to him, the Cardinal nodded his encouragement.

"I never imagined that anything I ever did," I read, "or anything that was ever done to me would attract so much attention. But something did happen. And there is attention.

"On some days when I am not feeling very well, I can get angry. But I have realized that anger is a wasted emotion, that I have to remember why I became a police officer. I'm sometimes angry at the teenage boy who shot me. But more often I feel sorry for him. I only hope that he can turn his life to helping and not hurting people. I forgive him and hope that he can find peace and purpose in his life."

Yes, that's Steven, I thought. With compassion like a Christ. Tears welled in my eyes, which I kept down on the three wrinkled sheets of paper. I didn't want to look at my husband, to be reminded again of what he'd lost, of what we all had lost.

"I have always had the love of my mom and dad, brothers and sisters, Patti Ann and now our son Conor Patrick," I continued, fighting sobs. "I never thought there could be anyone else in my life. The last months have proven me wrong. But let me tell you, there is more love in this city than there are street corners. Our lives have been touched by new friends, some we have met and some we will never know, who have brought us hope in times of despair, and joy out of tears. Each of my days is brightened by the cards, letters and visits from our new family."

Next to Steven, I could see Milton Petrie, the "Blue

Angel" who'd given hundreds of thousands of dollars to police widows and who, after Conor's birth, had created a trust fund so our son wouldn't have to worry whether he could afford to go to college. And Brian Mulheren. The Cardinal. Chief of department Bob Johnston. Cops. Family. They, too, were fighting tears.

"I thank the people of New York," I read, "for making me a part of their family, and for helping me more than I ever could have helped them, as much as I tried. Mayor Koch and Cardinal O'Connor have cheered and inspired me when I least expected it. And every day, Monsignor John Kowsky has prayed with me, and for me, and next to me. And the doctors, nurses and staff of Bellevue Hospital have been dedicated and tireless in their care beyond description. And, finally, there's a movie by Woody Allen, called *The Purple Rose of Cairo.* In the movie, the characters walk off a theatre's movie screen into the real life of a woman in the audience. I know the feeling."

My face was wet with tears, my emotions torn by the beauty of Steven's thoughts and the horror of his injury. I could barely see the final lines.

"One of my favorite movies is *The Quiet Man,* starring John Wayne and Maureen O'Hara," I concluded. "I have watched the movie many times over and over, and know many of its lines. So when Maureen O'Hara appeared in my room one day it was like a dream—as if she had jumped from the television set. She has become a good friend, and we are so happy that she is here to witness the christening of our baby boy.

"In closing, I thank you again. But I ask you to remember this. I chose the life of a police officer with all its risks. I believe that I am the luckiest man on the face of this earth. I only ask you to remember the less lucky, the less fortunate than I am who struggle for the dignity of life, without the attention and without the helping hands that have given me this life."

The less fortunate. The sound of Steven's respirator, like a metronome, filled the church. *Whoop-whoosh.*

"God bless you all," I wept. I turned and fell into the arms of Cardinal O'Connor.

There was silence as a room full of reporters dabbed the moistness from their eyes.

Bellevue, March 1, 1987

No one—not myself, not Brian, not Peter Johnson, certainly not Patti Ann—imagined the impact the statement would have. As Patti Ann embraced Cardinal O'Connor, I expected questions from the reporters. Nothing. The mayor was crying, the press was crying. Nobody could talk. Brian whispered to the Cardinal, "Somebody's got to do something," he said. "You've got to be up there and say something." But before the Cardinal could speak, the reporters began to applaud. "A radiant moment," Brian would say later, and the mayor would marvel at Patti Ann's presence. I was so proud of her.

Upstairs in the cafeteria, several hundred friends and relatives waited for us. As I came into the room, they crowded around me, congratulating me and asking Patti Ann how I could be so forgiving, why didn't I want Shavod Jones in jail for twenty-five years. "That's just how Steven is," Patti Ann told them.

I'd never been the center of attention for that many people at once, but I began to sense that my words had touched people deeply, unexpectedly and profoundly.

By the evening news, that impression was confirmed. The baptism, and Patti Ann's delivery of my speech, led most local newscasts. In the papers the next day, the story was page one, and even the New York *Times*—which rarely paid the attention to police officers that the other dailies did—ran a picture of Patti Ann, Conor, the Cardinal and myself.

In my hospital room the next morning, the media began calling, asking if I'd elaborate on my remarks. I refused. I hadn't agreed to the speech to become a media personality. I had said what I had to say and it was self-explanatory. "Fallen Hero Pens City A Moving Love Letter," one columnist wrote, and the *Times* editorialized, "If Officer McDonald had taken this opportunity to express anger, it would have been understandable—but not nearly as meaningful as words he actually voiced, again through his wife . . . Clearly, Officer McDonald has found peace and purpose in his own [life]."

My purpose in life was what it had been for the previous two years: to be a cop. I'd arrived in Bellevue a cop and I'd leave as one. My mind was undamaged and I had the compassion I'd always felt towards people who had to struggle to live. To some, that made me a hero. To me, I was just doing my duty.

Two weeks later, I lay in my bed, the television tuned to the St. Patrick's Day parade. In 1985, I'd marched in the parade for the first time, a member of the Emerald Society. Like my grandfather and father,

I'd walked up Fifth Avenue, snapping a salute to the review stand and trying to catch a glimpse of whatever celebrity was serving as grand marshal. This St. Patrick's Day was dedicated to the department's Medal of Honor winners and had a union chief as its grand marshal, but I thought it belonged to Maureen O'Hara. An interviewer from one of the TV stations put a microphone in her face as she walked by with the mayor and the police commissioner. "So many afternoons I sat over there in the stands," she said into the camera. "But today my name is Steve McDonald. Please, God, next year he'll be marching for himself."

"We're going to be thinking about him all through the afternoon," the commentator said.

"Hello, Steve," Maureen said. "Hello, Patti."

Patti Ann smiled as she changed Conor's diaper. I tried to smile, but it was hard. I wanted to be outside on the street with my fellow officers. As the parade continued, the 3,000 cops—out of 120,000 marchers—came by the same TV camera post. Spotting the microphone, they began chanting.

"Steven, Steven," they said, one line of blue after another, as they passed. "Steven, Steven."

Patti Ann, or the nurse—someone—wiped my tears.

With the birth and the baptism over, it was time to plan my future. Since the fall, Bellevue—in particular the neurosurgical chief, Dr. Ransohoff—had been proposing that I move to a rehabilitation center. I was enough of a political football, however, so that the hospital staff's hands were tied. With the mayor's, and the rest of the city's, keen interest, Bellevue couldn't throw me out, not when its annual budget depended on tens of millions of dollars of city funds.

But we'd all agreed that Bellevue was no long-term answer. I wanted to go home, to get away from hospital beds and hospital food and the narrow, circumscribed life of the sixth floor. The weaning had been a failure, and I still lacked a voice. Even using Dr. Fried's technique with the cuff trache, I couldn't handle talking more than thirty minutes a day, and the effort it took barely made it worthwhile to me, though I realized how grateful others were to hear me.

Brian had begun investigating rehabilitation centers in the fall. Dr. Ransohoff had been pushing for Goldwater, a rehab institute in Manhattan that specialized in patients on respirators. The reports we'd gotten on Goldwater, though, suggested it specialized in respirator patients with illnesses, not spinal cord problems. Brian had also looked into the Rusk Institute, a highly regarded New York City spinal cord recovery center and a member of the federal thirteen-center regional system. However, we discovered that Rusk wouldn't accept vent-dependents like myself.

The Miami Project, a Florida-based spinal cord program, wanted me badly. The Miami Project was less than ten years old and had been started by an ex-pro football linebacker-turned-attorney, former Miami Dolphin Nick Buoniconti, after his son Mark had been rendered quadriplegic making a tackle in a college football game. Buoniconti came to the city regularly on fundraising business and made a few phone calls to arrange to see me. Brian, however, had his doubts about the Miami Project's high tech approach to injuries as serious as mine. Nevertheless, Buoniconti thought he could sell me on Miami. And I'd wanted to meet him. As a football player, I'd thought he was one of the best.

One afternoon, he'd arrived at Bellevue's lobby. The cops at the hospital called Brian and he'd told them to stall Buoniconti long enough for he and Greg Fried to arrive. By the time they got to me, Buoniconti was in the room, very personable, describing the project, and telling me what they could do for me.

"You can get off the ventilator," he said. "What are you? A C-3? That's the level Mark's at. He's gotten off. You can do it." The project's medical chief, Dr. Bart Green, might consider removing the bullet still in my spine, Buoniconti said. I might even be able to walk again, he suggested.

I was confused enough to want Brian to look more closely at the Miami Project. No one at Bellevue, nor Dr. Fried, had suggested that the removal of the bullet might improve my situation without the risk of significantly more damage. And, given the level of my injury, no one knew exactly what my chances were of breathing on my own.

Brian continued calling—to the Yale University Medical School, the Sloan-Kettering Institute for Cancer Research, to Dallas, and to a regional spinal cord center in San Diego. All the indicators pointed towards a small Colorado hospital none of us had heard of before: Craig, in Englewood, a suburb of Denver. Jim Griffiths, who used to run the Secret Service contingent at the White House, was an old friend of Brian's now stationed at the Fitzsimmons Medical Center in another Denver suburb. Brian asked Griffiths to find out what he could about Craig. Griffiths reported back that it was a top facility, used a comprehensive team approach designed to give patients as much independence as they were capable of handling, and—since 1972—had been designated by the federal government as the Rocky Mountain Regional Spinal Injury Center, one of thirteen model centers across the country and one of the few with a substantial history of treating ventilator-dependent patients.

Finally, Brian called a doctor there, one he knew who also served on the Miami Project's board of directors. With Brian's typical good fortune, the doctor's son turned out to be a police officer, and even though they'd never met, they hit it off right away.

"Here's the case," Brian explained, telling the physician the extent of my injuries and how they'd happened. He explained we were considering the Miami Project, but that he had some doubts. "What do you recommend?"

They talked for a while and the doctor, who was affiliated with both institutions, confirmed what Brian had learned about Craig and the doubts he'd had about whether the Miami Project was appropriate for someone with my highly unusual injuries.

"If I were you," said the doctor, "I'd send Steven to Craig. Not because I have a relationship with it, but that's where he should go."

"No other place?" asked Brian.

"That's right," said the doctor.

Without hesitation, Brian dialed Craig's admissions office. Sue Nyre, the admissions director, said that she and a staff physician, Dr. Robert Menter, would be coming to New Jersey for a conference. "Why can't you stay here in Manhattan?" asked Brian. "We'll get you where you need to go." Eventually, Nyre was persuaded. Dr. Menter would evaluate my physical condition and Nyre would explain to us what Craig was all about.

Sue Nyre would tell us later that she wasn't entirely comfortable with the plan. "The police were running interference for Steven," she said, "and we'd never seen anything like that before. Brian wasn't inclined to take our protocol at face value, and I wondered if Steven and Patti Ann would be able to get direct access to us, and us to them."

Bellevue, March 26, 1987

At 8:30 in the morning, Dr. Menter and Sue Nyre arrived at Steven's room. They'd insisted that we ask everybody, even the cops who watched over him, to leave. Standard procedure for Craig included a one-on-one relationship with the patient and the patient's spouse. At dinner the night before, Brian had agreed to the arrangement. He'd become convinced Craig was the place for us. Both the doctor and Sue were pleasant and confident, which was reassuring to Steven and me. Too many people had faced Steven's injury as if it were bizarre and frightening. Dr. Menter and Sue had obviously seen patients like Steven—many of them.

Typically, Sue told us, patients like Steven were referred by their physicians. Our case, where we'd referred ourselves, required careful scrutiny of Steven's medical files and an examination by Dr. Menter himself.

After reviewing the x-rays, the doctor began a pinprick test on Steven, a simple way to confirm the level of injury, and how badly Steven's phrenic nerve —the nerve that controls the diaphragm, opening and closing it to allow air in and out—had been damaged. Steven's father had been studying research on phrenic pacemakers, which when implanted can open and close the diaphragm mechanically. A pacemaker, we'd hoped, could get Steven off the respirator immediately.

"No," Sue explained. "You have to keep the trache in, because the pacemaker can't operate twenty-four hours a day. It's not like a heart pacemaker."

Dr. Menter, meanwhile, had been studying Steven's pulmonary chart. The chart showed that Bellevue's weaning strategy had been to reduce the amount of air he was getting from the respirator from one thousand cubic centimeters per breath, to nine hundred, then eight hundred, forcing him—in theory—to compensate with his own efforts. Steven had been telling people all along it wasn't enough, that he was smothering, but Bellevue had not remedied his complaints.

"When you get out to Craig," Dr. Menter said, "I'm not sure exactly how everything is going to work, but we're going to raise you to eleven hundred cubic centimeters."

As soon as he said that, Steven told me later, he decided he had to get to Craig. He felt as though Bellevue was killing him, since they specialized in acute care, not in patients who are stable.

When the pinprick test was finished, though, Dr. Menter had some disappointing news. The central nervous system was as damaged as the x-rays suggested.

"It doesn't look like I can get you off the ventilator," he said. "Not completely, anyway. Maybe several hours a day, but I don't want to make you any promises."

At least we're getting straight answers, I thought. Sue Nyre began to discuss Steven's injury with me, covering ground I was already familiar with. "If I'd realized the press coverage they'd had," she'd say later, "I might have been intimidated. I told myself, 'This guy doesn't have a recent injury, but don't assume he's been told much about it.' They were relatively knowledgeable, though. And I thought they were brave, that they didn't want to let people down." When she reminded me of how much we were trying to cope with, I began to cry. She put her arms around me, as Steven watched.

"I don't know if you've had the privacy to grieve like this," she said, "but if I were you, I'd choose a place where I could."

Towards the middle of the afternoon, we invited the rest of our families, and Brian, into the room to watch a videotape that described Craig, its philosophy, and its programs. We saw patients outdoors, and in shopping malls, learning how to manage escalators and to get in and out of vans. We saw therapists dressed in jeans, and quadriplegics maneuvering through halls in motorized wheelchairs. We saw a spirit, a sense of hope that had never been apparent in Bellevue.

When the tape was over, Steven was ready to leave immediately. I was sold, too, except for the fact that it was so far away. The Craig program required that I spend several weeks there, in Colorado, learning how his wheelchair works, how to maintain his bowel program, how to supervise and evaluate his nurses, what he should eat, and when his position in bed should be changed. I'd depended on my family for support and at Craig I'd be thousands of miles away.

There'd been arguments, compelling ones, to stay

close to home. For months, ever since Dr. Ransohoff, Bellevue's chief neurologist, first recommended transferring Steven, Goldwater Memorial had been presented as the logical choice. Goldwater was in Manhattan and had patients on respirators, we'd been told. No one had told us about Colorado, and we'd never visited Goldwater, not realizing there'd be any place to compare it with. Now there was.

Thirty minutes after Sue Nyre and Dr. Menter left, the arguments for staying home were raised again. Some of Steven's family cringed at the thought of still another separation, this one a matter of thousands of miles. Goldwater's perfect, one of his siblings insisted. "We've gone there and looked around," I was told. "It's not as bad as it sounds."

I'd better see for myself, I decided.

Built on Roosevelt Island, a narrow strip in the East River just north of Bellevue, Goldwater looked forbidding and institutional from the outside. The inside wasn't any better.

My eyes told me all I wanted to know. I looked around and could picture Steven dying there. There were children on respirators who were sick, not injured. There were street people who'd been run over by cars. There were elderly patients, ancient enough for nursing homes, waiting for death. This was the rehab of last resort, an American Civil War hospital in the twentieth century. I could see nothing positive, nothing that could compete with the scenes we'd watched on the Craig tape. What had Steven's family seen? I wondered. What had they wanted to see?

"If that's not depressing," my father told me, "I don't know what is."

"I don't care if he stays in Bellevue the rest of his life," I agreed. "There's no way he's coming here."

If Steven and I had any future at all, I now knew, it would have to begin at the base of the foothills of the Rocky Mountains. At Craig Hospital.

Ten

Bellevue, April 1987

The media began reporting in early April that I'd decided to go to Craig. The stories focused on the possibility I'd get off the respirator, one quoting Craig's medical director, Dr. Daniel Lammertse, as saying Craig's treatment goal for patients like me was "to get someone to the point where he or she could be at home and could have the maximal quality of life."

For me, though, Craig was going to be a chance to go outdoors for the first time in nine months, to see the trees and grass I'd missed since Shavod Jones pulled the trigger on July 12, 1986.

Craig wasn't going to be cheap, but the city of New York and the unions had agreed that catastrophic injuries such as mine ought to be covered in full for both police officers and fire fighters if the injuries occurred on the job. At nearly $1,000 a day, Craig by itself would cost more than $150,000 for my stay. The Lear jet and flight nurse would be another $12,000. A motorized wheelchair, ordered in New York to be shipped to Colorado, would cost $17,000 more. A customized van, built out west, $30,000 more. Add to that the training for private nurses who'd care for me when I got home . . . well, the costs were staggering and I had to wonder how those without the coverage I had, and the support system, could ever hope to achieve their "maximal quality of life."

Until I'd been hurt, there'd been no formal process for reimbursement for costs generated by injuries like mine. But the mayor had made it clear to Brian he wanted the costs handled expeditiously. Greg Fried officially prescribed the trip to Craig, Patti Ann's presence there, the wheelchair, even the van, as part of my treatment. And that prescription would authorize the city to release funds. By taking care of my needs, the city created a system for caring for other New York City cops, particularly those on the mayoral "exempt" list—the dozen line-of-duty injured officers who will never heal completely enough to return to regular duties.

And they gave me the freedom to escape Bellevue.

We decided to leave New York two days after Easter. On Easter Sunday, both the Cardinal and the mayor celebrated Mass with us in the chapel, a Mass where the Cardinal told Patti Ann and me that Jesus arose from the tomb, and that Patti Ann and I had been in another tomb, waiting for an opening. "Bit by bit, inch by inch," said Cardinal O'Connor, "that rock will be moved from that tomb."

Patti Ann was frightened. She didn't like to fly, and she'd never been separated from Conor, who'd stay behind in Malverne while she spent four days at Craig, becoming oriented. As she packed the hats, the cards, the pictures and mementos in my room, she told her mother, "I don't know if I can do this." The hospital room had been a cocoon, a womb sheltering us from the rest of the world. Leaving it on the morning of April 21, 1987—a windy, cold, thoroughly miserable day—seemed as filled with risk as with reward.

The New York press turned out in force, and we held a brief press conference in the Bellevue lobby. Patti Ann, holding Conor, and Mayor Koch stood in front of a battery of microphones. I sat next to them, in a wheelchair. "On behalf of Steven and myself and Conor," Patti Ann told the reporters, "I want to thank everyone for everything they've done in the past nine months. We're going to keep on praying and keep the faith.

"This is the first step in getting Steven home again," she added. "We'll be a family again."

I couldn't help smiling at Conor, who was bouncing excitedly in Patti Ann's arms, looking in wonder at the cameras and lights in front of him. The press asked me for a comment. "I'm looking forward to the trip," I managed to say. "I want to be home with my wife, to be with my baby, to be a family again. This is a step closer to home."

Several attendants lifted me out of the chair, wrapped me in a long white blanket that looked like a body bag, and strapped me onto a gurney. Bellevue's nursing supervisor pushed me through the emergency room entrance. Photographers crowded around, and I tried to stay calm. "You were all alone," Dennis Breen would remind me later, "except for Patti Ann, Brian Mulheren, and nine thousand strangers."

"Aren't I good enough for the front door?" I joked with the nurse. "I came in the emergency room entrance, and now I'm going out the same way."

"In a hospital," she told me, "the emergency room is the front door."

Medical Emergency Room Vehicle 578—the same buslike ambulance that took me from Metropolitan Hospital to Bellevue nine months earlier—drove me to the 34th Street heliport, on the edge of the East River. A five-minute flight on the police helicopter took us to LaGuardia Airport, where I was wheeled onto Craig's private jet for the flight west. Everywhere we stopped, there were hundreds of people trying to catch a glimpse, wanting to wish us well. "Journey of Hope," the New York *Post* called it, and the paper's front page that afternoon consisted entirely of a photo of Patti Ann bending over me, as I lay in the helicopter, trying to understand what I was mouthing over the noise of the engines. The picture, I learned later, won a national award.

Moments after it was taken, we were airborne. Patti Ann, Brian and myself were headed to Colorado.

In the Lear jet, Brian had arranged for sandwiches, Coke and Seven-Up to be on board. He stood in the back of the plane, wearing his Irish walking hat and official-looking tan raincoat, his various beepers strapped to his belt and inside his suitcoat, and looking a little out of place. I couldn't see out the windows, so the flight nurse held a small pocket mirror in front of my face, at an angle, so I could catch the view. In Ohio, we refueled, then landed at Stapleton Airport in Denver.

At the Denver airport, we were greeted by a ten-man police honor guard, the press, and an old navy buddy, Les Moore, who was stationed at the Fitzsimmons Medical Center. I'd known Moore for eleven years: He'd named his daughter, Stephanie, after me. And for the first four months at Craig—Les then was transferred from Denver because he was entering officers' training—he visited me every day, feeding me candy when Patti Ann wasn't there, reading me letters, taking me to his house.

The New York press had preceded us to Craig. The night before we'd left, one reporter called Patti Ann. "You better bring winter clothing," he'd told her. "It's snowing." When she got out of the plane, bundled in her parka, it was sixty degrees, and the sun was shining.

The sun! I got barely a glimpse of it as Lieutenant John Weber of the Denver police leaned over me to say, "The people of the city of Denver want to welcome you with their love and respect." Then he turned to Patti Ann. "Anything you need or require," he said, "consider it done. We have fourteen hundred people at your service."

I was loaded into another ambulance, and a police escort took us to Craig, an unimposingly modern gray brick three-story building attached to a larger acute-care hospital, the Swedish Medical Center. While Patti Ann completed the paperwork for my admission, I was taken to the third floor. My bed was one of four in a room that had a curved, rotunda-like window with views of the Rockies. What a change. In Bellevue, when I finally was lifted out of bed and seated in a wheelchair, after months of being flat on my back, I'd get pushed to the lone window in my room and stare at the apartment houses lining the East River. At Bellevue, the outside world had seemed cloaked in grime; here, the world looked pristine, clean, fresh, beautiful. I felt like Dorothy must have in one of my favorite movies, when she landed in

Technicolor Oz having seen nothing all her life but black-and-white Kansas.

Emotionally, I was running the gamut: everything was new and exciting, but my family and baby were back in New York; Craig promised some hope, but the cops I'd been relying on for support weren't around; I'd left Bellevue on a dark, rainy, depressing morning, now I was in sunny Colorado.

The staffers introduced themselves. I tried to settle in.

Craig Hospital, Englewood, Colorado, April 1987

Steven may have been unusually severely injured for what Bellevue typically saw, but at Craig, he was closer to the norm. The hospital's chief administrator, Dennis O'Malley, said that he'd met at least ten other patients over the years with injuries similar to Steven's, and that the trend for higher and higher quadriplegics to survive would increase. Craig, O'Malley assured me, had probably the largest population of spinal cord-injured patients in America. And since 1978, when the federal government began directing funding for spinal cord rehabilitation to a network of thirteen specially designated centers, most ventilator-dependent patients had been choosing Craig, if they had a choice.

Craig had originally been a tent colony, I learned, a tuberculosis clinic for indigent patients. Most Colorado hospitals had begun that way. Eventually, the community gave Craig some property, and once TB was controlled, the founding physicians built a rehabilitation center for polio victims. Around the end of World War II, Craig started working with spinal cord patients like Steven. The insurance industry, I was told, had demanded some type of rehabilitation that would get patients out of expensive hospital beds—though most of those patients came from car accidents, and sports mishaps, especially diving. They still do.

For years, Dennis O'Malley told me, the state-of-the-art rehab center had been the Stoke-Manville Hospital, in England. Now there were six leading centers, he said, all in the United States. "It's a matter of money," he said. "Stoke-Manville, a few years back, invented a bed for spinal cord patients. I understand they currently can't afford to buy the latest version of that bed. We can."

But I could see it was a matter of attitude, too. Steven was going to be just one of sixty spinal cord patients—there were also twenty head-injured patients—and would have his own team of therapists and doctors. Some patients, the head-injured, could walk, but would be helped by attendants. Others were paraplegic, and could push their chairs through the halls. There were quadriplegics who could breathe on their own, and others who couldn't. A few patients wore "halos"—castlike structures that strapped around the chest and over the shoulders and that attached by steel rods to a metal ring fitted around the head—immobilizing the neck. Even some of the staff members, including our family counselor, Fred Freche, were paralyzed. We could sense there wasn't going to be any warehousing of patients here, nor any hands-off approach because of Steven's status as a public figure with powerful friends. Steven was just Steven McDonald, on the same level as everybody else.

Which meant Steven was about to become more independent. I'd known since Sue Nyre's visit to Bellevue that teaching independence was what Craig did best. Exactly how that would work, though, had escaped me. As I walked into Room 301, the methods started to register. There would be no night nurse on duty by his bedside, or anyone else watching over him. Instead, hanging above the pillow he'd sleep on, was a small rubber ball. Inside the ball was a mercury switch. If Steven needed a nurse, or any other kind of attention, he'd have to tap the ball with his head. That would send a signal to the nurses' station on the floor.

I wasn't sure I could deal with this. Was he going to get the attention when he needed it?

I began to hyperventilate. "It's going to be all right," Brian assured me. "Everything's okay."

He was right, but it took me a few days to realize that.

For that first week, the New York media wanted to talk with us every day. Craig's staff had never experienced anything like it. The former governor of Alabama, George Wallace, had been a patient there at one time and had generated a little attention. But the cameras and reporters Steven's presence attracted dwarfed anything the hospital had seen. Before Steven, Craig had not been covered at all in the Denver papers. For the six months he was there, there were dozens of stories as the Denver writers followed the New Yorkers' leads.

I didn't want the reporters to see my anxiety. When Mike Koleniak of the New York *Post* asked for my thoughts that first night, I was upbeat. "Steven is psyched," I told him as I unpacked in one of the apartments Craig maintained a block from the hospital for families of patients. "He's looking forward to seeing the improvements in himself. He wants to go home—to be out of the hospital, to get on with his life. At Bellevue, we had people coming in and out all the time. It was very nice, but a little crazy. Here, things will be a little bit calmer. We'll be able to be with each other more, and share much more time together."

In a week, I told Mike, I'd go back to New York and get Conor and return to Colorado. My son and I would stay in the apartment and, eventually, Steven would become an outpatient and move in with us. "It'll make us feel like a family unit for the first time," I said.

"We'll Be A Family Again!" headlined the *Post.* But Conor was in New York, with my mother. And I was with Steven, struggling to learn how to live our new lives.

Craig Hospital, April 1987

I had roommates, which I hadn't had at Bellevue. One, Chuck Horton, a twenty-eight-year-old from Altoona, Pennsylvania, had been injured in a car accident. He was a high-quad on a ventilator, too, who'd met with the New York press and told them I was coming to a place that would help me. I never developed a relationship with Chuck, but I did with Courtney Miller, a teenager—maybe sixteen or seventeen—from North Carolina, who'd also been in an automobile wreck and was also on a vent. Courtney's injuries weren't as high as mine and she was having lots of discomfort with her trache, from which they were weaning her. At night, when the nurses were at their station, I'd hear the air pressure alarm go off on her respirator, and her soft cries.

"Courtney," I'd call through the curtains that separated our beds, providing privacy but increasing our fear of being alone, a fear she and I, both helpless, felt acutely, "are you okay? Everything's going to be all right."

Then her panic would pass. I know the sound of my voice made her feel I was standing next to her, holding her hand.

We developed, over the months, a quiet understanding though not a tremendous intimacy. And she surprised me when on the day she left, she came to say good-bye with her mother and stepfather, bringing me flowers and a calendar. On the calendar, she'd had someone mark her birthday, her high school graduation day, and Conor's birthday.

At Craig, I developed a new network of friends. My therapists—Gail Galinsky, my occupational therapist, and Sharon Blackburn, my physical therapist—were the people I was closest to. But I also appreciated the company of Les Moore, my Navy buddy; Jim Griffiths, who'd sit by my bedside and tell me stories of the great forgers the Treasury Department used to hunt; and Carole Harrison, a local restaurateur and manager of the Denver Fire Museum, who arranged for a car for Patti Ann, and a crib and bassinet for

Conor. But other than Courtney, I never developed friendships with other patients, never quite had the need to gather with them at the nurses' desk to hang out.

That hanging out was the common practice, a daily routine for most of the patients on my floor. They'd get together after morning therapy, and again after the day's schedule ended, and shoot the bull and smoke cigarettes. I never wanted to do that, and I still don't know why, except that I was probably acting true to type. I was never much of a social butterfly before my injury. At work I would talk to people, but I wasn't one for hanging out, at least not frequently. The other patients felt the need to share—one had been shot by a female undercover officer posing as a prostitute, was paralyzed and had forgiven her assailant, much as I had Shavod Jones—but I was a private person and already more exposed in the press than I felt comfortable with. I also felt having injuries in common wasn't enough to create a friendship, although since I was so focused on returning home to as normal a life as I could lead, that feeling may have been a defense. Still I couldn't shake it.

Instead, I'd go back to my room in the evening, and either watch television, phone New York, or visit with friends from outside the hospital. Craig constantly tried to screen those visitors out. There was nothing like the traffic passing through my room in Bellevue. A Denver police officer would stop by on occasion, and, more rarely, a local priest, Brother John Fava. Brian, or Peter Johnson, or a family member might fly out for a few days. But the hospital discouraged the activity. Its philosophy was that since no patient was admitted who wasn't stable medically, we were here to work, to develop our skills. The fewer the distractions, the faster we'd progress to independence. When Carole Harrison began to show up regularly, a nurse told her, "Stop this. Steven's never going to get better unless everyone leaves him alone and lets him work."

Carole passed that along to Jim Griffiths, who told me. I immediately called Carole.

"Please keep coming," I said to her. "You're the only one who ever does, other than Patti Ann."

My first afternoon, when I'd been dressed and put into a chair—Craig wasn't going to let me stay in bed, and twenty-four hours after I'd been in Colorado, I'd spent more time sitting up than I had any day during the previous nine months—Gail Galinsky and Sharon Blackburn introduced themselves.

Both were attractive, athletic young women not much older than I, and I was especially drawn to Sharon. She was a thirty-eight-year-old triathlete and registered physical therapist who'd graduated from the University of Florida. After a short stint at Craig, she had worked with disabled students at the University of Wisconsin's Whitewater campus, teaching them independence, and then had rejoined the Craig staff in 1981 and become the therapist on Dr. Lammertse's team. Later I found out that Dr. Menter had recommended Sharon be assigned to me because of her experience. I always thought she'd been assigned because she'd once wanted to become a cop. "The problem was," she'd say, "there were only meter maids when I was growing up."

"Is there anything in particular you want to do?" Sharon asked me this first day.

"Outside," I mouthed.

"We'll do it," she said.

I was in a reclining chair. Because I sat in only one position in New York, I'd develop skin sores and was at risk of fainting because the blood would settle in my lower body. Sharon pushed me through the automatic doors leading to the back terrace. For nine months I'd been indoors; for two-thirds of a year, I'd breathed hospital smells and heard hospital sounds. My world had been a cramped, artificial harbor—safe, secure, but deadening.

From the terrace, I could see trees, a small grassy hill falling away from us, and the Rockies not far away. The sky was crystal blue, the sun shining, the air still, clean and dry. The sounds of a car's engine, a jackhammer, a jet engine overhead, broke the stillness from time to time. Beautiful. I sat and sighed. Great, I thought. Then I turned melancholy. Would I ever be able to enjoy days like this with any more freedom than I had now? Nine months earlier, I would have stretched out on that grass and rolled around with Patti Ann. Now I was stuck in a chair.

We stayed until the sun began to set behind the mountains. And, from then on, I'd ask Sharon every day to take me back out.

"Steven," she'd protest, "we have to do some *work!*"

Sharon's job was to exercise my arms and legs, to stretch and loosen all my joints, and to encourage me to use my neck muscles. During exploratory surgery that first day in Bellevue—an operation tracing the path of the bullet from where it entered my neck to the point it hit my spine—some of the muscles on the right side had been cut. They'd healed, but the weakness had made it tough for me to hold my head up at all. I'd need the strength in my neck to move my head so I could reach the controls of my motorized wheelchair.

The wheelchair was crucial to any independence Craig could teach me. Back in New York, an order had been placed for a sophisticated $17,000 model that would be shipped to Colorado to arrive when I did. The chair—which also came with hand controls useless to me—could be maneuvered by "sipping" and "puffing" into a pair of flexible plastic tubes that curved up from the computerized motor behind the backrest. The sipping and puffing was a simple enough idea: inhaling through the straw was a sip, and exhaling a puff. The sips and puffs controlled the chair's direction, its speed (there were three, although the first two were pretty slow and only good if you were in close quarters; in first, I always felt I was holding things up), and whether or not the back reclined or stayed upright (alternating those positions, I learned, lessened the chances of body sores developing). But this chair, we discovered, operated on a timing mechanism. Inhale a second too long, and I went right instead of left.

Gail set up orange rubber cones in Craig's gymnasium and I was to steer around them and between them, like driving test cars in those automobile ads on television. Only I felt like the inferior car, the one that couldn't stay between the lines, that knocked all the cones down. Gail remembers my language as colorful, but I was frustrated as hell. I'd go veering off in one direction, Gail running after me, Patti Ann and Conor sitting on the sidelines, watching and trying not to laugh too hard. The chair acted like a klunker and didn't seem built to my dimensions. The timing was impossible, and even Patti Ann and Gail couldn't figure it out. They could walk away from it, though. I couldn't and would bang my head against the back in frustration. After a couple of days, we gave up. Gail ordered a new chair, with a sip-and-puff system that operated on the amount of pressure I used rather than its duration.

Besides learning to drive a wheelchair, occupational therapy for a high quad was limited. Gail spent hours teaching me how to do word processing on a computer, entering the letters with sips and puffs, this time in Morse code, through another plastic straw. I started many letters to family, friends, well-wishers. But I only completed and mailed one letter, to Mayor Koch, a get-well card, after he'd suffered a slight stroke. "I was always trying to get him to finish a letter," Gail would say. "I'd tell the other therapists not to disturb us." I'd read, using a mouthstick—a piece of metal with a plastic bite I'd hold between my teeth to turn pages of a book or magazine propped on a stand angled over my head. Turning those pages was the only physical exercise I could do by myself. And I'd play simple games like vertical checkers, moving the pieces with the stick.

The computer desk was stuck in a far corner of the third floor therapy room, an airy though not particularly cheerful space that was bustling with activity in the early mornings and afternoons. Patients lay on two four-by-six-foot exercise mats—raised a foot off the ground on four narrow steel legs—for their daily range-of-motion work. Another patient might be erect, suspended in the standing stall, an upright steel frame with straps for feet, legs, torso and arms, and a desktop that fit against the chest. My first time in the standing stall was wrenching. "Boy, you're a tall drink of water," said Sharon, trying to keep the mood light, and I was glad the Craig staffers were seeing me the way I'd been—the six-two athlete, the cop. But Patti Ann was there, too, and I was looking at her as I had before, and remembering our loss.

Behind the desk, in an annex to the therapy room, was a row of airplane seats and the body of a car. Here, paraplegics and low quads were shown how to get in and out of their transportation. Not high quads, though. We would always need assistance. And in the training room around the corner from therapy, a bed, couch, toilet and bathtub were available to teach paraplegics how to cope with them. Again, this equipment wasn't for me.

Dr. Daniel Lammertse, a forty-ish, bearded, slender man with a preference for bow ties and tweeds, headed the team responsible for my case. He was a calm realist, discouraging us from hoping for a research breakthrough or unanticipated "cure" for cord damage, but encouraging us to believe my Craig stay could improve the quality of my life. "Patients here," he said, "are commonly inspired. In general, people do more than they think they can."

"One immediate issue," Dr. Lammertse would say later, "was to give Steve a voice. He wasn't a bad lip speaker, but he was frustrated he couldn't communicate better. Another was eating. Bellevue thought he needed a feeding tube, but he didn't. We wanted him to develop an appetite. And the third was education.

There were so many things for Steve, Patti, and their families to learn: the bowel program, bladder maintenance, suctioning, and how to respond if the ventilator goes haywire.

"There are between ninety and one hundred new ventilator-dependent, high-quad injuries a year," Dr. Lammertse would say. "That is, those who survive. Most in developing countries, for example, don't. Society simply doesn't put enough value on individual human life in many places. As a result, the technology necessary to support spinal-cord injuries—wheelchairs, prosthetics—isn't available.

"At Craig," Dr. Lammertse explained, "our longest surviving vent-dependent, high-quad patient has now lived eighteen years since first injured. And 70 percent of all in that category are alive after five years. Up until World War II, the presumption was that anyone with a spinal cord injury high enough on the spine to affect breathing was dead. Since then, however, emergency medical treatment has become so much more effective. Getting through the first couple of years is the toughest. You're very susceptible to pneumonia, because you can't cough or exhale to get rid of the secretions in your lungs. Those secretions are a place where bacteria grow, and if they're not removed regularly by suctioning, they can lead to the illness.

"So the life expectancy is somewhat reduced," Dr. Lammertse would say, "but, in fact, there are several thousand vent-dependent quads alive today."

The biggest problem, Dr. Lammertse would say, is the cost associated with living with such an injury. Most can't afford full-time attendants, and the burden of care falls on the patient's family. Health maintenance organizations—HMOs—don't, for the most part, cover this follow-up care at all. My notoriety, Dr. Lammertse told me, might cause some inconveniences for the hospital, and for me, but any media attention that could make the public more aware of the complications and continued expense stemming from these injuries was worth the tradeoff.

I'd think about that during the next few months. Few others at Craig could look for that kind of backing. One fellow I met on my floor was describing the excitement he felt about going home.

"Where do you live?" I asked. "What kind of place have you got?"

"Well, it's just a house trailer," he said, "but the sheriff's department is building me a ramp so I can get in and out."

Within a couple of days, my feeding tube had been pulled. Patti Ann returned to New York, picked up Conor, and came back to the apartment Carole Harrison outfitted. While she was gone, the hospital ran another series of phrenic nerve conduction tests to compare with the findings Dr. Menter got at Bellevue. Dr. Menter's conclusions were borne out: there was so little nerve activity, my diaphragm couldn't be stimulated. And without my diaphragm moving downward and creating suction to draw in air and expand the lungs, I couldn't breathe on my own.

Getting off the respirator completely, it might never happen. At least, according to the doctors, not according to me.

Three weeks into my stay, Dr. Lammertse ordered my trache changed. The cuff trache would be replaced with a Jackson trache, one that let air pass by my vocal cords. Where at Bellevue replacing the cuff trache had been painful and frightening, Craig handled the operation with assurance. I stayed calm and felt little discomfort. Patti Ann was waiting for me in my room when I was brought back.

"I love you," I told her. In my own voice, not the froggy croak I'd managed to say at Bellevue.

"I love you, too," she said, tears forming in her eyes.

I'd been waiting almost a year to say those words. When I'd left the apartment that July afternoon, we'd been struggling in our marriage. Our work days were out of sync, I was grabbing overtime, Patti was pregnant and needed my attention . . . the problems of a police marriage, the ones we were so sure wouldn't apply to us, had been hitting home.

All those small hurts had festered when I couldn't speak to her. I'd said "I love you" hundreds of times by mouthing the words, making empty sounds with my lips. But now, saying it in my own voice, seemed the most important task I could accomplish.

"I love you," I said. "I love you. I love you."

Patti Ann put her face next to mine and held me.

Malverne, May 1987

Steven would be coming home, I realized, to an apartment in Manhattan he'd never seen. We'd be separated from both our families, and I didn't think I could handle Conor and Steven and the nurses we'd need without my family close enough to help out.

Michel Court, the one-block street my parents had lived on since they'd moved to Malverne, was a dead end. Mom and Dad lived at the corner nearest Drake, the cross street, and earlier that spring, one of their neighbors had passed away. That house, across Michel Court and at the far end of the street was a small Cape. In another time or place, it might have been someone's starter house. But in the heated-up real estate market on Long Island, it was a $200,000 property. At least.

Even before Steven left Bellevue, I'd raised the subject with him. He knew the house—he'd seen the outside often enough when he was visiting me—and also understood its proximity to my parents. "Would living that close to my mother and father bother you?" I'd asked him.

"No," he'd mouthed, "it'd be no problem."

Now, with Steven in Colorado, I decided to tell my mother what I'd been thinking. Would they want us that near them?

My mother had been hoping I'd ask.

"Your father had the same idea," she said. "He thought it'd be perfect. I told him to keep it to himself, though. I didn't think we should interfere in your lives. I wanted to let you decide."

I'd contacted the son of the former owner. Yes, he'd sell, he told me. The asking price was $225,000.

And the house, we'd discover, was hardly perfect for our special needs.

I came back to New York in May to a series of events honoring Steven and myself. On May 16, the College of Mount St. Vincent awarded me its Elizabeth Seton Medal at the school's graduation. Of all the commemorations, this one touched me the deepest. Mother Seton's husband had died when she was twenty-nine, and she'd converted two years later and raised her five children as Catholics—despite her relatives' objections—and eventually founded the first American congregation of the Sisters of Charity. She'd refused to allow herself to become a victim, and once the shock and anger of my situation had begun to pass, I'd adopted that attitude too.

"Our public struggle," I told the graduates, "is the struggle of thousands of New Yorkers every day. They rarely get our attention, but they do deserve our prayers." Before I'd left Colorado, I said, I'd asked Steven what I should talk about.

"The streets," Steven had told me. "Tell them about the streets of New York." At Conor's baptism, Steven reminded me, he'd written, "There is more love in this city than there are street corners." And, I said to the Mount St. Vincent graduates, there was.

"If we believe the headlines of our daily newspapers," I said, "then New York City is but a city of victims: wrongdoers, and those done wrong alike. Some would argue that the boy who shot Steven McDonald was a victim of circumstances, of our societal ills. I know Steven was certainly a victim.

"Every day, thousands of New Yorkers are also victimized—by bad luck, ill health and crime. In today's society, victim is an easy role to assume. It can even be a comfortable one in a nation that prides itself on helping those who cannot help themselves. Mother Elizabeth Seton was a victim, too. A widow with five children, she was stranded, penniless and exhausted, in a country an ocean voyage away from her native

America. Her prospects were bleak, her future a dismal one. She was, as it is said, a victim of her circumstances.

"But for Elizabeth Seton, the role of victim became a benefit, not a burden. She became a victor, not the vanquished.

"When Steven was shot, he too was a victim. For a while, he didn't know if he'd live or die. Almost a year later, Steven is no longer a victim. He has placed himself in the hands of God, and has lifted himself out of the vise of circumstance. He is an example of strength, courage, faith in Jesus Christ, faith in the goodness of man, and, finally, a living example of the forgiving spirit.

"I leave you with one thought from Paul," I said, "in a letter to the Corinthians. 'We walk by faith, not by sight.' If we can follow the example of Mother Seton, then we need not be victims. No matter how dark the path, no matter how broken our limbs or our spirit, we walk by faith.

"Steven and I thank you for helping us walk the first steps."

I could barely finish, and both the mayor and the Cardinal, sitting on the auditorium stage, helped me to my seat.

As I'd spoken, I had realized my audience was composed of women not much younger than myself. Now, as the auditorium emptied, one graduate after another approached me and said how glad they were I'd come. They made me feel honored because, just a year before, I'd been one of them. I realized how much I'd changed, that those few seconds in which Shavod Jones shot my husband had drastically altered my life.

The words I'd just spoken, I knew, had not been empty, and I'd said what I meant. One after another, the girls told me they were praying for Steven. They could relate to me, they said, because I was one of them, and that hit home.

Two weeks later, eight thousand friends and wellwishers came to the Jacob Javits Convention Center for "A Benefit for Badge 15231," sponsored by the Patrolmen's Benevolent Association, the police officers' union. Steven's union trustee, Eddie Mahoney, a tireless and loyal advocate for cops had done a lot of the organizing—a police officer's benefit of this size was unprecedented, and both Mayor Koch and Maureen O'Hara agreed to appear onstage with our families—and, like so many others, would remain close to us. Mahoney's daughter, Tara, would join our Catholic Youth Organization basketball team a year and a half later.

Standing on the center's huge stage, looking over the crowd, I was reminded how many lives Steven had already touched. "The strength of Patti Ann and the strength of Steven," the mayor said, looking over towards me as I stood next to my parents, "is so enormous that they have taken us into their hands. It is not we who comfort them. It is they who comfort us." When it came time to respond, I lost my composure and began crying.

"When Steven says there is more love in this city than there are street corners," I said, recalling his statement at the baptism, "I know what he means. You make us proud to be New Yorkers."

In early June, the Police Department awarded Steven its Medal of Honor at Police Medal Day. While the May events had offered a joyous hope, Medal Day held a bittersweet melancholy. Four of the fifty honorees had been killed. "A tragic year," the police commissioner said. A police bugle sounded "Taps" for the dead officers, and forty-five cops stood motionless, saluting. In my lap, Conor played with the Medal of Honor hanging from a ribbon around my neck, oblivious to the pain of the moment.

As the ceremony began, I was handed an envelope with a Colorado postmark. Now, waiting for Monsignor John Kowsky's closing prayer, I opened it. "There are only two things in the world I need," the printed card read. "My dreams, and you."

At the card's bottom, in shaky, uncertain writing that could only have been made with a pen held by a mouthstick, were the words, "Love, Steven."

"May all your tours be safe," intoned the monsignor, in that soothing streets of New York voice that had become so familiar during the Bellevue months. "May all of our injured get well . . ."

Conor laughed as the medal caught the bright sun.

"May the Lord be gentle with all our dead," said the chaplain.

Conor and I flew back to Colorado for Father's Day. I'd been away from Steven for three weeks, our longest separation since we'd been married. We'd talk on the phone every night, and I knew he'd begun trying to breathe on his own off the respirator and was up to twenty-five minutes, four times a day.

As we walked through the jetway, I could see a cluster of people at the door of the terminal. In the middle of the group was a wheelchair. Steven. He'd decided to surprise me by meeting us at the airport.

"I'm relieved you're back," Steven said, as reporters' cameras clicked away, capturing the reunion. "I couldn't do it without you."

I held Conor close to his face, so Steven could kiss our son.

Craig Hospital, June 1987

There would be four Colorado cops killed in the line of duty while I was at Craig and I went to all their funerals. Jim Wier—shot trying to break up a family disturbance—was the first. Wier had been a rookie, younger than I, and left a wife and two small boys. I saw them crying at the cemetery. The widow came up to me. Her husband had been the hero, but she was holding my head and touching my chin thanking me. I could see loneliness in her face and I imagined Patti Ann and Conor in the same situation. For days, even weeks, no one had known if I'd live or die. But I'd survived, and Conor would know his father. Jim Wier's boys would be left with only a memory.

The Denver police officers and fire fighters had donated $1,500 to a fund Carole Harrison had helped establish for me in Colorado, and the New York Patrolmen's Benevolent Association reciprocated with a $5,000 check to the Wier family, as did one of our benefactors, Bear, Stearns partner Arthur Crames. That pleased me. I was in Denver to learn enough skills to be able to go home, but I was still a cop. If I could help others, somehow, then I was doing my job. When Dale Koski, a Denver policewoman who'd been seriously injured while on duty, told me she'd been forced to retire on two-thirds of her salary, I told her that I'd publicize her situation and compare it with my own. The media coverage hasn't pressured the Denver mayor into changing the department's catastrophic care plan yet, but the Denver department says that, now, it's just a matter of time. "Steven's a constant reminder," said the Denver chief of detectives, Jerry Kennedy, after I left. "While he was here, a number of officers were killed. They're dead and buried. Steven McDonald is not, but every day he's alive, he knows he's paid the supreme price."

While Patti Ann was in New York, Sharon Blackburn and other Craig staffers continued to get me ready for the rest of my life. Sharon had an enthusiasm and energy I could easily relate to. Before my injury, I was a manic sports fan, the kind of guy who rubs the television screen to jinx an opponent; I was a huge rock fan, especially of bands like U2 and the Rolling Stones; and I loved good food. When I'd go on outings from the hospital, Sharon would indulge me in all three. She'd talk sports and make sure the radio was tuned to the right station. "You're the only person I know," she'd say, "who'd order lobster in Denver." Then she'd make me explain to her how to pick the meat out of the shell, dip it in butter, and feed it to me. "I don't know how to do lobster," she said.

The outings were recreational therapy—a program which included, for many patients, painting, photography, gardening, drawing, even hunting and fishing. For those with lower spinal cord injuries, there's almost no limit to what Craig shows you you're capable of doing. But the furthest I could go was to get back out into society: going to restaurants, to movies, to sports events and concerts.

I had to get used to the preparations involved. Someone had to wash me. Someone had to dress me. Someone had to get a pass for me and pack my medicine. Someone had to arrange for transportation and make certain I was back at the hospital an hour or two before 10:00 P.M. That was what we called the witching hour, when the orderlies ended their shift. At Craig, the hospital bed was a foot higher off the ground than my wheelchair—at home in Malverne, now, they're at the same level—and it took two men, or three women, to transfer me to bed. If we missed the orderlies, we had to wait for the night shift, a skeleton crew, to get to me. And that could take quite a while.

At first, going out of the hospital felt awkward and uncomfortable. Claudia Muldoon and her husband, Fred Betts, a local businessman, invited me to a cookout at their home—steaks, burgers, kids running on the grass—and I felt like an outsider, an intruder in a distinctly family affair, unable to circulate among the guests. Other times, Sharon would call for the ambu-cab, a taxi service for Craig patients, and we'd go to a local mall to see a movie and to eat. In the theatre's darkness, I'd try to lose myself in the film; around me, the audience would hear the sound of the respirator and turn to stare at the source of that distracting Darth Vader voice. In Denver's mall corridors, people didn't know who I was, and children would come up to me, in wonderment, as if I were E.T.

"What's that tube going down your throat?" they'd

ask. "What are those tubes you blow into? Why does the wheelchair go up and down?"

Adults I passed were different. They'd attempt not to look, eyeing the sky or the ground, then probably sneak a peek as I went past. I still remembered myself as before; they saw me as an oddity.

And I was.

On that first trip to the mall, I wanted to eat a taco. But as I was being fed, I could sense the stares of the other customers. I felt like a baby, an infant all over again, needing help to bathe, to urinate, to empty my bowels.

The dependency would depress me some days, particularly those when Patti Ann was away. The more I learned about myself, the more I realized how much I'd always have to rely on others.

The bowel program was the worst. As a hospital corpsman, when I was in the Navy, I had had to deal with others' feces. Other than facing death, it was as revolting as the duty got. So I hated shitting in my helpless condition, knowing that someone else had to take care of mine.

At Bellevue, where there was no commode chair, I'd wait days. Then they'd use an enema. They had no concept—no one had taught those nurses—of how to set up a program. The enema was not only messy and unpleasant, but often insufficient so that one of the nurses would have to insert her gloved finger up my anus to stimulate me further. I'd wait forever to avoid subjecting myself to that whole procedure. Unconsciousness would have been preferable. At Craig, and later at home, I'd be lifted into a commode chair every other day. A nurse would place a suppository in my anus which would stimulate the lower bowels. Then she would stimulate me digitally. The regularity, the gravity, and the lack of an enema tidied the process up. But when the doctors at Craig tried to teach Patti Ann the program, she got sick. She couldn't do it.

I vowed then that she'd never be in a situation where she had to. Our medical insurance would provide me with twenty-four hour nursing, and I'd insist the agency maintain that schedule once we got home. Absences and illnesses have to be covered. But, even if they weren't, I'd pay somebody an absurd amount to empty my bowels before I'd let Patti Ann do it. I'd always respected nurses. Today no one respects and revers them more than I do. Too often, low paid and ignored, they deserve to command our appreciation and love.

When I got home—and, as my third month in Colorado ended, I hoped it would be soon—Patti and I would not be nurse and patient. We were husband and wife. And I'd do whatever I could to make certain we remained husband and wife.

WITNESS:

Sharon Blackburn

Steven arrived at Craig Hospital on a Tuesday. I'd taken that Monday off, to stay home and watch the Boston Marathon on television. Some of the other therapists called me that night. "Every reporter in the world is here," they told me. "How are you going to handle him?"

Dr. Menter, who'd evaluated Steven in New York City, had recommended I be assigned as Steven's physical therapist. His reasoning, I heard, was I'd been at the hospital a long time. I'd started working at Craig in 1978, then left the next year for the University of Wisconsin's Whitewater campus. In June 1981 I'd come back to Craig and worked there until September 1987. In that time, we'd occasionally get an important person as a patient, but no one had had the amount of publicity Steven had. My philosophy was that spinal cord injuries are the great equalizer, though, and I told the other therapists that.

"I don't see treating this man," I said, "any differently than I treat anyone else."

My first impression, when I saw him the next day, was that of a good-looking guy in a sad situation. I'd had maybe five or six patients as seriously injured. One woman, who came to Craig a few months later, had a higher injury—her neck had been broken at the brain stem, in a car crash caused by a driver who registered .3 on a breathalyzer—and she had neither neck muscles nor facial muscles. She couldn't chew, swallow or talk. Still, Steven was unfortunate. Most high-quads are injured at the C-3 or C-4 level and can eventually get off their respirators. With his cord half-severed between the C-2 and C-3 level, Steven never could.

Usually, the therapists and aides get closer to the patients than the doctors and nurses do. On the exercise mats, especially, the patients really open up. Steven was no different. As I exercised his arms and legs, he'd sometimes talk about how badly he felt, and he did have his rough days.

"Aaah!" he'd all of a sudden exclaim.

"Want to talk about it?" I'd ask.

"It's not fair," he'd say. "My family's home. My baby's growing. All I want to do is hold him. And I can't."

We'd encourage that reaction, because you can't get past it unless you let it out. Towards the end of his stay, we were watching the CBS "Morning Show." Patti was a guest, with two police widows, as I remember. One widow described how long it took her to overcome her grief. Steven got upset. Patti Ann got the raw end of the deal, he said.

"If I had died," he told me, "she could mourn, then meet someone else, and remarry."

Steven had a spirit about him, and I never got as close to a patient as I did to him. I came to think of him as a brother, and even when I left Craig that September, two months before he was discharged, I'd come by once a week to take him out. My roommate and I would transfer him to the car and then we'd drive him over to our house to play music and watch videos.

"Oh, no, Sharon," Steven would protest as we wheeled him out, "it's too much trouble, too much trouble."

"Naw," I said, "we can't always depend on the ambu-cab."

One morning, in early September, we drove him eighty miles to the Scottish Highland Games in Rocky Mountain National Park. Christine and I had the transfer down slick by then—we'd take the respirator and its tray off the chair, lift Steven into the seat, put the respirator in, and fold the chair up. Then we'd be off. To the accompaniment of an Eagles tape in the cassette deck, we'd haul up those winding roads, with Steven laughing, singing along, and saying—every now and then, as we came around a sharp curve—"Ooh, Sharon, maybe this isn't such a good idea."

One of Steven's New York friends, Father Mychal Judge, decided to pay a surprise visit on his way from California. That afternoon, however, the International Police Association was having a picnic at the Cherry Creek Reservoir to which Steven had decided to go. The priest got directions at the hospital and somehow found us out in the woods. When Steven saw him—miles from nowhere, completely out of context and totally unexpected—he couldn't remember Father Judge's name. He had never said it out loud before.

"Father," he said, "what are you doing here?"

But the priest was equally astonished. In the

months he'd known Steven at Bellevue, Steven had never spoken. He never realized Steven was groping for his name.

"Oh Steven," was all he could say, "I've never heard you speak. You have a beautiful voice."

I'd heard from Steven and Patti Ann that they'd regularly have Mass said for them at Bellevue Hospital. But that didn't happen at Craig. The administrators, particularly the public relations director, Marlene Casini, kept outside visitors to a minimum. One day, an older Catholic priest walked in. He said he'd tried to see Steven seven different times, but that Marlene had always told him, "Steven doesn't want to see you." Steven was furious. No one had asked him what he'd wanted. But Craig wanted to control his rehabilitation, and not have Steven dictate to them.

On another occasion, when a different priest visited Steven got worried. A couple of the New York cops—Dave Martelli and Steve Fuchs, I believe—had put a photo on his wall of the two of them mooning the camera at Pike's Peak. "I hope he doesn't look at it," Steven kept repeating, "I hope he doesn't look at it." If the priest did notice it, though, he kept his thoughts to himself.

Most of the patients at Craig were takers, asking you to invest in them emotionally. Not Steven. He was a giver. In August, I competed in a triathlon, and Steven told me he'd be there. He got an occupational therapist to go with him, and he watched the entire event.

Not only was he a giver, but he had a sweet, quiet sense of humor. In October, we went to the Notre Dame-Air Force Academy football game, his first outing in his new van. We drove in a back way, taking us right through the corps of cadets in the Air Force band. Steven was decked out in Notre Dame clothing from head to foot and had this huge Notre Dame banner stuck to the van. Everyone started booing, saying things, and I got a little nervous.

"Hey," I told him. "Maybe we should put on trenchcoats."

"It's okay," he said with a smile, the boos raining down on the van, "we've got God on our side."

When he left Craig, I felt like my best friend was leaving. For weeks after he'd gotten back to New York, we'd talk on the phone every night. I knew he was having trouble adjusting to being at home, but I didn't doubt that was where he wanted to be. "Sharon," he'd say, "you just can't get good pizza in Colorado."

Eleven

New York City, July 1987

If we were to move to a new home by the time Steven returned from Craig, I realized I had to make some decisions. The more I considered the small Cape at the end of Michel Court, the more sense it made. With the addition of a ramp in the front, and the widening of some halls and doorways, we could make the first floor accessible. Conor could sleep on the second. Steven wouldn't be able to see him there—there wouldn't be any way for him to get up and down the stairs—but I expected compromises like that would entangle the rest of our lives.

The Foundation created in Steven's name by the Patrolmen's Benevolent Association had over $200,000 in it, and close to $40,000 had been generated by the May benefit at the Javits Center. Could we use that money to pay for the house? I asked Brian. He said he'd arrange a lunch meeting with the Foundation's accountant, and with Dickie Fay, at the office of Bear, Stearns, a Wall Street brokerage house where

Dickie had been a partner for twenty-one years. We'd discuss it there, Brian said.

Dickie and Pat Fay, his wife, had been regular Bellevue visitors, sometimes accompanying Dickie's brother John, who suffered from cancer and was receiving chemotherapy at another hospital. Some afternoons, after his treatment, John would visit Steven too, to give him a pep talk. Steven was at his lowest those days.

John Fay and his brother tried to speak to Steven's doubts.

"I'm fighting," John would tell Steven, "and I *know* I'm dying." And he was. John's death would come before Steven made it home.

Both Dickie and John had been benefactors of the Police Department and the Fire Department for years, and Dickie was co-chairman of the Widows' and Children's Benefit Fund of the two departments. As a director of Bear, Stearns, company policy demanded that he give to charity a large chunk of his income. "These men put on a uniform every day and when they leave their homes, their wives and children don't know if they're coming back." He'd been a fund-raiser for Catholic Charities, served as financial advisor to the archdiocese. Dickie, a small, gentle man approaching his fiftieth birthday, had seemed an obvious choice to run the Steven McDonald Foundation, and I'd been pleased when he accepted.

Now, his advice on how to proceed with buying a house would be valuable. After we'd been seated in the corporate dining room, Brian and I outlined the plan. Dickie thought for a moment, then excused himself. He wanted to speak with Arthur Crames, he said, another Bear, Stearns partner who'd helped see us through the Bellevue times. After a few minutes, Dickie asked us to join Crames.

"You don't need to use the Foundation funds," Dickie said. "We'll buy you the house."

I felt embarrassed.

"Oh no," I said, "that's not what Steven and I want you to do at all. You've been so good to us already."

Dickie Fay was adamant. The case was closed. The two men would purchase the house, and Brian Mulheren, through the auspices of the mayor's office, would help coordinate its renovation. That evening, I called Steven with the news. He sounded as excited as I felt. After I finished describing the conversation, I began singing to him. Ever since he'd been in the hospital, and had been strong enough to listen to a phone call, I'd sung to him at night, before he and I went to sleep. As he'd regained his voice, he'd sung to me too.

"I'll be loving you," he began, "always."

"With a love that's true," I returned, "always."

Steven had taught me the song. He'd learned it from watching the movie, *The Lou Gehrig Story.*

At Craig, Steven's progress had been great. He was off the respirator for a half-hour at a time, his face was tanned, and he and his therapists had taken several outings into the foothills and mountains surrounding Denver. But, he told me, he was ready to leave the hospital. He'd been there nearly three months, and a typical stay lasted no more than four.

"When we finish the house," I told him, "it'll be time to come back." Brian promised the renovations would be done by Christmas, perhaps even Thanksgiving. As soon as possible, Steven urged us. The walls of a hospital, even one as supportive and optimistic as Craig, can be stifling and kill any hope, he reminded me.

On July 8, 1987, we decided to demonstrate how far Steven had come. A press conference was arranged in the hospital gym, and—as the video cameras ran—Steven drove himself into the room. "Craig has given me back my independence," he told the reporters, "but things are still tough. It's difficult when you wake up in the morning, and the only thing you can move is your head." For the cameras, he typed on a computer, "Cops are tops."

"How do you feel now about Shavod Jones?" one journalist asked.

"Maybe Shavod Jones feels really badly," Steven said. "Maybe I could talk to him, and tell him that it's all right. Maybe no one's done that for him."

Then Steven mentioned he'd hoped we'd have a large family. "Six kids," he said.

"I'd do it again and again," I said with a smile. "But six?"

Craig Hospital, July 1987

By the end of July, Patti Ann and Conor were to return to New York. Patti had to sign the papers to buy our new house and get the renovations started. Before she left, though, she and Conor drove with me to the Mother Cabrini Shrine, a chapel in the woods twenty-five miles west of Denver.

I'd thought long and hard about why I needed the church. There was a saying I'd heard before I'd been shot, that the church is full of hypocrites. But it's also full of sinners, and that's how I saw myself. My tragedy was a test, a trial, that was forming my faith. And, at the Mother Cabrini Shrine and in the churches where I'd worship in New York, that faith was being shaped and structured.

The priest at the Mass—Father Peter Smith—had, as an infant, recovered from an acid-induced blindness and fatally high fever when doctors held no hope for him. The recovery had followed forty-eight hours of prayer to the saint, and the priest told me afterward, "I, for one, know the age of miracles hasn't passed."

Both Patti Ann and I continued to pray and have faith that something would change. At night, as I lay in bed, I would try to move my toes, my fingers, anything. I imagined I was John Wayne in the movie, *Wings of Eagles.* Wayne is married to Maureen O'Hara—yes, my favorite film couple—and is home from the navy. His children cry, and—not being used to the sound—he assumes something terrible has happened and rushes to the stairs. The bannister breaks, he takes a fall, and is paralyzed. Although at first he can't handle his situation, and alienates Maureen, his wife, he eventually tries to motivate himself to work towards a recovery. "I'm going to move this toe. I'm going to move this toe," Wayne tells himself, over and over.

Many of my nights would pass the same way. Move that toe, I'd think. Move that toe.

Help me, God, to move that toe.

But this wasn't a movie. And all there'd be were the pins and the needles. Always the pins and needles.

I seemed to be attracting all the bad luck allocated to my family. Of David and Anita McDonald's eight kids, I was the only one in and out of hospitals. I'd had an appendectomy, a couple of hernias, and now this. I'm serving my penance on earth, I'd think. I'll be able to skip purgatory and go right to heaven when it's time.

What I didn't expect was that lightning would keep striking. But it did, on Thursday, July 23, 1987.

Dinner was over, and one of the nurses' aides, Paula Jacobs, had brought me back to my room. I was watching television when the phone rang and Paula answered. She sounded concerned and brought the receiver to me. Before she placed it to my ear, she warned, "Conor's sick."

Two thousand miles away, I could hear Patti Ann, crying out of control.

Conor had been hospitalized, she told me, and the doctors said he had meningitis. His fever was 105 degrees. She'd stay with him in the hospital, and our families, the Cardinal, and friends would be there for support.

Once again I felt helpless. Patti Ann needed her husband. Our son needed me. And I couldn't be there to help them get through this trial.

Paula tried to console me. Meningitis is serious, she said. But it's not usually fatal any longer. If it's caught early, there aren't any after-effects, either. I began to calm down. Weeks later, I found a way to repay her kindness. Paula lived alone, and one of her cats—they were like children to her—died. I asked another aide to buy a Persian cat to replace it, and I presented the animal to her one night as a surprise. She started crying, and said she'd name it Bailey, after the Irish cream liqueur.

Bailey's since mated and had kittens, so I suppose I left a small part of me in Colorado. But, more importantly, Conor recovered. The antibiotics broke his fever the next day, and a week later, he was released from Mercy Hospital. I was elated.

Malverne, New York, August 1987

In those first few hours, as my baby lay suffering, I felt my faith tested beyond human limits. Conor was burning with fever, and I was yelling to God. "What are you doing to me?" I shouted, between sobs. "I've got Steven in Colorado. Isn't that enough?"

When the crisis passed and we'd returned to my mother's a week later, I grew anxious again. Conor's meningitis had reminded me that there were problems and battles ahead of us, that life hadn't been put on hold while Steven was in Craig. The house closing was scheduled for early August, and once we owned it, Brian would be able to assemble the team put together by Mayor Koch's office to coordinate the renovations.

The papers were to be signed at a lawyer's office in Huntington. Sitting there, while the attorneys reviewed the documents, I noticed a rash on my wrist. I tried to ignore it, but I was really, really nervous.

This is final, I thought as I picked up the pen. This is a commitment.

By the time I'd finished my signature, my body was covered in hives. Panic was setting in again.

In Colorado, Steven said he had only one request.

"All I want," he told me, "is no pukey walls and fluorescent light bulbs. Otherwise, it's going to remind me of the hospital."

My assumption was there wouldn't be too much work to do on the house. When the builders and the architect took a look, they told me I was wrong. Brian arranged that first meeting in early August. He'd made quite a few calls around City Hall, and by the time we'd gotten together in Malverne, deputy mayor Bob Esnard, the city Building Maintenance Department, and architect Thomas Gibson had all been enlisted on the project. So had Peter Lehrer, one of the partners in the huge construction company of Lehrer McGovern Bovis, which had supervised the multi-million-dollar restoration of the Statue of Liberty. Lehrer sent Stephen Karafiol and Bob Arnzen of Target Builders, a Lehrer McGovern Bovis subsidiary, to join the city crew.

With Brian leading the way, we walked through the house.

"Steven and I will sleep downstairs," I said. "We'll need to widen the front door, the doors leading into the kitchen and the bathroom, a couple of the hallways, and . . ."

"Don't you want to be with Conor?" asked Karafiol. "Won't Steven want to be able to see him put to bed, and be there when he wakes?"

Of course I wanted that, I said, but it would be impossible. Even if we could get Steven up the stairs through some kind of lift arrangement, the slant of the roof wouldn't allow him to get all the way into the upstairs bedroom. As I spoke, Karafiol and Arnzen filmed the interior with a portable video camera. For an hour, we looked at every inch of the house. The architect, Tom Gibson, came to what struck me as a gloomy conclusion.

"We've really got to rip this place apart," he said, "and start from scratch."

To my surprise, Arnzen and Karafiol agreed. In the short time he'd been inside, Stephen Karafiol had already visualized a new, expanded floor plan: an elevator to the second floor, a bigger upstairs, a treatment room on the first floor. Brian had been listening quietly. Greg Fried would have to approve any renovations before the city—as the mayor's office had committed to—would pay for them. "Okay," he decided, "let's do it."

For a month, the architect and the builders researched what Steven's needs would be. Craig doctors reminded them that Steven couldn't sense heat or cold, and that the furnace, air conditioning and humidity levels would have to be electronically monitored to give him true independence. He would need a bathroom and shower accessible to a wheelchair, counters that he could fit underneath while seated in his chair, and—ideally—access ramps that wouldn't ice over in winter.

Each day, I'd walk across the street from my parents' house and look at the renovations on ours. Already laborers had begun to gut the inside. The amount of building to be done seemed staggering, and I wondered if it could possibly be finished by Christmas. Steven was ready right now to leave Colorado. He could stay off the respirator for ninety minutes at a time, and the Craig therapists had told me there wasn't much chance of improving on that. He'd rather be on the respirator, Steven himself had said to me. His voice—growing stronger every day as he got used to exercising his vocal cords again—had no strength when he was taking in air on his own. But he couldn't come home until there was a place for him to return to.

"Don't worry," Bob Arnzen told me. "Christmas is no problem. We'll be ready by Thanksgiving." Brian said we'd hold another press conference to acknowledge the city's efforts, a media event to dedicate our new house. All right with me, I said, but I began to wonder: will this house ever feel like our home? At my parents' home, I found a bouquet of roses waiting, with a card.

"There's no place like home," it read. "Love, Steven."

On September 21, the plans were finished. Mayor Koch came to Malverne to introduce the press to the project managers: Karafiol; Arnzen; the electrical engineers from Syska & Hennessey who'd install the two backup generators Brian had decided we had to have; and interior decorator Melanie Nathan. All were donating their services as were a dozen other suppliers.

Monsignor Kowsky said a blessing, the one item the architects and builders couldn't provide. And the one—God's protection—our family needs most of all.

"Again and again," I said, "the people of New York have opened their hearts to us. For those people, we dedicate our home and open its doors wide.

"There will be no more holidays in the hospital," I

announced. "We're planning the biggest Thanksgiving in history." Mayor Koch, who'd later joke he expected to annex our Malverne lot to the City of New York, tried to explain why the city had stretched so far to help us. "The McDonald family," he said, "has come to symbolize more than themselves. They represent extraordinary courage and faith."

The eight weeks of construction were a frantic blur. I was playing sidewalk superintendent—bringing over cookies and soda from my parents' home, reviewing sketches and floor plans, and consulting with Melanie Nathan on the decoration. Like Steven, I wanted no sense of hospital inside. Before construction started, I'd hired a Malverne company to recover two sofas, two chairs, and an ottoman in a jade-and-rose flowered chintz. Those five pieces of furniture, and the living room fireplace, were all that would be left of the original house and its furnishings. The original owner, Mrs. Recogzin, had left these pieces of furniture to us. She was one of my role models as a young girl and always kind to Steven and me. The furniture is a small reminder of her influence on me and her generosity to our family.

Arnzen and Karafiol were doing a masterful job of scheduling and juggling. With so many different contractors involved and so little time allotted, there might be thirty workers on the job at any one time. I'd make my way through the maze of sawhorses, sheetrock, lumber and paint, encouraging the men and taking pictures. I wanted Steven to be able to follow the progress; it was his house, and many of the questions I was trying to answer were decisions he would have made if he'd been there.

Not everything went exactly according to plan. I wanted a smooth wood floor, or tile, with throw rugs for warmth in some rooms. Craig suggested that wall-to-wall carpeting would be preferable; the throw rugs, we were told, could get tangled in the wheelchair's mechanism. I already knew that a similar kind of accident could easily occur. In Colorado, shortly after we'd arrived, a late spring snowstorm hit while Steven, my brother Billy, and I were all outside. I thought the respirator might be damaged by the precipitation and took off my shawl to cover it. "Don't put that thing on," Billy warned. He was right. The fabric caught in the chair's wheels and the chair froze up. I was near tears when an attendant came and helped us in. Not Steven though. He and Billy were laughing—good news, when I thought about it later. Steven's sense of humor had returned.

Every few weeks, I'd return to Colorado. The elevator's in, I'd tell Steven. Or the therapy room's finished. Or the brickface is completed. Before the final trip, in November, when we'd celebrate our second wedding anniversary, then pack for the trip home, I took a last look. The interior still resembled a construction site, and Michel Court was rutted and potholed from the traffic. Still, I had the sense that our house wouldn't be institutional, but homelike. A week later, when Steven and I returned, I'd know for sure. If, that was, the work could be completed in a week.

Don't worry, Arnzen and Karafiol reassured me, don't worry.

Craig, November 1987

The city had ordered a van built in Denver. Starting with a basic Ford Econoline, the customizers raised its roof, added a hydraulic lift to its rear so that whoever was driving me could raise me into the vehicle through the back doors, and built bench seats along one side panel to accommodate passengers other than my nurse. The van would be assigned to the New York City Police Department's fleet. So I began to get nervous when Brian told me he was having them install a compact disc player, and air conditioning.

"I don't know, Brian," I said.

"Look, Steven," Brian countered, "you're going to be using this every day and spending a lot of your time in it. You're going to live in it, if you want to know what I think. The city's not going to pay for that other stuff. We've got private donations—more than a thousand dollars from the Denver police alone—that are going to pay for those extras."

And he was right. I use the CD player all the time.

The van was delivered in the middle of October, just before the Notre Dame-Air Force Academy football game. I noted with pleasure that a big red apple surrounded by the words, "New York, New York," had been painted on the rear-door compartment holding the spare tire. I'd been looking forward to seeing Notre Dame play ever since I'd heard the game was scheduled. Brian and others had made the arrangements, and I was going to sit on the sidelines near the Notre Dame bench where the Notre Dame coach, Lou Holtz, would meet me before the game. We put together a convoy of cars—the van in the lead, with Patti Ann and Sharon Blackburn accompanying me, and others following, including Brian and Barbara Goldy, the public relations director of the Sheraton Tech Center (the hotel used by the New York press and many of our friends)—but, as was often the case when I had to travel, we left late. Patti Ann was nervous—she hadn't been with me on a lot of the outings Sharon and I had taken, and didn't realize the independence I'd developed. She feared that the roundtrip and the game itself might be too much for me to handle.

But I wasn't worried. Arriving in Colorado Springs almost an hour and a half after we were expected, we found that the traffic to the stadium was at a standstill. We were directed off the main road and onto an unpaved shortcut that, eventually, took us into the stadium through the entire Academy corps of cadets, a sea of blue. As we crept through, they peered inside and saw me dressed—head-to-toe—in Notre Dame's blue and gold. Hisses, boos and whistles rose from the crowd, and Sharon began to worry they'd tip the van over. I told her to relax, that God was on our side.

When I made it to the field, the game was about to begin. Coach Holtz rushed over to me, surrounded by photographers and reporters. He'd planned to give me a monogrammed blanket, but it had been forgotten in the hustle. Instead, he took my cap off my head and replaced it with his.

Everything was rush-rush, and the coach just had time to say he thought I had a lot of bravery, strength his team could use for inspiration. "I wish my team had half your courage," Coach Holtz said.

"You're going to win, aren't you?" I asked.

"You can bet your bottom dollar on *that!*" he said.

And the Fighting Irish did. But the game was frustrating for me, too. With the press all around, I had trouble following the action and I realized again how difficult maintaining my privacy had become. By the fourth quarter, I said to Sharon, "Think the media can leave me alone long enough so I can watch the game?" I got worried, too, about the noise. If something went wrong, I feared, no one would be able to hear the alarm on the respirator or my cries for help. At the game's end, the media and the fans who numbered in the thousands crowded around me and onto the field. Like Moses parting the Red Sea, Lou Holtz raced back onto the field and awarded me the game ball that the team had voted to give me. I felt like getting up and walking to the van.

After, as I was being loaded back into the van, Barbara Goldy began to scream. The lift operated in such a way that it appeared my feet, as I rose, would be trapped under a piece of metal extending from the van's floor. Barbara didn't know the lift platform slid backwards a few inches before it stopped rising. She gave an embarrassed apology when she saw I was fine; though, I sensed that people who hadn't known me for a long time would constantly be uneasy around me, unable to get beyond the equipment keeping me alive and supporting my day-to-day existence. "It was nerve-wracking," Barbara would say later. "Every step was a learning experience."

It was difficult for me to play the role of the teacher.

On November 9, 1987, our second wedding anniversary, Father Mychal Judge flew to Craig to say

Mass and to renew our wedding vows. Actually, in the excitement (and in another media swarm), Father Mike rushed through the vow-renewal part of the ceremony, but we forgave him. (Both the *Daily News* and the *Post,* which sent reporters to cover the Mass, published stories saying the vows had been spoken.) One New York radio station even broadcast from the tiny ten-seat Craig chapel.

We hadn't been certain Father Mike would be able to make it. For several months he'd thought he was going to be dispatched to Japan for missionary work there. When Patti Ann would speak to him on the phone, she'd end the conversation with, "Sayonara, Father." He himself said he'd been looking for some sign, some indication from God the Father as to what he should do, and that fall he'd found it. His superior at the Friary asked him to counsel AIDS victims in New York City and he'd accepted the assignment eagerly. Such a selfless task suited his temperament perfectly and allowed him to maintain his other New York ties, which included serving as a member of the board of trustees of Siena College, upstate near Albany.

Like Peter Johnson, Brian, and my family, Father Mike had been a lifeline to New York while I'd been at Craig. I'll never forget the night he called me and started to apologize when the sirens at the fire station on 31st Street just across the street from St. Francis began to blare. "Oh, Steven," he'd said, "I'm sorry."

"Father," I'd told him, "that's music to my ears."

And he'd taken the receiver and held it out the window, so I could hear the street symphony more clearly.

The wedding anniversary was the last important

moment we had at Craig and I wanted it to be special. I kept the plans from Patti Ann until she flew from New York. Three weeks earlier on Halloween, I'd let the therapists dress me as Tarzan—they'd even wrapped plastic vines around my wheelchair—for the hospital costume party. Then another patient made up as a policewoman came and arrested me. Up until then, I hadn't participated much in hospital activities. At the midsummer Field Day, I'd stayed on the sidelines and watched the others run the relays and the obstacle courses. Most of my outings had been with friends and one of my therapists who became a friend, Sharon Blackburn. But as my departure grew closer, I was more outgoing and expansive.

In fact, I felt confident enough to accept Barbara Goldy's offer of a room for the night at the Sheraton after our wedding anniversary Mass and dinner. In October, I'd told Barbara that I wanted to be home for the anniversary—after all, I had already been at Craig longer than most patients—but Brian had told me the house wouldn't be ready. "If it's okay with your doctors," Barbara had said, "you could celebrate here."

"That's not why I brought it up," I told her.

"I know," she said, "but we have the rooms and we'd love to have you."

So it would be that our wedding anniversary night was the first Patti Ann and I spent together outside a hospital (since the shooting a year and a half earlier). The Mass moved both of us to tears, as Father Mike's reading of the gospel often did. "Thank you for the beautiful faith that you've given us," he said. "Just seeing the difference from last year, when you didn't know what the future would bring, is beautiful." At the end, as he had the year before, Father Mike sang.

"When Irish eyes are smiling," he warbled, "the whole world smiles with you."

Our tradition, I thought. Forty of our closest friends joined us at Carole Harrison's Firehouse Museum restaurant for a reception, where a three-piece band played "New York, New York."

The evening, though, wasn't what I'd hoped. It had been a stressful day for Patti Ann. I'd spent a lot of time talking about the future and going home, and she knew there was still much work to be done on the house. Conor was in New York and had had a doctor's appointment. When Patti Ann phoned her mother in the morning, she'd been told that Dr. Martin wouldn't give Conor the shot he'd been scheduled to get, because the baby was running a fever. The meningitis scare was still on her mind and she wept off and on until early afternoon, when Dr. Martin reached her to say the fever was low-grade and that postponing the shot was routine.

Back at the hotel, we ate dinner with the Goldys, Brian, and Father Mike. Then we went upstairs. By arrangement, Sharon Blackburn took the room next to ours. Although she was a therapist, she'd had a lot of hands-on nursing experience when she was at the University of Wisconsin. If any crisis arose, our thinking went, she'd be just a few steps away.

The dryness of the room was brutal on my lungs. Because I can't cough or blow my nose, the congestion built up and I had to be suctioned throughout the night. At midnight, Sharon and Patti Ann put me into bed, and Sharon left. For the rest of the night, every forty-five minutes or so, Patti would have to remove my trache, attach a tube connected to a small vacuum pump to the opening in my throat, and clean out the mucus. Not very romantic.

For Patti Ann, it was a bit of a revelation. I don't think she'd completely considered how our home life was going to be. As she said later, "I had to do a lot that night, a lot of the medical procedures I was just learning. It was like, wow, this is what it's going to be like when we get home. I didn't get any sleep at all. And the thing of being there, alone, with Steven, was weird. A nice weird, but . . . different. After over a year of getting used to not sleeping with someone, being in bed with Steven felt strange." The *whoop-whoosh* of the respirator, a sound I'd never fully gotten comfortable with, filled the hotel room.

About nine the next morning, we called Sharon and told her it was time for breakfast. How had it gone? she asked. I was scared, I told her, but we'd gotten through it. Then I fell asleep. Sharon and Patti Ann, they told me later, watched *Dirty Dancing* on a pay station while I snoozed.

The Teamsters Local 808 in Woodside, Long Island volunteered to drive the van to New York, and on November 20, 1987, four of them, including John Mahoney and Ed Martinez, both retired cops, left Englewood. They'd have the van at Kennedy Airport, the plan went, when I landed the afternoon of the following day—a thirty-four hour, non-stop trip.

The chief executive officer of Federal Express, Fred Smith, agreed to loan his corporate jet to take Patti Ann and me. A former Marine, as I'd been told, helping out a former Navy corpsman. The Marine Corps motto, "Semper Fidelis" never seemed more real to me. When we got to Stapleton Airport in Denver, though, we discovered that no one had anticipated how we'd get into the plane. The door was narrow, and there wasn't an aisle chair once we got inside. Sharon and others had to take the respirator off my chair, and holding it to one side, lift me and my manual chair into the plane. Then I had to be taken out of the chair and seated with the respirator on the floor next to me.

Brian had joined us for the flight. He'd been in Malverne the day before, making sure the house was finished. That day had been unseasonably warm, near sixty, and he'd had no doubts the final aspect of the project—the repaving of Michel Court—would be completed as we crossed the continent. But, minutes before we drove to the airport, Brian had called home and been told the paving couldn't be done. The temperature had dropped, the contractor said, and the asphalt wouldn't soften enough.

"What are you talking about?" Brian had screamed. He'd worked sixteen-hour days to complete our house and bring us home, gotten roughly a half-million dollars worth of donated material and labor, and now some road builder was telling him he couldn't lay down pavement when he, Brian, knew the air had felt more like mid-spring than late fall. "I don't care what it takes," he'd shouted, "I want that road done by the time our van pulls onto it."

Now, weighed down with beepers and radios, Brian seethed. Reporters, cameramen, the mayor and his aides, the first deputy police commissioner—they were all going to be on our doorstep. Sure, the contractor was donating his services, but everyone else had pushed to finish. This one guy could ruin the perfect scenario Brian had spent nine weeks constructing. And because it was too cold? How, Brian wondered, could it be too cold?

When we landed, we found out. Getting off the plane felt like stepping into an arctic freezer. The wind whipped across the tarmac, and the twenty degrees felt like minus twenty. If I could have, I would have gotten down and kissed the ground. I was that glad to be back in New York. But, of course, I couldn't. The van was waiting, and I was hustled inside. Twenty minutes later, we were in Malverne.

I'm not sure what I expected, coming home. I'd seen the pictures on the construction, heard Patti Ann's descriptions, but as we turned onto Michel Court, the anticipation frightened me as much as it cheered me. I could hear the sirens of police vehicles and, more softly, the bagpipe strains of "The Minstrel Boy" and "The Wearin' of the Green." Then, through the windows, I saw the crowds. Hundreds of neighbors and friends. Scores of cops, more than a hundred, lined both sides of the street, standing stiffly at salute. The freshly paved street, Brian noted with relief. A contingent from the Central Park precinct stood nearest the house, and my heart sang. God, I wanted to be with them!

And the house! What had been a modest brick Cape now stood as a beautiful two-story colonial. The United States and Irish flags hung by the door. On the ramp leading to the front door—a ramp I'd learn later that was electrically heated so it wouldn't freeze over in cold temperatures—waited Mayor Koch, Deputy Commissioner Condon, Dick Fay, Steve Karafiol, Bob Arnzen, Peter and Chris Johnson, the mayor of Malverne, the chief executive of Nassau County, our families, police brass, even the ex-Mets outfielder Rusty Staub, who owned one of my favorite Manhattan restaurants. The Emerald Society's Pipers were shivering in their kilts and everyone looked blue with cold. Over the doorway hung a huge red, white and blue banner: "Welcome Home Steven, Patti Ann & Conor."

The crowd parted to make way for us, and the mayor hugged Patti Ann and kissed me on the head. He handed us a gold key and, thankfully from what I could see of the frozen onlookers, said, "It's too cold for a speech. God bless this house."

Patti Ann held the microphone for me.

"It's been a long time," I said. "Patti Ann and Conor and I . . . well, it's very difficult to express our feelings. I worked so hard for this moment. It's just overwhelming. You can see that *this* is really the city of brotherly love, not just Philadelphia. The next time anyone wants to bad-mouth a cop or a New Yorker, they should take a turn down Michel Court and they'll see exactly what it is to be a cop, what it is to be a New Yorker.

"I love New York," I said. "I love you all."

The door to the house slid open, and Patti Ann and I turned and went inside. Patti Ann screamed with joy and surprise, so much had been done. Oh my God, I thought, as I took in the living room, the stairway to the second floor, the kitchen and dining area, and the sliding glass door to the rear deck. I never expected the house to be like *this!* There was no hint of hospital about it, nothing suggesting the institutions I'd spent the last fifteen months of my life in. This home didn't say "handicapped." Instead, it looked like an Irish gentleman's country house.

For those days and weeks at Bellevue and at Craig, I'd been trying to lose myself in the movies a nurse or therapist or friend or loved one would plug into a VCR. For all that time, I'd tried to escape into the characters and plot lines others had created—to imagine myself John Wayne's "Quiet Man." Now I was Natalie Wood in *Miracle on 34th Street,* the girl who gets her dream house, the one she'd asked Santa Claus for.

I'd been wishing for a home to return to. And, through the kindness of friends and strangers alike, my wish had been granted.

Patti was weak with excitement, too. And Brian beamed as we *oohed* and *aahed.* "You went bananas," he'd say later, "and, to me, that moment made the previous nine weeks worth it."

Too soon, we had to leave, to go to the Malverne firehouse for a thank-you reception in honor of everyone who'd lent a hand in the renovations. I was exhausted but happy to see the guys from the precinct. My shield was hanging proudly around my neck, my wife and son were with me, and my life was beginning anew.

"How do you feel?" Mayor Koch asked me.

"I'm 1098," I told him with a smile. That was the police code for "ready to resume patrol." But, I added, "Obviously I just can't climb back into the radio car."

"You will!" my friends in the firehouse shouted. "You will!"

WITNESS:

Richard Fay

My grandfather had been a cop, and from my mother I'd heard stories about families left destitute after officers had been killed. Cops aren't financial wizards; most live month-to-month on their paychecks and their overtime. So I'd made a habit of ensuring that the widows would have money for clothing for the funeral, and for food at their homes afterwards. Most were Catholic, and hosting visitors was the practice. And, I knew, whatever pension money they would receive would take two or three months to arrive.

I had never contributed to an injured officer, however. The monsignor and Brian told me this was a special case and they asked me to visit him, with my brother John.

John had cancer, a terminal case, and was already getting chemotherapy when we first went to Steven's room. John didn't have the financial resources I had, but he'd always helped cops too, and at his printing business would run off tickets, posters and programs —whatever they needed. Steven was still out of it when I first saw him and was introduced to Patti Ann. She seemed as young as my own kids, a little girl whose world had fallen apart. But her faith was remarkable, the embodiment of everything a parochial school taught its students. And she wasn't mad at the guy who shot him! I'm an eye-for-an-eye guy, and that drove me crazy. But her faith was so strong, and she was so forgiving, my own faith became stronger. Today, I love her like a daughter.

My brother Johnny would sit by Steven's bed, and I'd visit with Patti Ann. Steven and Johnny seemed to get strength from each other. Johnny would encourage Steven, telling him that it didn't matter how he lived, just that he *lived.* "Where there's life, there's hope," Johnny would say. "There could be a cure for spinal cord injury some day." When Johnny died, and Steven was still at Craig, he called me.

"We both lost a good pal," Steven said. "We have to think how much better off he'll be in heaven than he was suffering here on earth." It was the first time, I think, I'd heard Steven speak in his own, full voice.

We discovered that Steven's wheelchair wouldn't be able to get in and out of the Stuyvesant Town apartment. Patti Ann was looking for a house to move into when he got back from Colorado, but I was concerned. I didn't want her to spend all the money that had been raised for them on a home. If the city changed its policy, and Steven was no longer on the payroll, they'd need that money and the interest it was earning, to survive.

I arranged for them to put the funds into government bonds and asked my accountant to straighten out their finances. Then Patti said she'd found the house she wanted, on Michel Court in Malverne, across the street from her parents.

We were at the Bear, Stearns office when she told

me, and I excused myself to discuss it with Artie Crames, another partner and, like me, a regular Bellevue visitor. Artie and I agreed we'd buy the house for them, and I returned and told her. "Don't worry about it," I said. She was so moved, so upset that I might have thought that had been what she was asking.

"That's something we'll do," I told her, "but you've got to promise me that the money taken in through the PBA, and the Javits Center fundraiser, will stay intact. Tell me that you won't draw on it, and that you'll live on the police salary."

Patti agreed.

The first time I ever saw the house, in person, was the day Steven came home. My wife Pat, our daughter Sarah and I were there, at the front door with the mayor and the builders and the families, to greet Steven. I'd seen some pictures, which Patti would send or bring by, but as long as she was satisfied, I hadn't needed to see it myself. I hadn't seen Steven since he'd left Bellevue, either. Brian Mulheren asked me to go to Colorado, but I'd thought it almost an invasion of Steven's privacy.

"No," I told Brian. "He's out there for one reason. To rehabilitate himself and get healthy."

When I did see the house, I was thrilled. It looked so normal inside, like the typical newly married couple's home. The interior, which Patti had decorated so beautifully, was warm, with no feeling that a handicapped person lived there. I told Steven how happy it made me. "I'm sorry it's not twice as big," I said. "And I'll always be here to help you."

I'm not an emotional guy. My first wife died, my brother died, and I learned not to cry in front of my children. But I had chills when I heard Steven speak the day he returned, and it wasn't because of the cold. There but for the grace of God, I thought, goes my child.

I've known priests, even Cardinals, in my life. I've never seen the faith exhibited by these two kids. It's genuine, not phony. After my brother died, I suffered a stroke. I lost sensation on my left side, and whenever I felt sorry for myself, I'd talk to Steven. He was my therapy, my medicine.

"Hey, pal," I tell him, "you make me feel *good.*"

Twelve

Malverne, November 1987

Like Steven, I treasured the house as more than I'd ever hoped for. But, in those first days, the normal family life I'd imagined we'd lead wasn't there. Reporters, family and friends were constant visitors and the blessing Father Mike had bestowed upon us at our wedding anniversary—"Give these two privacy"—seemed an elusive wish.

Before we'd left Craig, Dr. Lammertse told us the adjustment would be difficult. "Disability in the hospital is a norm," he'd warned. "Outside, you're back in the real world, where it isn't." I was understanding that better. At night, lying in our bed, I'd hear the respirator pushing the air into Steven. After a couple of hours, I'd have to leave and climb into the bed in the spare room across from Conor's. There, by myself, I'd freeze in one position, motionless, and try to imagine what Steven was experiencing. After a minute or two, I'd give up. My pillow would be damp with tears.

During the day, as the visitors came and went, I'd feel uncomfortable, as if it wasn't even my home, and I'd take Conor across the street to my mother's. Sometimes, I'd leave him with her and climb into the car, and drive. Anywhere, just to be by myself.

I'd hoped we'd be able to call friends over for dinner, to go out and get Chinese food or take in a movie. But there were endless demands on our time. Steven's schedule, and the insomnia he was suffering each night—he'd stay up until three or four in the morning, letting the night nurse, Mary Horton, read the letters that came in the mail that morning, or watching old movies—meant that most mornings he stayed in bed. Every other day, the morning shift nurse would administer his bowel program and he often wouldn't be dressed and in his chair until early afternoon. When I'd retreat to my mother's, she'd remind me things could be worse, that we had Conor, that the miracle we prayed for every night could come at any moment.

When Thanksgiving came, our first together at home in two years, I held that thought. And I prayed to the Blessed Mother, as I did every night, that Steven would walk again.

Give us our miracle, I said to myself as the family clasped hands together in grace over the holiday feast, and someone else can have this beautiful house. We'll walk away from it, just like that. In front of me, hanging on the wall, was the Irish blessing that read "May the road rise to meet you. May the wind be always at your back. May the sun shine warm upon your face; the rain soft upon your fields. And until we meet again, may God hold you in the palm of his hand."

Amen, I thought, hearing the lines in my mind.

"Amen," whispered the family around the table, as each finished his own meditation.

Malverne, November 1987

Normalcy was coming with difficulty to Patti Ann and me, and—it seemed to me—in odd ways. Late at night I'd snack, sending the night nurse downstairs to the kitchen for cheese, meat, whatever was in the refrigerator. I'd call friends in Colorado and then describe the pizza I'd had for dinner, and I'd spend Saturdays and Sundays watching football on television—Notre Dame, if the team was on, and the Giants and the Jets. Phil Simms's jersey and a game ball signed by his teammates held a prominent place in the cabinet in the second-floor guest room, as did the baseball glove worn by Met pitcher Jesse Orosco in the seventh game of the 1986 World Series, and a turn-of-the-century history of the Police Department, a gift from the police commissioner himself, Ben Ward. Requests for us to appear at breakfasts, church groups, fundraisers poured into the house. Behind many of the invitations, I began to sense, was the presumption I'd improved, that my injuries were no longer serious. Occasionally, I'd get an odd look from an individual I'd just been introduced to when I'd make no gesture to grasp his outstretched hand.

But, my return home notwithstanding, I was as seriously hurt as the moment after Shavod Jones's bullet cut into my spine. There had been no neurological improvement, although there was improvement in my overall medical condition. And these shattered pieces of lead could still be seen on the x-rays, lodged below the second vertebra. I wanted to go back to work in some capacity, to counsel and advise other officers, but it would have to be on my own schedule. "There was a department perception," Dr. Fried would say, "that Steven had a transient condition, that he'd regained movement. And that perception led to some complaints—nothing public, just small pockets of simmering resentment—that Steven had gotten special treatment, and extra media attention. But when he was shot, he was the most seriously injured-in-the-line-of-duty cop to survive, and those injuries and the complications they present, haven't changed."

I wanted to respond in a thoughtful way to the homecoming—my mind was as keen as ever and using it was one thing I still had to look forward to—and Peter Johnson contacted the *Daily News* for me. The paper would be happy to publish a piece, he said.

"Where should we begin?" Peter asked me.

I thought back to Thanksgiving Day 1985, when I'd been assigned to the Central Park Precinct. The sun had been setting and the parade and game watchers were sitting down to dinner. The park had been left to me and to the homeless people, snuggled like babies on their beds of wood bench.

I'd been sad, even lonely, that night, watching how their day had ended. Guilty, I'd imagined the turkey and sweet potatoes that awaited me—and not them—at my parents' home. Praying silently for them, as I continued my patrol, I thanked God for his blessings.

Now it was two years later. Some things had changed, I told Peter, but others had not.

"What do you mean?" Peter asked, puzzled, his pencil paused in mid-air.

"I can't walk," I said, "but I still can be moved. I can't touch, but I can still feel. And I thank God every day for his blessings on me and my family."

I hadn't been to Central Park since the day I'd been shot. But the others I'd been with that first Thanksgiving, many of them, were still there. And my sadness and guilt remained, too.

My second Thanksgiving as a cop had been in Bellevue. Brian had arranged for dinner in the hospital cafeteria for myself and the six heroic cops who'd been wounded in a Bronx shootout earlier in the year. A lot of us, and our families, had cried that day. But we were so grateful to be alive and to be needed by the ones we loved.

"Peter," I said, "you know I'd fantasize about Thanksgiving in New York when I was at Craig. I'd dream about the times when I was a small boy and I'd watch the clowns from Macy's, and the huge floating balloons of Superman and Mickey Mouse jiggling gently in the air above Broadway, like cartoon clouds in a concrete canyon. But what I remember best was staring at my father—he was a sergeant then—standing at attention. Stiff blue tunic, dress gray gloves. And he'd smile at me, with a sly wink, like we had something that only little boys and cops could understand."

"How did you feel on days like that?" Peter asked. "Don't you feel differently today?"

How did I feel? Good. I felt good, especially when

Grandpa Conway was by my side, his hand on my shoulder. Good, warm, at home. And knowing that, someday, I wanted to be in that uniform, too. "No," I said, "today isn't different. It's better. Patti Ann's made my family bigger and stronger. Hundreds of New Yorkers, who have written letters and offered prayers, have given me a new sense of home. And I still want to help people, to be a police officer."

A year later, I wasn't sure I'd live. Or, some nights, that I wanted to live. I knew now, though, that I had a purpose. Conor, nine months old and just beginning to toddle, pushed a toy truck towards Peter. "I want to roll down Broadway," I said, "with him in my lap." Conor would see, like I'd seen, the department store windows with their elves and reindeer, the magic that signals the start of the Christmas season in Manhattan. Later, when he was old enough to understand, I'd tell him how the people of the city had reached out to me.

"You know what's funny, Peter?" I said. "It's ironic that this has made it so clear to me how blessed Conor is to have loving, caring parents." As a police officer, I'd seen the torment and abuse that's inflicted on children. Sometimes, the babies died; others would grow to adolescence and become dealers or muggers, carrying guns or knives and delivering the same hurt and suffering they'd received.

Peter watched Conor playing with his toy. "It's like your life has begun again," he said.

"That's right," I agreed. I knew the chance of walking again was minimal, that going back on patrol, feeling the adrenalin rush of pursuit, was an against-all-odds long-shot. But I owed it to Conor, to this small, smiling boy—and to the children he'd have—to make New York a better place to live.

"End the article this way," I told Peter. "Say, 'On this day, I thank all of you for holding me in your hearts and minds and prayers. As we all sit at our Thanksgiving tables, let us give thanks for our good fortune. Let us remember that for all of us, the greatest gift is to feel. Not touch. And the hardest task is not to move. But to be moved.'"

Conor laughed at some private baby joke. I blew into a straw, so my wheelchair would turn and give me a better look at him.

Malverne, December 1987

Ethel Bass, one of the top producers for ABC's "20/20," had approached us, asking for permission to interview us at home for a show to air just before Christmas. Barbara Walters, she said, would be the interviewer, and Steven and I agreed. Both Brian and Dr. Fried had urged Steven to take control of the media spotlight he'd be in, coming out of Craig—they'd said the same when he'd left Bellevue—and to use that platform to speak about issues important to him. Why the public ought to respect police officers, for example, and the nature of spinal cord injuries. We respected Walters and liked the idea of telling our story from beginning to end. She'd get it right, we thought, and be sensitive to the topics Steven wanted to raise.

On December 3, the "20/20" crew arrived at the

house. I don't know what I expected—a producer, a camera, Walters maybe—but Bass brought enough equipment and technicians to outfit a local station. Our garage looked like a small studio, with monitors, sound boards and tape machines, and bright strobe lights and cameras filled the living room.

The morning had passed by the time Walters arrived. She was assertive from the first, which reminded me that she was a tough, attractive lady who didn't get where she is by smiling. She made Bass rearrange the set-up a few minutes after she'd walked in, and when Steven's face began to sweat a little, she insisted the lights be turned down immediately. We'd seen her on ABC a lot, and the command she had over her crew—the way they jumped for her—was surprising. You didn't get that sense, watching her on the screen.

Bass said that Steven would be interviewed, then me. As Walters led him through questions about the day he was shot, why he'd become a police officer, and how he'd been able to forgive Shavod Jones, I stayed upstairs with Conor, who was grumpy and crying. Steven quickly got tired—neither his voice nor his neck muscles were as strong as they are today—and smiled only once, after Walters said, "You amaze me." When my turn came, Steven rode the elevator up to the family room to take my place.

Neither Steven nor I had discussed what we were going to say. We hadn't felt the need to. It had been best when what we had to say came from the heart, when people could hear how we really felt, but I knew I was nervous. As I sat, Walters told me to relax. She began by asking me about the day of the shooting, and I told her how I'd been driven from Pennsylvania, ignorant of the extent of Steven's injuries. When I saw him, I told her, "I said to God, 'How can you do this to Steven? He's such a good person.'" Reliving that day I could feel the tears start to come. I looked across at Barbara. She seemed cool.

Then she asked me about our relationship, how it had changed physically. I hesitated. Steven was the same person I'd always loved, and he was still attractive to me. How could I get that message across?

"Do you know what's hard?" I said, almost forgetting the camera was on me. "Seeing other people as a family. And that'll never go away. Because, if it does, it means that my feelings for Steven have gone. I want him to hold my hand, to touch me. If I could turn the clock back, and have him hold me once again . . ."

I broke off. Barbara Walters looked uncomfortable. A year later, she said in an interview that it was the one time in her career she'd lost her composure. "[Patti Ann] had tears," she said, "and I had tears."

When the interviews were finished, she came up to the family room to spend ten minutes with Steven and myself. "I think your love and forgiveness is the essence of Christmas," she told us, and we felt flattered.

Two weeks later, on December 18, the segment aired. Four of us—Brian, Rose Garibaldi (one of Steven's nurses), Steven and myself—watched. The piece opened with a photo of our Christmas card, a family portrait without Steven's trache tube showing. "Eighty-five police officers are killed each year, on average, in the United States," Barbara Walters said, "and hundreds more are injured. This is dedicated to all of them." Then she described our card. "Picture perfect," she said with irony, as the screen filled with a close-up of Steven, in his dark blue dress uniform, wearing his medal of honor, trache tube in, saying with great effort why he'd become a cop.

"It had been," Steven said, "my ambition, my dream to help others."

No more than five minutes into the segment, I had to leave the room. Steven was describing the shooting. And I didn't want to relive that day still another time.

I've never seen the entire show. I doubt I ever will. But Ethel Bass called to say it had been nominated for an Emmy Award. And Peter Johnson guessed it had not only raised $20,000 for Steven's fund in contributions from viewers across the country but raised the consciousness of all who saw it.

Don't give up hope, don't give up faith, I'd told Barbara Walters, and something good will happen. According to Ethel and to Peter, that message had rung true.

Malverne, March 1988

Brian watched the "20/20" show with me after Patti Ann walked out. "Well done," was his judgment, but I was unhappy. There'd been the contrast between the Christmas card and the reality of my condition—and I hated to be reminded how hurt I was. (We have a family portrait hanging on the wall behind the dinner table, a photograph taken after I'd come home, and there's no trache showing there either.) I'd gotten tired as I was talking, and it had showed. But, more importantly, the point I'd been trying to make that I was nothing special, that most cops felt the way I did about the job, had been lost.

"After you made an arrest of a youngster," said Barbara Walters on the show, "you'd go to the families, and counsel the kids in your off-hours?"

"Yeah," I answered, "I did."

"And you'd give them your phone number?" she said.

"Yeah," I said, "in case they wanted to do something, to play basketball, or wanted someone to talk to."

During the December 3, 1987, taping, I'd added that this had been a technique I'd learned from other cops on the job. That's got to be the first step, I explained, because after a boy or girl is arrested, the parents become responsible. When I—or any other police officer—goes knocking on a door to follow up, I'm just being a cop. "For two years," I told Walters, "I had great teachers. I picked it up from them."

None of that was televised. I wished there had been time in the segment to show more of the way I felt about being a cop, and less time spent on my current condition, but I knew television's limitations. That material ended up on the cutting room floor.

After I'd been home a few weeks, I'd gotten a letter from Dennis O'Malley, the director of Craig Hospital. This will be the most difficult time, he'd warned, when all your expectations crash into your reality. He was right. At Bellevue, and at Craig, I'd thought about the life I'd lead when I got home, the tasks I'd be able to accomplish, the trips I'd take. But the dependence was too great, like a crushing weight on Patti Ann and me.

One afternoon, when Dr. Fried was visiting, I told him I might be better off dead.

"Doc," I said, "if anything were to happen to me, I'd just as soon you didn't rush to help."

"Never would I take a life," Dr. Fried said. "I'm Jewish, but I don't believe in euthanasia or abortion. To me, there's no such thing as mercy killing. You want to kill somebody, you know how to do it. You don't need a doctor."

"What if I get worse?" I asked.

"How am I going to know?" the doctor asked. "You'll never get me to do you in. Because two seconds after you're gone the news bulletin comes along that they've figured out all you gotta do to fix the spinal cord is take vitamin G."

Every day, I'd spend some time—a few minutes, or an hour—listening to a police radio in my therapy room. There was usually a second radio in the van, a handheld one that was the property of whichever officer was assigned to drive me that day. I'd get excited following the calls, wishing I could somehow respond. Then depression would set in. What, I'd wonder, could my police role possibly be?

One was suggested by another injured cop. Richie Pastorella had asked me to join the Self-Support Group and attend its monthly meetings in Queens.

The Self-Support Group had been founded by Pastorella—a detective assigned to the Bomb Squad—in 1983, a year after a New Year's Eve bomb planted by a Puerto Rican terrorist group, the FALN, had blown up in Pastorella's face. At the time, Pastorella—married with two teen-aged children—

had been with the Bomb Squad eighteen months. He'd handled about seventy-five calls, usually to confiscate illegal fireworks or to conduct a post-blast investigation. That New Year's Eve had been the only time Pastorella and his partner Tony Senft had ever confronted a live device.

Pastorella, a big, handsome man with a lot of confidence, would visit the Police Academy and the precinct houses with other injured officers and lecture recruits and patrolmen and women alike on the importance of protecting themselves. I can remember him once describing his personal night of horror.

"I'd joined the Bomb Squad," he'd said, "because I wanted to be more than just one of twenty-seven thousand. Remember Tom Wolfe's *The Right Stuff*? And how there were pilots, and pilots? Well, I wanted to distinguish myself. First, I became a forensic technician, one of just seventy-three in the department; then I joined the Bomb Squad, one of twenty-six. I was trying to reach the pinnacle of my profession.

"A few minutes before 9:30 P.M. on December 31, 1982, my partner Tony and our German shepherd High Hat responded to a call that a bomb had gone off at 26 Federal Plaza. By the time we got there, the radio reported a second had exploded at police headquarters, three blocks away. We rushed over.

"An officer, Rocco Pascarella, was on the ground. One of his legs was missing, just below the knee. He wanted to talk—'brown paper bag,' he said a couple of times—and raised himself up on his elbow to be better understood. I threw my coat over his leg so he wouldn't know it was gone.

"His name was so like mine, I was afraid my family

would hear a news broadcast and assume it was me. Then High Hat pulled Tony towards two support columns not far away. There were two paper bags and High Hat sat between both. In the meantime, passers-by were gathering and there weren't enough cops to keep them back. I was screaming, 'Get away!' and people were coming closer to see what I was talking about. Because of the holiday, we were the only members of the squad on duty. We'd have a long wait before any expert backup support would arrive. But we didn't have much equipment to work with: just armored suits, and special "blankets" to cover the bombs.

"'Look, Tony,' I said, 'we have to do something quick. Someone could get killed.' With Tony behind me, I approached one of the bags. Kneeling, I began to lift the blanket. The bomb—four sticks of dynamite—exploded, driving the plate on the front of my suit up into my face."

Pastorella lost both eyes, 75 percent of his hearing, the fingers of his right hand, and suffered bad, bad burns on his right arm and face. Senft, behind him, lost one eye and most of his hearing. The fourth bomb never blew up; its firing mechanism didn't work. Months later, after his face had been reconstructed by plastic surgeons and he'd been discharged from the hospital, Pastorella felt adrift at home, alone, wondering if learning to dress himself and to cook were all life held for him. His wife and Senft both reminded him he wasn't the only injured cop.

"We have problems, too," Senft told Pastorella. "It's not all that's left, unless you want it to be."

Pastorella had contacted the employee relations section of the department and asked for a list of all line-of-duty injured officers who hadn't been able to return to the job. He got twelve names and a promise of office space. Those twelve became the core of the Police Department's Self-Support Group, meeting once a month to talk to each other, visiting newly injured cops and their families, negotiating on their behalf with doctors and psychologists, and reaching out to healthy cops to remind them of the toll the job can take. "The Police Department doesn't send us," Pastorella would say. "We go on a voluntary basis. We are the only fraternal organization within the Police Department that seeks no new membership.

"We do not want you," he'd tell recruits, "to join us."

Nevertheless, by the time I was released from Craig, the Self-Support Group's membership had swelled to thirty-two, twelve of whom were—like me—on the mayoral exempt list, paid at full salary by the department but, at the moment, unable to return to duty in any capacity.

What I liked about the Self-Support Group was its effort to comfort and help the families of other officers, even those whose injuries had happened off-duty. There'd been two other spinal-cord-injured officers in Bellevue when I was there. One, Tom Mann, hurt himself in a diving accident off-duty. The other, Al Cortez, had crashed in his patrol car. Both had been paralyzed and both needed support. Their circumstances had been different from mine: Mann was off-duty, and Cortez was under investigation, though never charged, by the department's internal affairs section in the Seventy-seventh Precinct's Buddy Boys scandal. That had made their needs more acute, and Pastorella's group had been very helpful. It also helped me define my role in the department.

A quote from a famous American came to mind after my first meeting with the Self-Support Group and those brave police officers who have gone on to their next patrol, that is, "uncommon valor was their common virtue." Their sacrifices are too quickly forgotten.

On February 26, 1988, Eddie Byrne, a rookie cop, was assassinated by Queens crack dealers as he sat in his car in front of the house of a witness in a drug case. He was twenty-two years old and the first of seven officers who'd die in 1988 on the job on New York streets. On television, I'd watched the suspects' taped confession. "I saw his hair stand up," the alleged shooter said. "It was like someone put his head under a hair dryer."

That perp's not of this world, I thought. Then I corrected myself. No, he's too much of this world. This material world, where a leather jacket and a new pair of sneakers can be worth a young man's life. I told Brian I wanted to go to the Byrne funeral. In Colorado, being with other cops, showing solidarity by attending funerals, had been my lifeline to New York City.

At the church, Eddie's father and mother were distraught, and I ached with their hurt. But it seemed Eddie Byrne's death was already being used as a political opportunity by some officials and clergy. I couldn't stop thinking about the parents he'd left behind; I wondered what the politicians were thinking.

* * *

On Christmas Eve, I'd gotten to Midnight Mass and been awed by the beauty of the celebration. As I'd looked up at the Gothic arches, I'd said a prayer for improvement, some sign that my body was getting better. My eyes caught the symbols of the Holy Spirit, and they said to me, don't give up. But there'd been nothing. On Sundays at Mass, I'd say the same prayer. And every evening at home, when a Eucharistic minister would stop by to give Patti Ann and me holy communion, I'd pray some more.

Let me move my hands. My toes. Anything.

St. Patrick's Day came and I drove the length of Fifth Avenue in my wheelchair, puffing until I felt ready to pass out, correcting the chair's steering as it veered to one side or the other. Then it was the Easter season. When I'd been in Bellevue the year before, a month prior to flying to Craig, I'd received an unsigned letter just before Ash Wednesday. Both Patti Ann and I had received thousands of letters from friends and strangers alike, but this one—I thought as one of the nurses read it to me that night—was special. "Dear Steven," the writer had begun, "I am writing to you because I need your strength and faith for what I am undertaking. I decided that I would give up drinking for Lent, and forever, and I am having a hard time trying to kick the habit. I have been drinking for about thirty years, every night, night after night, for no reason at all.

"I have made a commitment to give up drinking and I credit my abstinence so far (I have not had a drink for six days now), to thinking about you and your wife Patti and your sweet baby Conor.

"I think of you all the time. I go to Mass every morning, and I light a candle for you so that you might walk again, and by doing this, I find the strength to take each day at a time and try to stay sober. I am doing this for myself, but I need your faith and your strength that you have in God and I know that if I keep you in my heart and prayers, surely God is going to help me kick my drinking habit.

"I want you to know that I am praying for your recovery and I will be writing to you from time to time to keep you posted. I read about you all the time in the newspapers and I have cut out your pictures to keep me going. I will not tell you my full name, but it is Anne.

"Thinking of you and remembering you with warmest thoughts and prayers . . ."

When the nurse had finished, I'd asked her to fold the three sheets of purple paper and save them. Twenty other letters had come in the mail that day, but I didn't want to hear any more. Anne's words had stayed with me, through the night, the next day, for the entire year. A week or two later, she'd written again. "I made it through Easter," she said. "Thank God and thank you and Patti Ann for giving me the strength." The second letter had reinforced the high the first gave me; I felt I was rising off the bed.

Now it was another Ash Wednesday, and Patti Ann and I were going to Mass at St. Agnes, the Rockville Centre church I'd attended as a kid. As Bob Dalia was lowering me on the van's lift, I remembered the days I'd sneak off to the pizza parlor, grabbing a church bulletin so I could tell my mother who'd said the Mass. That seemed so long ago. A few friends came up, said hello, touched my hands . . . and we were inside. The organ's chords and the choir's sweet voices filled the space. Patti Ann, holding Conor, bowed her head in prayer. Near her sat her father, and brother Billy.

I began, again, to remember Anne's letter. "I think of you all the time," she'd said. "I need your faith and your strength . . ."

Idly, I looked at my left hand. Its fingers were stretched out, suspended above the chair's arm, like a diver's about to enter the water. Not unusual. They'd look that way after a spasm, and Patti Ann or a nurse or someone else who knew enough to keep the joints and bones in proper position, would gently bend the fingers forward. As I'd tried so many times before, I willed my fingers to close.

Amazingly, they did. I watched as I made a loose fist. Had Patti Ann seen? I looked up. No, she was preoccupied with Conor. Could I unfold the fist? No. I'd have to wait for another spasm. Would I be able to do it again? I didn't know, but for a moment I'd gotten something back.

Outside the church, I tried to get Patti's attention. "Pat," I said, "I've got something to tell you." But she was surrounded.

It wasn't until that evening that Patti Ann and I were finally alone, and I could show her. "Look at my left hand," I said. Then I made my fist.

"You did that?" she said. "You made that happen?"

She held the closed fist, gently caressing the fingers. "Thank God," she said.

I did thank God, but I also thought of Anne, whoever she was.

Malverne, April 1988

As I watched Steven close his hand, I knew something was still going on inside him, that my prayers to the Blessed Mother had been heard. But the doctors weren't overly optimistic. I'd called Craig and spoken to Dr. Lammertse. How much more can we hope for? I'd asked.

"Sometimes people get better," he'd answered, "but that little function isn't a likely omen."

That stung.

"If you don't want to say it means anything," I told Dr. Lammertse, "that's fine. But don't take it away from us. That's something we're going to hold onto. It took nearly two years to get it."

Who's to say something else won't return in another six, or eight, or ten months? If it happens, I thought, it happens. If it doesn't, it doesn't. But I could keep reaching for it.

Two weeks later, Steven could move the toes of his left foot. Since then, there's been nothing.

I can't give up, I'd tell myself. It's not easy. But I can't.

The best moments were those we'd share with children. Steven became a regular visitor to St. Mary's Hospital for Children, a Long Island institution whose kids would show Steven their homework, draw pictures for him, and laugh with excitement when he'd roll into their ward. After driving him over there one afternoon, Bob Dalia told me, "You know, he reminds me of Mickey Rooney in that movie where he's the mayor of Boys Town. At St. Mary's, Steven knows everybody and likes everybody and tries to touch each kid he sees."

Together, we'd talk to schoolchildren. One spring Sunday, we drove over to Rockville Centre to visit the St. Agnes High School CCD class. Steven wanted to tell them about Ash Wednesday and remind them that he shared their background. "Why did it happen at Mass?" he wondered out loud, as the students sat silently. "I'm not supposed to be able to move anything. I wish it was the ability to breathe, but I'll take that. The most important thing I can say, the most important thing you can do, is believe in prayer. I just know that some day I'm going to be able to breathe without this respirator and to hold Patti and Conor again."

Steven reminded the students, and me, that he'd been visited in Bellevue by a man who'd gone to the Yugoslavian village of Medjugorje, where six teenagers—the Visionaries—were witnessing each day the apparition of the Blessed Mother. That man had showed a videotape of the teenagers praying, and had urged Steven himself to pray to the Blessed Mother, to say seven Our Fathers, Hail Marys and Glory Be's. "I guess we have always prayed," Steven told these children, "but I don't think we had ever been given direction like that. Patti Ann will always say, 'Say your seven sevens.' I just believe that the Blessed Mother had so much to do with my being able to move my hand.

"I don't know you," Steven continued, "but I grew

up in this town. I went to your school and I can just imagine you're a lot like me. Being a cop, I saw a lot of kids your age in Central Park and on 42nd Street. I know you may want to give up and do whatever because you get upset with your parents, but you have to believe in prayer. I could have given up a long time ago. Patti Ann and other people always told me to keep on praying, that something will happen. If I didn't believe that, I may never have lived to see my fingers move. I don't know what that means. Maybe a month, a year, or ten years, I'll be able to move the rest of me."

Steven paused, and I could tell he wanted to rest. One of the students raised her hand. "How do you feel?" she asked me. I wanted to give an answer as straight, as real as Steven's. I held his hand and spoke quickly. "Steven had no choice," I said. "The suffering is his. I couldn't believe God would do this. I'd always done everything the right way. I got into trouble like everybody else—I was normal—but I did what my parents told me to do. I wasn't into drugs or drinking. So I couldn't understand why, when the doctor said, 'He's paralyzed.' I felt like running somewhere, to get away.

"When my cousin, Father Seamus O'Boyle, came here from England after the shooting, on a visit, he'd talked to me about God's love. 'He had no part in that devilish act,' Seamus told me, 'but He's there to help you pull together the rest of the way.'

"But there've been miracles," I said. "That's what I hold onto. I love Steven very much. There's been a lot of goodness with the bad. I get upset to see Steven the way he is, but they never thought he would sit in a chair. It's not easy, but you go on."

I explained we were getting out more, going to restaurants and movies, trying not to isolate ourselves and dwell on self-pity. But, I said, sometimes the stress led me to explode at Conor over a carelessly thrown toy, or at my family down the street. "She takes a lot out on me, too," Steven interjected. The kids laughed as we smiled at each other.

"Your faith's special," one student said. "Is it because of the shooting? Or has it always been a part of your lives?"

Steven answered the question. "I don't want to scare you," he said, "but until something happens in your life like this, you don't think about it. You don't want to think about it. You don't want to be tested. But when it happens, you can't ignore whatever it is. You lean on your faith a lot more than you would have had it not happened."

He was tired again and had to pause more often. He stared directly at the boy who'd asked. "*You,*" he emphasized, "don't have to wait till something happens . . ."

Steven halted.

". . . Your relationship with God, with Jesus, with Mary . . ."

With effort, he continued.

". . . No matter what happens, it's a very good thing . . ."

". . . It's not extraordinary, it's all yours. I'm not the exception . . ."

". . . I just happen to be a cop doing my job. I'm not extraordinary."

Steven was too tired to finish. "You've done fine," I turned to him and said. Behind me, the students stirred. Then one spoke clearly from the back of the room. "We're going to be praying for that miracle to happen," she said.

Thirteen

Malverne, June 1988

Every day's mail would bring more invitations and awards. Both Steven and I would be honored as one of the national Fathers and Mothers of the Year. Schools, police groups, and Sunday school classes wanted us to speak. I was feeling distant from my old friends; Steven's and my lives had accelerated—for all the wrong reasons—into a whirl of black-tie invitations, celebrity events, and influential friends. A girlfriend I hadn't seen for months would call, and I felt as if we lived in different countries. We'd gone to high school and college together, hung out on the weekends with each other, and now—when I tried to explain to her what I'd been doing with my free time—I worried she'd think I was trying to impress her. But I wasn't.

"You know," another friend told me one afternoon, "some people are jealous of you."

I was stung and didn't know what to say. Sensing my hurt at her comment, realizing what she'd said, she mumbled an apology and hung up.

How could anyone understand our lives without living them? The press had suggested, for one, that our house would be a technological marvel, that a computer named HAL would be programmed to respond to Steven's voice and would be controlled by a wireless microphone mounted on his chair. "The fourth member of the family," the *Daily News* had called it, and they published a diagram suggesting that the TV, the phone, the lights, the front door, the elevator, and the house's heat, air-conditioning and humidity would all be directed by Steven's commands to the computer. This wasn't the first time others had assumed high tech could give Steven unusual freedom. At Bellevue, a University of Virginia professor had installed a computer that was supposed to respond to commands given by eyesight—that is, Steven could look in a certain direction on the screen and tell the computer what he wanted it to do. But the professor and his assistant could never stay long enough to correct a problem when something went wrong, and the cops and nurses didn't know enough to be any help. Eventually, they took the machine out. Steven never did have any success with it.

HAL didn't help us, either. The system, a jumble of interconnected wires and boxes, was in the first-floor therapy room. The keyboard and monitor were on a table, but the plugs and connectors were on the floor. Within a couple of days, Conor had crawled underneath and pulled everything apart. I had no idea how to put it back together and neither did anyone else around the house. "Don't bother," Steven told me, "don't worry about it. I'm always going to have someone with me."

Conor would scramble up on the chair, kiss and

touch his daddy's face and play with Steven's trache, occasionally pulling it out. Or he'd punch the buttons on the respirator, setting off its alarm. For those first months, I'd pay attention when they were together, worried that Conor might accidentally hurt Steven. But I'd never keep Conor away. I wanted him to love his father, to understand that when he wanted to share his cookie with Steven, he'd have to feed it to him, and when he wanted to go for a ride, he'd have to climb into his father's lap himself.

One afternoon, the three of us were upstairs. I was making the beds and Conor and Steven were in the family room, watching television. As I tucked in a blanket, I heard Conor scream, a cry of terror. I ran to him and saw he'd gotten behind Steven, out of his sight, and had become curious about the chair's wheels. As Steven had tried to turn the chair around to see what Conor was doing, Conor's hand caught in one of the wheels and was being twisted by the metal spokes. Thank God Steven had stopped as soon as he heard Conor wail. I tried to pull it out. No way. It was jammed, already turning red.

"Oh no," I cried, "Steven. His hand's pinned. Move forward! Move forward!"

The chair's motor was powerful enough to sever Conor's hand. If Steven blew the wrong way into his tube, the damage might be permanent. He grabbed the plastic straw with his lips, and puffed. The chair inched forward, and I scooped our baby up and rushed downstairs to Pat Dillon, the nurse on duty. Conor was all right, she said. The hand was bruised, but the skin was not broken and he could move it. Then I realized I'd left Steven. I went upstairs to tell him, and he was crying.

"I'm sorry," he said. "I didn't know he was there. I'm sorry."

"It's all right," I told him, wiping my own tears. "Everything's okay."

Publicly, we kept sending a message of hope and faith. At the Mother of the Year Award, I shared a few words with Ivana Trump, developer Donald Trump's gracious wife. Like me, she was an honoree. We'd first spoken at the Midnight Mass Christmas Eve where the Trumps had been introduced to us by one of the Cardinal's aides. She'd seemed warm and natural then and at the awards ceremony she greeted me like an old friend. That wasn't always the case with the celebrities we'd meet. At the Father of the Year ceremony, two weeks later, singer Kris Kristofferson made a point of inviting us to hear him at the Bottom Line, a Manhattan nightclub where he was performing a few days after the luncheon. We accepted and the club manager greeted us and made sure we had excellent seats. Afterwards, I went backstage to thank Kristofferson. Several other women were with him, and as I walked into his dressing room, he stared at me like I was an intruder. He could not remember who I was until the club manager jogged his memory. I quickly left, more than a little embarrassed.

Despite all the activity, the meeting with the St. Agnes elementary school students and Steven's words about Medjugorje had stayed with me. I had always dreamed of going on a pilgrimage and had prayed to the Blessed Mother ever since I had received my first Holy Communion. And once Steven was injured, our families had talked about seeking a miracle through travel. As far back as January 1987, there'd been the possibility that Steven would go to Lourdes. Monsignor Kowsky knew—as we did—that Steven was in danger of dying.

The monsignor had ruined his health with the schedule he kept for us—he was a diabetic with a weak heart—because Steven, in a way, became his miracle, the vindication of his faith, the personification of his Catholic values. Worried that Steven was going to weaken in Bellevue, he called Peter Johnson and said, "I don't know how we could do this, but if Steven could fly, maybe we could get him to Lourdes."

Peter had asked the monsignor to check with the doctors to make sure that altitude wouldn't create new problems. The monsignor called back and said it wouldn't. "It'll be difficult on a commercial airliner, though," the monsignor said. "He'll need a nurse to travel with him, if not a doctor."

Peter then called Guy Hawtin, an editor at the New York *Post* who was close to Rupert Murdoch, the newspaper's owner. "Does Murdoch have a jet?" Peter asked. Hawtin said he did. "Can you get it for Steven McDonald?" asked Peter. Hawtin said he'd see.

Peter, the monsignor and Hawtin agreed to meet for lunch, and Hawtin—who was studying to become a deacon in the Anglican Church—said he recalled that Murdoch's wife, Anna, had taken an interest in our plight. If we can use the plane, Peter told him, we'll agree to having you and a *Post* photographer accompany us. But nothing can be printed until Steven returns to New York. Two days later, Hawtin said that the Murdoch jet was ours.

That trip never happened. Steven wasn't going to

leave until after Conor's birth, and the plans to go to Craig began to fall into place. But I'd never forgotten the promise of hope that that pilgrimage had made.

And the presence of the Blessed Mother in Medjugorje was even more immediate and alive. Perhaps in Yugoslavia, I'd begun to think, I could find the answers to the questions my faith was posing.

At home, Steven would grow especially frustrated when he saw someone throw Conor a ball or help him shoot baskets. Steven had been a good athlete and loved sports, and he'd always imagined teaching our children how to run and to catch. At the Father of the Year luncheon, he'd met Willie Randolph, then the second baseman for the New York Yankees, and Randolph and Yankees owner George Steinbrenner, who invited Steven to Yankee Stadium.

After the Yankee game, Steven was asked if he wanted to go into the clubhouse to meet the team. He seemed uncomfortable at first, and I knew the meetings with athletes at Bellevue had sometimes been awkward. One night, the New York Rangers general manager, Phil Esposito, had stopped by. When Steven was a boy, he'd tell me later, he'd idolized Esposito and, in his street hockey games, would practice the center's moves around the goal. The night Esposito visited Steven in the hospital, he'd brought another player, Dave Maloney, with him. When the Rangers lost to the Islanders in the playoffs, Steven said afterwards, one newspaper had run a picture of Maloney, weeping, in his dressing room. Steven had cut it out and pasted it in his scrapbook.

Steven had tried to tell Esposito and Maloney that he'd really been touched by Maloney's sensitivity. But he couldn't be understood. "I was freaking," he'd said later.

I wondered if being surrounded by Yankee players might depress him. Once Steven got into the locker room, however, the meeting went well. Lou Pinella, Dave Winfield and Ricky Henderson all had a few words with him, and one of the coaches, Gene Michael, never left his side. "He was like a kid," Steven said, "asking me about the chair, how it went forwards or backwards, left or right, and how the machine helped me breathe."

But Steven wished the ballplayers had known him before the injury, just as he wished someday Conor could see him as he had been. At Conor's first birthday party, Steven had been feeling especially sorry for himself. There were a lot of couples at the house and they were enjoying themselves and admiring our son. Steven got really down. One of the men there, the husband of one of our nurses, came over to him. "Steven, maybe ten years from now you'll have your cure," he said. "What will you be then? Forty? And what will Conor be? Eleven?"

"He was right," Steven told me later. "That wouldn't be bad at all."

Steven gradually came to realize he could do for physically challenged athletes what men like Phil Esposito and Willie Randolph had done for him. That is, become a source of inspiration. At Craig, he hadn't wanted to participate in the hospital's Field Day wheelchair relays and races, but wheeling himself down Fifth Avenue on St. Patrick's Day had given him a boost of confidence. When he was invited to be the keynote speaker at the 1988 New York State Games for the Physically Challenged at the Nassau Community College's track, he agreed. On June 2, speaking before about one thousand athletes, their families, and volunteers, he explained that the accomplishments of the athletes could mean as much as those of any Ranger or Met. The boys and girls, some blind, others on crutches or in chairs, still others missing limbs, listened intently.

"Like you, I am physically challenged," he said. "I wasn't always challenged. Two years ago, as a New York City cop, I could chase and even catch the fastest bad guys. Today, I cannot walk, I cannot run, and I have trouble breathing on my own.

"Many of you have similar challenges. Some of you cannot see, or hear, or move as well as those who are not physically challenged. And you are often reminded of those limitations by people in our society who speak and point and stare without thinking. Surely, the days can be difficult. All of us, at one time or another, say, 'Why should I get out of bed today?'

"By being here, you show you have determination, strength and faith in your own ability to succeed, no matter what the odds are.

"Two years ago, if I had been here at all, I would have been merely a spectator. Today, I am a fan, a physically challenged man who understands the long hours and hard work that has brought you here. You are not only athletes, you are not only competitors, you are heroes. You show us the power of hope, the power of love. The power of the challenged is great indeed.

"You inspire me," Steven said. "I look to you for your prayers and your best wishes so that I can do the same thing. In closing, I want to tell you this: life is a great thing, a great gift. We have an obligation to our Creator and ourselves to make our lives the best we can. But we also have a duty to help those who are less fortunate than ourselves. There are many people like that. I know you are those kind of people who will help, be guardian angels and helpers to others who may not be as strong and happy as you are.

"Be like Clarence, the angel in the movie *It's A Wonderful Life,* the angel who convinced Jimmy Stewart, in spite of all his burdens and challenges and disabilities, to choose life. As Clarence says to him, 'Yes, it can be a wonderful life because of friends like you. You make the difference. I love you. God bless you.'"

Steven finished to cheers, and the races began. Conor sat on his daddy's lap, and for a while we watched. Then Steven signalled it was time to go. As we headed towards the van, Susan Gordon Ryan, the director of the Games, approached. "Listen, Steven, there's a little boy who wants to meet you," she said. The boy's name was Bobby Mohammed, he was eleven-years-old, and he had spent the past ten years at St. Mary's Hospital on Long Island, where children with severe birth defects were cared for. Bobby had been abandoned by his parents when he was a year old, Susan said. "He told me that he knows Steven loves him, and he knows Patti does too. 'How could you know that?' I asked. 'Because Steven has a trache,' Bobby said, 'and Patti loves him, doesn't she?' 'Yes,' I told him. 'And I have a trache,' Bobby said, 'so Patti must love me.'"

In July, Steven saw Bobby Mohammed for the first time at St. Mary's and began to visit him regularly. Each time Steven would visit, Bobby would show him his homework and writing, as if Steven were a surrogate father. Then we got truly wonderful news: Bobby was being adopted. He'd have a family of his own again.

New York City, August 1988

"Joe Doherty?" Dennis Breen said in astonishment. "Steve, he shot a British officer. That's us. Once you put a uniform on, you're a part of everybody. When a freedom fighter, or a terrorist, shoots a uniform, that's us."

I'd just asked Dennis to drive me to a Free Joe Doherty rally in Thomas Paine Park, a small patch of green in the shadow of the Manhattan Corrections Center, the high-rise federal prison a couple of blocks from Police Headquarters. Doherty had been held there for six years after an informant had tipped investigators he was tending bar in the city. The authorities then arrested him on fugitive charges for fleeing Northern Ireland after he and other colleagues had shot a British army captain named Wes Maycott. The Justice Department wanted to extradite him and had interred him upstate at Otisville; Cardinal O'Connor had interceded and he'd been brought back to the city. Joe and I had begun to communicate early in the year by mail. What I was reading in these letters was not what was being released by the media in Northern Ireland, which was controlled by the British government. I had to do more. Someone had to listen to Joe.

"You don't understand," I'd told Dennis. "Joe

Doherty exists because the British government in Northern Ireland is oppressive. If there were no DIPLOCK courts, there would be no need for the Joe Dohertys. The British don't belong there."

Reluctantly, Dennis agreed. We couldn't wear uniforms, he'd pointed out. The patrol guide prohibited it. We were going as private citizens, he said. Or I was. He was just driving.

I'd become more and more outspoken in defense of Catholics in Ulster ever since the Republic of Ireland bestowed citizenship upon me in April. That had taken an extraordinary vote of the Dail and the Seanad, the two branches of the Irish legislature. Technically, I hadn't been eligible to become an Irish citizen; I was third-generation removed from Eire. But the Prime Minister himself, Taoiseach Charles J. Haughey, had interceded. And on August 21, he'd taken time out from a trip to the United Nations to personally confer the honor upon me. "The Irish have made a unique contribution to this great country, the United States," he'd said, as my family and Mayor Koch listened with pride, "in many fields of endeavor, but I don't think there is any area in which they have made a more significant or courageous contribution than in the police service."

I imagined Grandpa Conway on his Bronx beat, and my father in his black-and-white, and remained lost in those dreams until the mayor broke my reverie. "If I had my choice," Mayor Koch said, "and couldn't come back as a Jewish person, I would like to come back as an Irish person. I say this because I admire the Irish qualities of courage, patriotism and loyalty. Other groups have the traits, but the Irish have them in a special way."

The mayor chose his words well. Irish Catholic cops, I'd always felt, were especially sensitive to the problems of minorities in New York. Black community leaders try to say white cops are racist, that they represent and defend a different class. But we remember our roots, too. My family had come to America without anything, driven from their homeland because the British had confiscated everything of value. I'd read the stories of women and children who'd died by the sides of country roads, their mouths stained with the grass they'd eaten trying to keep themselves alive. One of my great-grandmothers had been an indentured servant just a century ago, the only position she could find. And my father's family had emigrated after the First Famine, carrying almost nothing with them across the Atlantic, on the coffin ships. My family's story is that of many Irish Catholics who found a haven in the Police Department. Much of that has not changed for newly arrived Irish citizens.

Oh sure, there are cops who don't give a damn about people. It's a fact of life—the NYPD is bigger than the United States Coast Guard—that, from top to bottom, you can find insensitive people. But they're a small minority compared with the cops on the job who care. And one reason is that we're all well aware of the troubles in Northern Ireland, and what they've done to our people. We've watched, on television, Protestant leader Ian Paisley stand up in a Papal audience in France and accuse the Holy Father of being the Anti-Christ.

Some black community leaders like to suggest that the police are their supporters' enemies, that there is a kind of war raging on the city streets fueled by economic injustice. On a television talk show, I watched a teenaged black girl, explaining why she refused to salute or pledge allegiance to the flag, say, "This country has been built on the backs of black people." As if they've been the only ones who ever suffered. Listening to her reminded me of a quote my father once told me, from Alexis de Tocqueville, a French minister who'd come to America in 1849 to look at our country's prison system. "De Tocqueville wrote," my father had said, "that the blacks in America, the slaves, were treated better than the Irish in Ireland." When Jesse Jackson spoke at the Democratic Convention in Atlanta, he seemed to be making the same point. "We came over in different ships," he'd said, "but we're all in the same boat now." I'd agree that blacks haven't been treated well by this society, that they haven't been integrated. But the people who point fingers at Irish cops are wrong. Because my people have gone through the same discrimination. For eight hundred years, they've been segregated in Northern Ireland, and it's happening today.

Any claim that the confrontations in East New York or the South Bronx are similar to the fighting on the streets of Belfast is absurd. Just absurd. We don't have a shoot-to-kill policy, like the SAS forces under the direction of the British government, or the Royal Ulster Constabulary, which represents the Protestant government. In those Irish neighborhoods, there is war. And, I believe, Irish Catholic citizens—and I can now proudly include myself—have to take stands. Joe Doherty signs his letters, "Irish Republican Army Prisoner of War."

I believe that to be true.

Even before I became an Irish citizen, I'd spoken

my mind—while Brian would shake his head in disapproval—at a couple of Irish-American affairs I'd been invited to. At the Holy Name Society, I'd quoted Roger Casement: "Ireland has outlived the failure of all her hopes—and yet she still hopes," and then I said, "We hope for an Ireland united in the spirit of life, not divided by the spirit of death and dissension. We dream for an Ireland where civility, not barbarity, is the order of the day." When a reporter had asked me if I was speaking to the Thatcher government's support of the ruling Protestants, I'd said, bluntly, "The British should get out."

Since I'd been in the Navy, I'd been following the politics of Northern Ireland in the *Irish Echo,* a tabloid published weekly in New York. One Navy friend, Bob McGrath, and I would spend long nights rehashing the news about the provisional Irish Republican Army's attacks, and the Protestant responses. In a way, the Troubles and my friendship with Bob became tangled up; years ago when I walked away from him as he was dying, it seemed as if I was walking away from everything I believed in. I was out of the Navy, but not yet a cop, when the cancer took its toll on him. Bob was a hulking guy—and seeing him waste away in a darkened room in the Vets Hospital on 23rd Street had been too painful. I didn't—couldn't—spend the time I should have. I was his closest friend, I felt a lot of responsibility to be there, but the last time I went I was smothered by the scent of decay. I opened the door to his room, and could smell . . . death. It scared me, and I ran. And I never returned.

When I first learned about Joe Doherty—how he'd

devoted his life, since he was eighteen, to the cause of reunifying north and south Ireland—I thought of Bob McGrath and the inconsistencies in my own life. I'd never done as well in high school as I might've. I'd never committed myself to a cause or ideal. As a cop, I'd sometimes been lazy. But Joe Doherty had never done that. He hadn't married, hadn't had any children, and had given his whole life fighting the sins of others. And, as a result, for the past six years, he's lived in a room half the size of my bedroom, a cubicle deliberately painted a depressing gray, without windows to see the blue sky or the stars at night.

When I first let friends and other police officers know how I felt, many were shocked. Like Dennis, they wondered how I could sympathize with a man who'd been convicted of killing a British officer. I don't pretend to understand the killing, I'd say. I think of the inconsistencies and the injustices in the legal system in the heart of Ireland where a British soldier, Private Ian Thain, convicted of murdering a Catholic citizen of the north, was released after two years and returned to active duty. I grieve for Captain Wes Maycott's widow and children. They're the innocent ones, like Patti Ann and Conor. But what happened to me and what happened to that Army officer are two separate situations. The situation in Northern Ireland is intolerable. Joe Doherty, the men he was with when Captain Wes Maycott died, and all the Catholics in Northern Ireland have the right to expect they'll be made a part of what's going on there and not be excluded by the British.

Indeed, I wish I could have lived my whole life the way he's lived his. If I had, I don't think I would have run from Bob McGrath as he lay dying. So, when I'd read there'd be a rally for Joe Doherty, I knew I had to go, no matter what the risk was.

As the van drew closer to Thomas Payne Park, I told Dennis to park a block away. I thought we could quietly sneak in and avoid attention. When we got to the corner behind the grandstand, my ex-lieutenant-in-charge when I first came on the job, Jerry Frye, spotted me. Now Captain Frye, commanding officer of the Fifth Precinct, he was observing the goings-on to ensure there were no problems.

"Hey, Mac," he said, "how you doing?"

I could see that Dennis was nervous.

Then, from the speakers' platform, former Special Prosecutor Charles Hynes's voice boomed over the crowd of several hundred. I caught the words, ". . . brave officer McDonald . . ." Whatever anonymity I might have had was completely blown.

The speeches left me with mixed feelings. Doherty's mother and sister stirred the soul with their words, but another speaker had sympathetic comments for the Puerto Ricans' FALN, whose 1982 New Year's Eve bombs had maimed three of our officers, including, as I said previously, Richie Pastorella, the head of the department's Self-Support Group for injured cops. Did others at the rally link the two? I didn't know. Did Joe himself? I didn't know that either. But I hoped he shared my belief: that a terrorist attack against New Yorkers and their police had nothing in common with freedom fighting in Ireland.

After the speeches, we marched past the federal prison. As we passed what we were told was Joe's cell window, we raised our heads to shout, "Free Joe

Doherty! Free Joe Doherty!" Around us, I could see guys talking into their lapels. Someone's gonna have a picture of me after this, I thought.

I'd never been one for demonstrations. My first had been in the spring of 1985. I'd joined ten thousand other cops—the first time I'd really felt myself a member of the Blue Wall—at the Bronx County Courthouse, protesting the indictment of Detective Stephen Sullivan after he'd shot a black woman named Eleanor Bumpers, who'd come at him with a kitchen knife while she was being evicted. Sullivan was eventually cleared, but the Bronx would continue to be a hard place for cops to receive respect.

That was hammered home by the Larry Davis trial. As we bore witness to Joe Doherty's imprisonment, witnesses in the Bronx were describing Larry Davis's shooting of six cops in November 1986 to a jury that would somehow conclude that Davis, a twenty-two-year-old convicted drug dealer, had been acting in self-defense when he unleashed his arsenal. He'd escaped that day and had been on the loose for almost three weeks when he was finally caught. In the Bronx, some had made him into a folk hero, but I thought he was a bad guy, a criminal who couldn't care less about any of the twelve sitting in judgment of him. The cops Larry Davis had hurt had been there to protect the people of the Bronx, and the citizens didn't care. They'd decide it was more important to clear Larry Davis.

I'd gone to the Davis trial as a spectator on its first day, and Davis's lawyer, William Kunstler, had told the judge my respirator and appearance would influence the jury, and—to reporters—accused me of being "a pawn" of the Patrolmen's Benevolent Association. It had been my own idea to attend, though, and when I'd told Peter Johnson, he'd suggested I go every day if I was going to go at all. But Kunstler's attack had made Phil Caruso, the PBA president, uncomfortable, especially when a *Daily News* columnist named Gail Collins wrote, "There could not be two more different cop-shooting cases . . . This case is not about what happened to Steven McDonald."

When the Davis verdict came down, one cop called to tell me about another rally at the Bronx courthouse. "If I could afford to," he'd said, "I'd leave the job tomorrow."

The "Free Joe!" chants were scattering now, and Dennis and I knew it was time to leave. A middle-aged woman approached me. Joe's mother. "I just wanted to thank you," she said, "for being here."

"Tell Joe," I asked her, "to get in touch with me. I'd like to hear from him."

Several days later, a Sunday as I recall, the phone rang at home while we were eating a pizza. Our niece Devon, who was spending the weekend with us, answered and began making funny faces as if a whacko was on the other end. "Patti," Devon said, "I don't know *what* this person is saying."

Patti put down her plate and took the receiver.

"Joe Flaherty?" she said. "Joe what? Oh, *oh.* Joe Doherty. Oh, Mr. Doherty, I couldn't hear well. I'm so sorry."

Joe was calling collect from prison. I was tongue-tied as I wheeled to the phone. I had so much I wanted to tell him, to ask him: about his life, about his favorite sport, about his parents and his loves . . .

A couple of minutes later, I could hear an alarm ringing at Joe's end. We'd barely gotten started. I'd asked about prison life and told him I'd met his mother. He asked about Conor and Patti Ann, and said from the pictures he'd seen they seemed a beautiful family. Then, over the bells in the background, he'd apologized. "Some kind of fight," he said. "They're shutting the stalls down. I'll have to go."

The line went dead. But I could still hear his brogue. I felt close to him, an intimacy that felt as right as anything I'd done.

Reaching out to Shavod Jones brought less success. When I was at Craig, I decided that contacting him was a priority. From what I'd learned from the trial, he seemed to me a throwaway, a kid who never had much attention and love. If I could show him that I cared, even after what had happened, maybe I could change his life. I didn't find *him* evil; we had been caught in an evil moment. The biggest tragedy of this situation would be if he went out and committed more crimes. I'm not a cop, I'd tell myself, he can walk away from and forget about.

I knew I needed a go-between, someone who could represent me without seeming to be on police business and who had both the street smarts and the intelligence to relate to Jones's family and to his lawyer. I decided on Mike Koleniak. As I've said previously, Koleniak was a New York *Post* reporter who'd been covering our story since the fall of 1986, when he'd told his editors he'd rather go to Bellevue to interview Patti Ann than write about the Mets World Series victory parade. More importantly, he'd been a cop for three years, retiring when the scooter he was patrolling in had been broadsided by a cab running a red light. The accident had left him with spinal injuries—not nearly as serious as mine—and a short-term paralysis that had left him, in the first minutes after the crash, unable to speak. Koleniak, better than most, knew where I was coming from and what I was going through. There came a moment at Bellevue when Mike broke down sobbing, wishing that he could trade places with me, and questioning why he was so lucky and I was not. Our friendship was born then.

He'd visited me twice in Colorado, once bringing his family out to spend Father's Day with us, the second time to write an article about my trip to the Notre Dame-Air Force Academy football game. The day after that game, a few hours before he'd been scheduled to fly out, he came up to my room to say good-bye.

"Is there anything I can do for you when I get back to the city?" he'd asked. Do you need newspapers, I imagined he was thinking, or books?

"I want you to do me a favor," I said. "I'd like you to talk to Shavod Jones's lawyer to see if I can go see Jones."

Koleniak and I had an easy relationship. We'd trade war stories, and when we ran out of our own, we'd talk about our fathers'. Like mine, Koleniak's dad had been on the police force. But I could see he was getting uneasy.

"Well," Koleniak hesitated, "that might send the wrong signal to other cops. And it's a lot to ask of Patti Ann . . ."

Cops, Koleniak and I both knew, aren't the most forgiving people. But this follow-up was no different from what I'd been taught to do by people like Bobby Reid, my field training officer when I got out of the

Police Academy, and Peter King, my sergeant in the Central Park Precinct.

"You know," I'd told him, "as far as I'm concerned, I'm still on the job. I've got seventeen years until I retire. I'd like to try and arrange some way to speak with Jones. This is a terrible thing, but something good can be made out of it. I don't want to destroy two lives. I don't want him to think his life is over because he's done this to me."

Koleniak said he'd try. "I'll do everything I can," he told me, "to set it up."

When Koleniak got back to New York, he called the prosecutor in the case, Dave Drucker, to get Jones's lawyer's number. "Peter Zeiler still represents Jones, doesn't he?" Koleniak had asked. No, Drucker told him. Zeiler had drowned in a swimming accident in Brazil. Zeiler's wife, Regina Darby, was now representing Jones. Koleniak called her and they agreed some kind of meeting might be possible.

By the time I'd come home, there hadn't been any more progress in setting up the meeting. At a party in Malverne, I asked Koleniak in a private moment to buy some stationery and a book of stamps and to deliver them to Darby to give to Jones. With them, I dictated a brief note for the boy: "Let's carry on a dialogue," I told Koleniak to write. "Please write if you have time."

A few days later, Darby called me at home. "I don't think it would be a good idea for Shavod to respond," she said. There was an appeal still going on and any contact with me might complicate it. Perhaps I could meet with Jones's mother, she suggested. I agreed. It was a first step.

This will be private, I told Koleniak. He could come, of course, but I didn't want any press coverage. (I would unwittingly leak the news myself when I inadvertently mentioned the meeting following a speech to the graduating students at a Queens elementary school. A *Daily News* reporter covering the address passed along my remarks to an editor who told Mike Santangelo. And Santangelo wrote a story.) He agreed, and on a hot sunny afternoon, Koleniak, my driver Bob Dalia, my nurse Pat Dillon, and I stepped out of an elevator and into a law office crowded with attorneys and legal secretaries.

Regina Darby was waiting for us with Jones's mother, an attractive, plainly dressed middle-aged women named Sharon Harris whose face was an unexpressive mask. She showed no emotion as we introduced ourselves. And she had no response to our hellos. Occasionally, her eyes would glance towards me. For the most part, she looked at the wall or at the top of Regina Darby's desk.

"Mrs. Harris," said Darby, "would like to know your intentions."

My intentions? Why, I wondered, did I have to prove myself to her? I was the victim and I wanted to forgive. What more did she need to know?

To talk to her son, I said. To see if there's a direction I can point him towards, an activity I can help him get involved in. I watched Mrs. Harris for encouragement; there was none. Not a nod, not a shake of her head.

"I'll speak with Shavod," Darby said, "and see if something can be set up."

I decided to talk to his mother directly.

"Something good can be made out of something

bad," I told her. "Shavod can start over and make something out of his life."

Her face tightened, but still there was no response. Then Darby's phone rang. The call was for Mrs. Harris and, her back turned to us, she spoke in a quiet, stern voice.

From what I could tell, the person calling her was going through a tough time. "Yes," she'd say. "No." Not only does she have to deal with what her son did to me, I thought, and where he is now, but this person she's talking with on the phone is in a crisis too. Amazing. Even though Sharon Harris was closed to me, seeing her trying to cope with difficulties in her life made her seem sympathetic. Maybe Shavod's life hadn't been that different from mine—my father had worked two jobs, my mother had raised us almost by herself—and if it hadn't, I knew how difficult that adolescence could be.

No, I told myself, I doubt I could understand what Shavod's family had been through. And in my condition, I probably couldn't be much help to him. Even if I could, it didn't look like his mother wanted to let me do much.

Her call ended and Mrs. Harris turned back to look at us, impassively. Your son and I are both failures, aren't we? I thought. Society's failures. I'm a cripple . . . no, not a cripple. That's too pejorative. I'm a ventilator-dependent quadriplegic young man with a family that's hurting. And Shavod Jones is institutionalized once again. If someone doesn't help your son when he comes out, I wanted to say, he'll become another Larry Davis.

I held my tongue and there was a momentary silence. Then Regina Darby thanked us for coming.

As we left, Mrs. Harris stayed where she was, seated, looking perturbed. On the street, Koleniak turned to me and said, "The way her face was set, it was as if she thought it's your fault her son is in jail."

I didn't want to talk. I'd seen the same expression. If I'd just found the gun, arrested him for possession of a weapon and, after booking him, given Shavod Jones my phone number, our lives would be very different. Ifs, ands, and buts. And a mother who faced me as if I were the enemy.

"Let me know if she calls you," I told Koleniak. And I asked Dalia to help me find a phone to tell Patti Ann my frustration.

Fourteen

Greenwich Village, August 1988

As a kid, I'd loved basketball almost as much as football. In the Navy, I'd played on teams wherever I was stationed, and had helped coach a Catholic Youth Organization girls' squad. I was a schoolyard kind of player, a little undisciplined, who liked to rebound, play defense and leave the scoring to others. In Colorado, I'd been reminded how much I missed the ball in my hands when, one Sunday, we went to church and I saw a boy dribbling in a park next door. "You know, I always like to do that," I'd blurted out, and immediately wished I hadn't. Brian Mulheren, who'd flown in from New York to be with me, looked stricken with guilt. It was the same look, I now realize, that people sometimes get when they pick Conor up in front of me.

At Craig, I'd reminisce about New York City with whomever wanted to stay up and talk. When Brian was there, I'd look forward to the emergency calls that would come into the hospital switchboard for him:

fires in midtown, bridge rescues, shootings. Not that I delighted in tragedy, but they were a way of keeping me in touch with the city. When Peter Johnson flew out, we'd talk about Greenwich Village, where he lived. I loved to hang out in the Village on weekends, listening to music, sipping milk shakes, taking in the street scene. There was a sense of community, but also of great freedom. And I thought Peter was lucky to be able to live there.

There's a great pick-up basketball game on Waverly Place and 3rd Street, I once told him. Semipro level, with guys who could have played pro if they had been taller. The teams were mostly street kids, and there was a lot of betting on the sidelines. It was great ball, and I'd stop by and watch when I was off-duty. "When you get back," Peter had said, "let's go."

We didn't keep that date until eight months later, when I'd driven into the city for a newspaper interview and some shopping at the Police Academy store. Peter had joined me for the interview, and afterwards suggested we check out the 3rd Street court, too.

I asked the driver to park around the corner. Getting me out of the van can be a bit of a spectacle, and I'd come to prefer to do it with as much privacy as possible. Having strangers watch as Patti Ann, or the nurse, or the driver unhooks my wheelchair from its restraints, pulls and pushes me backwards up the sloping floor of the van to the platform, and lowers me gently to the ground as if I were a fragile cargo of easily bruised fruit did nothing to enhance my sense of independence. And when I was out in the city, I wanted as much of that as I could get.

My excursions in public—unlike those first uneasy trips to the mall in Colorado, where I felt like an alien as passersby took in the chair, the respirator, and the tube coming out of my throat—had always gone well up to now. At Christmas, a month after I'd come home, we'd driven to Rockefeller Center to see its famous tree and lights. We'd pulled up onto the plaza itself—Brian was with us to make sure there'd be no problem—and opened the side door so I could look without getting out. A group of young kids carrying a boom box and a blanket came up to the van, curious at who was inside. When they saw me, they asked if they could break-dance for us. It turned out they were being chased off the property by security personnel. Brian interceded and asked some anti-crime guys to clear an area. The kids were great and the crowd that gathered around them applauded. Bobby Vinton, the singer, walked by and Brian asked him to come over. He did, and Bob Dalia went nuts, starting to sing "Roses are red, my love . . ." When they'd finished, an Hispanic girl walked up to Patti Ann and handed her a rose. "My boyfriend just gave me this flower," she said, "and I'd like you to have it."

Strangers would come up and touch my arm, or hand, saying, "We know who you are. And we're praying for you." After church one Sunday, on the sidewalk by the front door, I saw the people around me looking down at my feet. I raised my chair back to see better myself and realized a woman was kneeling on the ground, kissing my feet. "You're going to be a saint some day," she told me as she stood. Embarrassed, I stammered, "Have a nice day." At Flutie's, a restaurant on the downtown waterfront, waitresses told Patti and I we were inspirations. As I'd been shown before I left for Colorado, New York was far from a cold city.

Now, as we drew closer to the basketball court, I didn't expect the reaction to be much different. I never felt comfortable with the praise—I'd been an average cop, shot doing regular police work, and lived because of the strength, faith and support of Patti Ann and others—but no longer held hope I could blend into the crowd.

It was about 5:30 P.M. and the sidewalk was crowded with commuters streaming in and out of the West 4th Street subway station. The fence around the court was packed with spectators dressed in shorts, tank tops, and bright new Nikes and Reeboks flitted on the fringes like honeybees, taking bets and, possibly, making other kinds of deals. One guy—his eyes artificially wide and his walk less than steady—stepped towards my chair. He fixed on the respirator and stuck his hand out as if he wanted to touch it. Peter and Bob Dalia quickly stepped between him and me. "I think he's tripping," Peter whispered.

"Hey," the man said menacingly, "you were at Larry Davis's trial, weren't you?"

I nodded yes.

He smiled, then walked quickly back to the fence, whispering to several others. I couldn't hear what they said. But some began pointing at me. And laughing.

Peter and Bob got uncomfortable, but I didn't. At the fence I just kept turning my head back and forth, assuming that, sooner or later, someone would make room for me. And they did.

Before the summer was over, Monsignor Kowsky died. With his passing, I lost my guardian angel. He'd been Clarence to my George Bailey, the one person who would keep assuring Patti Ann and me we'd get our miracle. Our families would pray for us, every day, but it was the monsignor whose strength made me want to fight to live, to continue to be a police officer.

He died at home, peacefully, though we'd seen less and less of him after coming home. Before I'd been discharged from Bellevue, he'd had a heart attack—he was a diabetic who couldn't get himself to stay away from sweets—and his schedule of saying Mass at my bedside six nights a week, in addition to all his other police chaplain duties, had weakened him and left him without the stamina to ever fully recover. When I'd seen him over Thanksgiving and Christmas, he'd seemed pale and frail.

I'd assumed the department would turn out in force for the monsignor, and that the funeral Mass would fill the arches of St. Patrick's. But, instead, the mourners were told to go to St. Peter's, a beautiful chapel in lower Manhattan that, nevertheless, lacked the grandeur and symbolism of the Cardinal's own church. We have to get there early, I'd warned everybody. The crowds of uniformed cops would be as large as those for a slain comrade, wouldn't they? Hadn't the monsignor selflessly given himself to all the street cops in need, not just me? Didn't he use his spare time to counsel officers in Rockland or Westchester who'd begun to be crushed by the stress of the job? But, as we drove to the church, I realized I was wrong. There were more bosses mourning—sergeants, lieutenants, captains, deputy inspectors and chiefs—than there were patrolmen. The Cardinal and the mayor were there, but not the Blue Wall. Not that the monsignor would have cared. Yet I felt ashamed, ashamed of the police as a group because they hadn't shown up. The monsignor was at every funeral and at every hospital. He was the only chaplain in the department who was on hand for every crisis. For him, I expected thousands of cops, and a representation from the Army as a tribute to his combat service in Vietnam. Instead, nothing.

Later, I'd hear it was because he hadn't died in the line of duty. He did, though. He was working until the day he died, then went home to Far Rockaway to his family, knowing, I suspect, that the end was near. He went to sleep, and never woke.

Conor came with me to the funeral, and I wondered if he was as in awe of the badges, the uniforms and the buttons as I'd been when my father brought me, as a young boy, to a funeral. After the Mass, friends brought me down the church steps to the street, carrying me and the chair. And Conor came running over, and climbed into my lap. He took it all in, his eyes wide with excitement. Yes, I thought, I'd been the same way. We went to the cemetery, where the monsignor was buried next to his parents. An old soldier I thought, fading away.

And then we drove away, leaving the monsignor's casket there, alone.

That wasn't the way he did his job, I thought. He never left anyone alone.

Later, as my grief began to pass, Brian cheered me with a story I hadn't heard. We were at the Waldorf-Astoria Hotel, for a lunch honoring the late Terence Cardinal Cooke. At the time, some supporters of his in the Archdiocese were making efforts to have him canonized. The evening Cardinal Cooke died, Brian was saying, Monsignor Kowsky had been standing on Madison Avenue, at the foot of the steps leading to the Cardinal's residence.

"What's going on inside?" a persistent reporter from the New York *Times* kept asking. The monsignor tried to be helpful, though he knew as little as anyone else.

"Can't you give me more than that?" the reporter said, but Monsignor Kowsky, pipe sticking out of his mouth, black cap perched on his head, said he couldn't.

"Well, what's your name anyway?" the reporter said, pen poised over notebook.

"Ah, my name," the monsignor mused for a moment. He drew deeply on his pipe, then answered carefully. "Oh, I'm Cardinal Spellman. I came back to make sure that Cardinal Cooke doesn't get more than I did."

All funerals were hard for me, now. Two others would die before autumn—Sergeant John McCormick and Police officer Joseph Galapo—and I'd join thousands of other cops to pay my respects. Just getting dressed for their funerals was difficult and heartbreaking. Sometimes it would seem the only time I'd put my uniform on was to mourn, and looking at the sharp blue creases and the black shine of the shoes would remind me of the brave police officers we'd never see again. Those mornings are a struggle, an emotional turmoil.

Driving to the Mass, we'd pass buses and cars filled with other cops, some in uniform, some in plainclothes. All were in mourning, too, lost in deep thought for a fallen comrade. At the church or synagogue, we'd line up, saying hello to friends from the academy days or from precinct assignments. A sergeant from the ceremonial unit would call us to attention and, hands in white gloves, we'd wait, stiffly, silently, while the funeral cortege and the motorcycle escort, its thunder muffling all other sound, approached.

If there was room inside, we'd file in. If our hearts had not already been breaking, then sitting through the service and watching the faces of the officer's family would do the job. At the service's conclusion, we'd reassemble outside. A lone bagpiper's wail would pierce the air. Drums, muffled by purple cloth, would echo like a shared heartbeat. Then "Taps" would be played, the final blow.

I could see the anguish of each and every person on his or her face, worn like a flag, with pride and dignity, and with the knowledge of the deep sacrifice needed to keep that flag flying. At the McCormick funeral, the sergeant's young son J.C. was proudly holding his dad's shield and ribbons. He seemed so proud, unaware that his father would never return to wear them, to hold him and to share another moment of joy.

When I saw J.C., I broke down and wept uncontrollably. So many of us were being hurt: fathers, mothers, sons and daughters. I thought of a quote from the Bible, where Paul is addressing the Corinthians. "If one part suffers," he writes, "all parts suffer. If one part is honored, all parts share in the joy." We were hurting. Not just the department, but all nine million New Yorkers. Police families are the city's families. And society should feel the pain we feel.

New York–Fatima–Lourdes–Rome, October 1988

Steven wanted me to go on a pilgrimage, and with Monsignor Kowsky gone, there seemed even greater urgency. A stranger had called in September to say she'd paid for a place for Steven on an eighteen-day trip to Europe, a tour that would visit Fatima, in Portugal; Lourdes, in France; the Vatican, in Rome; and Medjugorje, in Yugoslavia. At both Lourdes and Fatima, Mary had appeared and spoken years ago to a young girl named Bernadette. In Medjugorje, the Blessed Mother was still appearing, as she had since 1981, and speaking to three of the six young men and women who'd first witnessed her—the Visionaries—every evening at 5:40 P.M. in the choir loft above the Church of St. James.

I believed something was out there for Steven. That was my faith. And I'd always prayed to the Blessed Mother. Steven couldn't go on such a journey—bus rides, overnight train trips—but, and he insisted, I could. We asked Father Mychal Judge, whose Franciscan order oversaw the Medjugorje church, to accompany me. With no hesitation, he agreed. And on October 11, 1988, Steven and Conor accompanied us to Kennedy Airport for the first leg of the flight to Lisbon, Portugal. Thirty-six hours later, Father Mike and I were in the midst of thousands and thousands of candles flickering in the Campanile, lighting Our Lady of Fatima's statue as tens of thousands of men and women held hands and sang hymns over the gentle tinkle of hanging bells.

I'd thought my faith strong, but the faith here was of a kind I'd never seen.

A seventeen-hour train ride took us to Lourdes, and Father Mike and I spent most of it talking and sleeping. When we got to the French town, we walked straight to the Basilica, through the main entrance, into the commune, and then to the grotto, where Our Lady had appeared to St. Bernadette. A woman from our group had already gone into the baths. When she saw Father Mike, she fell into his arms and began to cry. So much pain was released. Later, I'd learn her son had been killed in April . . . by a policeman's bullet.

In the Chapel of St. Michael, the patron saint of police officers, Father Mike said Mass. "Everyone on this pilgrimage," he told our group, "is looking for something. Whether we find that something or not, we will return home feeling different. Not miraculously different, but changed by the experiences and the people we've met." Then, that night, another procession by candlelight. After, we walked to the grotto and sat and prayed, watching the crowds. I found a pay telephone and called Steven. If he can't be with me physically, I thought, letting him hear the singing and the bells would share part of the experience.

But, thousands of miles away, he was distracted. "Oh no," I heard him exclaim.

"What's wrong?" I asked.

"Notre Dame just fumbled," he said.

Unbelievable, I thought. He's watching a football game, as if I was calling from Boston. But hearing his voice meant so much. I hung up and, when most of the people left the square, I gathered the few articles I'd brought—the ring, a picture of the three of us, and the cloth relic Steven's mother would bring to Bellevue—and touched them to the grotto's stone wall. Then I knelt and prayed for movement to come to Steven's body. When I finished, I turned to see Father Mike's face streaked with tears. "What a beautiful sight of faith," he told me.

Ever since I was a child, I'd imagined bathing in the waters of Lourdes. But the following afternoon when my opportunity came at last, I felt scared as I waited, together with about forty other women, to step into one of the five simple tubs. The water was cold, but my prayers quickly made me forget. When Father Mike found me afterwards, he said that he, too, hadn't noticed the chill. "And as I was putting on my habit," he said, "my body was already dry."

Rome. After a stopover in Nice, we reached the first city we'd been in since Lisbon. Noisy, crowded and frustrating. Cardinal O'Connor had told us, before we'd left, that he'd arrange for tickets for a papal audience, but the hotel had nothing. We called Steven, who called the archdiocese, who called . . . who knew? Meanwhile, Father Mike was studying our itinerary. The hotel we were staying at, we realized, wasn't the Hotel Pineta Palace, the printed destination. On a hunch, we walked to the Pineta Palace. In luck! The tickets were there.

At a little pizzeria late that night, over ziti and chicken, I confessed to Father Mike that the papal audience was a wish I'd had for more than two years. "I've wanted this every day since Steven was injured," I said.

October 19, 1988, was Audience Day, as we'd call it.

A taxi took us to the Vatican, an idea five thousand other worshipers had, and at the gates, I saw nuns—*nuns*—pushing and shoving their way to the front. "What's going on here?" I asked Father Mike.

"They'll do anything," he said, "to get near the Holy Father."

The skies switched from drizzle to blue and back again, but as we made our way to our seats, it didn't matter. Closer and closer to the throne itself we went, until—with a final wave of a Swiss Guard's hand—we found ourselves in the front row. Standing in awe, we took it all in: St. Peter's Square, the Papal Balcony, the statues, the podium . . . There was so much to see. At 11:05 A.M. the Pope's car drove in, slowly circling the entire square. What a tremendous feeling, seeing him. I wished Steven and our families could be with me, sensing this presence of strength and serenity. A photographer approached, asking our names and where we were staying. We were in The Row. A Milanese couple next to us showed their tape recorder; whatever was said, they'd capture.

Priests stood at the podium and read the messages John Paul II had for each person in his native tongue. The English message was about pain and suffering, which fit into why I was there. After the greetings were read, the Holy Father walked slowly down our row, shaking hands with everyone in each of the front boxes. As he got closer to us, I lost control of my emotions and began to cry, telling Father Mike to speak for both of us. Then he was in front of me, his eyes taking in my tears, Father Mike's obeisances, and the picture of Steven, Conor and myself that I held in my arms.

"Holy Father," said Father Mike, "Cardinal

O'Connor of New York sent us here. Her husband is sick . . ."

"Yes," I said. "He is a cop. He was shot."

The Pope's expression changed, softening into a sympathetic smile.

"He is a young man," the Holy Father said.

"Please, your Holiness," said Father Mike, "would you touch his ring?" The Pope reached towards Steven's wedding ring, and blessed it. Then he signed me on my forehead with his thumb, saying, "I will pray for you." I was weak with joy and accomplishment . . . a dream I'd never expected to realize had come true.

The Pope moved to the next group, and Father Mike and I stood, calm, blessed, tearful and fulfilled. When Steven had been shot, more than two years earlier, I'd asked my cousin Seamus, the priest who'd married us, to get in touch with the Holy Father because I'd figured he had the closest contact with God. And now we had the Holy Father's prayers ourselves.

That night, Father Mike and I returned to the Trevi Fountain, and threw in three coins each. I would return, I promised myself. But the peace and joy I'd felt that morning was already tempered with sadness. On the telephone, Steven had told me about the latest police tragedy in New York: the night before, in two separate incidents only a few hours apart, two officers had been shot and killed. One had been twenty-six years old, the other twenty-four.

"It's the worst day for the department," Steven had said. "The worst." Mention them in your prayers at Medjugorje, he said. Mention the whole department.

When will this madness, I wondered, ever end?

Queens, New York, October 1988

Chris Hoban had been working narcotics, undercover, making a buy on the upper West Side when one of the dealers pulled a gun. Michael Buczek had been responding to a medical emergency, a woman having chest pains, and saw—outside her apartment building—what he suspected was a crack deal going down. He and his partner chased the guys, and one perp turned and shot him. Both had been good, brave cops; for the first time in forty years, two had died in the line of duty on the same night.

The shootings helped crystallize my view on the death penalty. Everyone's life is sacred, that I've always believed. But the blue uniform means more; if a cop is killed, everyone should take it personally. It's not a life for a life. If police officers felt that way, we'd have death squads, like El Salvador did, exacting retribution for the government. The death penalty has to be judiciously used, but the threat to the criminal may, just may, convince him to throw down his gun. How many officers would be alive today if perps had surrendered instead of shot? How many widows and children would have fathers to grow with, to love and to hold? I don't know, but if the death penalty had saved one, I'd consider it a success.

The presidential campaign was heating up in New York when Hoban and Buczek fell, and the Republicans seized the opportunity afforded by the killings. Our governor, Mario Cuomo, opposed such a penalty and had cited studies like one done in England saying the death penalty wouldn't stop murderers or reduce the number of murders. He supported life imprisonment without parole instead. Though I personally liked him and respected his accomplishments, I disagreed with him on this issue. What about the families? I thought. At least they'd find solace. And who was to say that a dirtball, being chased, wouldn't refrain from firing his gun at a pursuing officer if he knew that a death sentence might be one of the consequences.

Was there a conflict between this position and my forgiveness of Shavod Jones? I didn't see it. Jones was a boy, fifteen, living through a crucial time in his life. The death penalty wasn't applicable to him, and to other children like him. Yes, they were kids with access to weapons and drugs. But they didn't know how to judge right from wrong, I believed. They couldn't be held accountable in the same way. Jones, and children like him, had little support at home, and society wasn't helping them. If Shavod Jones had been twenty-five, instead of fifteen, I might have felt differently. But he wasn't.

The Democratic candidate, Mike Dukakis, had followed Cuomo's lead and refused to endorse the death penalty. George Bush, on the other hand, had been supporting it ever since he entered the race. The Boston police union had already endorsed him. On the day the Hoban and Buczek shootings were reported in the papers, our PBA president, Phil Caruso, called. The PBA would be endorsing Bush the following afternoon, at Christ the King High School in Queens. "We'd like you to be on stage with him," Phil said. "Matt Byrne, Eddie's father, will be there too."

A few hours later, a lawyer named Robert McMillan phoned. He was the Republican candidate for the

Senate, he said, running against Daniel Patrick Moynihan. Could he come to the house before the rally, he asked.

There was only one question on my mind. "Do you support the death penalty?" I asked.

"I do," he said. I told him to come by.

That night, like the others since Patti Ann had left, was hard. Conor was staying across the street with his grandparents. Mary, the night nurse, and I were alone. After I'd gotten tired of watching TV, at about 2:00 A.M., I asked her to pull the blanket over my head. Sometimes I can sleep better that way, by shutting out the respirator and its *whoop-whoosh.*

Patti Ann was supposed to call at 5:00 A.M. and I dozed, then woke in panic. I couldn't see, forgot why, and yelled, "Mary, Mary!" Silence. I yelled again. More silence. It seemed like forever, trapped in the darkness, alone. A blanket over my head, and I was blind.

"Steven, I hear you," she finally responded. "I'm coming. I was in the basement."

"What time is it?" I asked. She said it was 3:30 A.M. Could I have only been sleeping that little? I was wide awake, frightened and lonely. "Let's turn on the TV," I said.

On the screen, as if I'd willed it, John Wayne, Maureen O'Hara, and the lush green hillsides of *The Quiet Man* came into focus.

"Mary," I said, "you know, I feel great now. Everything's in sync. *The Quiet Man* is on, and I know Patti Ann's okay."

* * *

Christ the King was familiar turf. I'd spent some of my childhood in the Middle Village section of Queens, and in June had spoken to the graduating class. I wasn't finished getting dressed when McMillan, with two aides, came to the door. Dressed in a dark suit and looking like a guy who knew his campaign was hopeless, he brought a book for me, the autobiography of a Catholic priest living in exile in Russia. The candidate wanted to ride in the van with us, but Bob Dalia said there wouldn't be room. Just as well, I thought. Although all the cops in attendance would be there on their own time, my van was a department vehicle. Taking a candidate to a rally in it was more than likely prohibited by the patrol guide.

The streets leading to the school had been blocked off by the time we approached, and Bob turned on the flashing red light on the dashboard. With only brief hesitation, we were waved through every intersection. Cops, peering inside, would wave and yell, "Hey, Steve!" when they saw me in back, my chair buckled to the floor.

We pulled into the parking lot minutes before the Bush entourage arrived, and were waiting for him in the lobby. I'd never met a politician on that level and haven't since then. But in the phone call I'd gotten from Ronald Reagan at Bellevue, and in a couple of letters the White House had sent, I'd felt more warmth and genuine emotion than George Bush expressed as he rushed in, trailing Secret Service agents and aides. "Hi, how ya doin'," he said quickly, patting my strapped-down hand, then walked into an office where he met, I guess, with school administrators and other officials.

I wheeled into the auditorium filled with faculty, students, family and the press. A bank of TV cameras was stretched along the wall opposite the stage, and filling the bleachers behind the stage were hundreds of uniforms. Even if the Bush rhetoric was familiar, I thought, the tableau of the cops framing his remarks would make a strong, indelible impression on TV that night. As I concentrated on steering my chair down the narrow aisle to the ramp leading to the stage, I was aware of cheers, and my name being chanted. The students were standing, screaming, "Steven, Steven," and I felt a little embarrassed. I hadn't known what to expect, but it wasn't that.

My place on the platform would be between Bush and Matt Byrne, Eddie Byrne's father, a former New York cop. Then the vice-president took the stage and after other dignitaries were introduced—including McMillan—Bush spoke.

As I'd expected, the rhetoric was unmemorable. He supported the death penalty and the need to continue the war against drugs. I'd heard it before. Matt Byrne presented Bush with his son's shield, which I felt was more dramatic than anything the vice-president had done. I'd like to think that George Bush, now that he's the president, has put that shield somewhere he can see it, every day, maybe on a desk, or bookshelf, or bedside table, to remind himself of the toll this war on drugs is taking.

Bush finished, and hurried off to his next engagement. A few minutes later, we followed, rolling slowly through the lines of plainclothed and uniformed officers at the foot of the stage. As I passed, they stood back to let me through, and clapped, reaching out to touch my hands and arms.

The Bush endorsement, and the fact that the department seemed under greater political pressure than I could ever remember, caused me to reflect that night on the department's image. In the bleachers behind the stage had been officers of all races and all colors, men and women. Yet a few self-appointed black community representatives had been saying publicly for over a year that the citizens of their communities didn't appreciate the cops' presence on the job whether or not police action was taken. The Eleanor Bumpers case, where officer Stephen Sullivan had shot and killed the woman when she came at him with a knife while others were trying to evict her, had been just one example. But the city had been ready to take Sullivan's job and put him in jail. Sullivan, and the Police Department, hadn't failed Eleanor Bumpers. Before it ever ended up in our hands, she'd been failed by too many others.

The self-appointed community representatives and others are wrong. Police officers and city residents help each other prevent crime. If there are people who don't believe that, then they're ignoring the reality of who we are.

To say, I thought as I lay in bed that night, that the New York City Police Department is insensitive to the issue of racism and brutality is incorrect and irresponsible. In a city where color and ethnicity run the spectrum, there will be, on occasion, some negative feeling by an officer, but it's neither the norm nor is it condoned or accepted. That's a fact, not my opinion. And the greatest injustice is that the groups who've acted irresponsibly towards the police are those who've gained the most. The TV stations and the newspapers find new viewers and readers through such distortions, and that only encourages the distortions to continue.

At community board meetings I've been to, seen on television, and read about, people would talk about the need for the department to become more representative of the city's population. I understand that. But the police officer never thinks he doesn't represent and protect all. Sure, there'll always be a bad apple who slips through the application process. But the police aren't Nazis. We care about the individuals we serve and we represent the people we serve in every way.

Some of the best cops I know happen to be black. Commissioner Ben Ward is a dedicated and good cop who hasn't forgotten his own distinguished service as a radio car patrolman, Chief David Scott, the Chief of Patrol, and Chief DeForest Taylor, Chief of Personnel are true field generals. Watching Chief Scott on the Fourth of July, 1985, in Central Park, dispatching officers and giving orders, I understood how you command respect by example rather than force. Jimmy Secreto and Jimmy Johnson are two of the finest sergeants I have ever worked under.

It comes down to due process. Due process should apply to cops as well as criminals. But, as the system's evolved, it doesn't. Unsubstantiated complaints are kept in our files, and that accounts for 90 percent of all complaints made against New York City police officers. Nine out of ten complaints with nothing backing them up, and they're a permanent black mark. A criminal won't serve a day in jail on hearsay evidence, but a police officer can lose his job.

It was this damn concern with image, I thought.

When Buczek and Hoban went down, one reporter said it had been because the bosses encouraged cops to be passive, that officers my age had been taught a good cop doesn't initiate, he waits and reacts to a situation. No, I thought, that's not it. It's overeager reporters, journalists and lawyers getting department commanders to second-guess themselves and change policies before the ink was dry on the old ones. We're not undersupervised, overmanaged and paralyzed, like that writer suggested; we're hamstrung by how the media portrays us, and by how overzealous lawyers want to prosecute us.

Finally, I grew tired. Patti Ann would be home soon. Maybe the Blessed Mother will have touched her, maybe Jesus will have made a sign. I remembered words I'd said at Christ the King in June, when I'd been with Patti Ann and not George Bush. "If people really want someone to pattern their lives after," I'd said, "they should look to my mother, and to Patti Ann. *They* are true followers in the footpaths of Christ." I wondered what the Pope had said to her. "Alloo, Patti Ann," he'd say in that broad, Polish accent, "how's the babee . . ."

I missed Patti Ann terribly.

Medjugorje, Yugoslavia, October 1988

I was very nervous. I didn't know why, but it was making me sick. At breakfast, before we left the hotel in Rome to drive to the ferry that would take us across the Adriatic Sea to Yugoslavia, I told Father Mike about my uneasiness. "If the town is good enough for our Blessed Mother to come to every day for years," he said, "it will be fine for us."

"I guess so," I told him.

I just didn't know what to expect. For over two years, I'd been praying for Steven's healing. Now I was going to ask the Blessed Mother to heal both of us: me spiritually, and Steven physically. Let my faith be strong enough, I prayed.

From the coast, we drove through the mountains. At the edges of cliffs a thousand feet high, eagles flew alongside our bus. The mountain road led into a valley, new construction everywhere, mud roads, and, then, the twin steeples of St. James, standing over the tiny peasant village. Our tour group of fifty would be staying in four local homes, and Father Mike and I waited quietly. We'd learned to keep our mouths shut, and not get pushy when others were. And we got to stay in the cleanest, nicest home. Then we went to Mass.

The church was crowded, and at 4:00 P.M. the priest asked the English-speaking tour members to leave so the Italians could come in. "Patti," Father Mike said, "if we leave we are finished. We will never get seats for the Rosary at 5:00 P.M. and the Visions at 5:40." So I stayed. A couple of minutes before 5:40, the Visionaries stepped through a door to the choir loft.

The church lights dimmed, then lights like lightning started to flash all around us. Not camera flashes, but powerful lights, which—we were told later—shown on Podbrdo Hill when Our Lady first began to appear to the children in 1981. After the lights, a Mass.

Father Philip Popovich spoke of fear—fear of God, of religion, of living and dying. I watched the faces of the Visionaries Ivan and Marija, and prayed.

For two more days, I tried to find my miracle. We climbed the hill, and I stared long and hard at the simple mound of rocks topped with a cross, where the Blessed Mother had first been seen. We walked to Marija's house, and she came outside and greeted us, taking questions. It was a primitive scene, chickens behind her, smoke curling from a chimney, and I had an uncomfortable feeling we all wanted a piece of her. Father Mike asked the first question. "Is there something that Our Lady has said recently that is good for us to hear this morning, that you are free to share with us?"

"Yes," Marija said, "last Monday the Lady spoke of family prayer and said when the family prays together, there comes joy and peace."

"Does the Lady's face change from happy to sad?"

"No. It is always the same. But it becomes more beautiful every day."

"Can you tell us the best vision you have had?"

"Tonight's will be the best. I must leave you now," she told us, smiling. "You see, my family is all at Mass, and today is Sunday, my day to cook. Soon they'll be home, and I have nothing prepared."

She appeared distracted for a moment, then left. I was a little relieved. I'd heard some Americans try to ask if there was a message for the United States. And I'd heard a group of English men and women complain that the message wasn't designated to their area of the world.

Father Mike and I returned to the church. He spoke with Father Philip after Mass, and asked the priest if it would be all right for Father Mike to go into the choir loft with the Visionaries that evening. Of course, Father Philip had said, Father Mike was a Friar, and all he had to do was be at the door at the base of the tower at 4:40 P.M. Father Mike was excited. "That was it!" he told me. "One, two, three, and he was gone."

I asked Father Mike to take our ring and picture with him. He agreed. Later, when he rejoined me, he told me what happened.

"The door opened," Father Mike said. "Philip signaled me in. Up the stairs after him I went. There were boxes on the side, some other things, then I was to the doorway. 'You sit over there on that bench,' Philip said, pointing at the only seat in the loft, 'and they will come for the Rosary at 5:00 P.M. Just stay there and when it is over, you can come down to celebrate. You'll want to do that.' And he was gone!

"The choir loft was bare except for the bench, a little kneeler at the end of it—just a kneeler, not a prie-dieu—and a chair sitting against the door opposite the one I'd entered. I sat, my black sack at my feet. Then I looked at the wall of apparition. A simple, but beautiful painting of the Gospa, Mary, about four by three feet hung there. Below it was a simple table—maybe the size of a speaker lying on its side. The altar. A plant, some silk flowers, and a pot with a vine of red plastic flowers were to the side.

"On the floor, leaning against the altar and wall, were the petitions we'd given Marija. I took my bag, opened it, and lay it next to them. Right at Our Lady's feet. Then I put Steven's wedding ring on the altar. For a moment, I had a strange feeling. What if Our Lady says it shouldn't be there? I laughed to myself.

"The Visionaries arrived. I didn't look around to see them. How many? The Rosary began. We moved to the second Rosary—it must have been during the third decade as I was kneeling facing the wall, the lights started and I had the feeling of movement. Ivan moved in front of me, an arm's length, then turned to see if Marija was following. She did. They knelt, signed themselves, then Ivan shook his head with a 'yes' three times. Marija nodded 'no' once.

"A scent, flowers, beautiful flowers, filled the loft. I swallowed and tried to exhale, but the flowers were everywhere. Downstairs, the church began the Rosary again. Ivan and Marija signed in unison, and began to pray. The night before, Ivan's voice had sounded deep, manly. Now I heard a young boy's. They finished praying, rose and left.

"I stayed until I felt a tap on the shoulder. It was Ivan, signalling me to come. I took the bag and the ring, and followed him down. At the door, I shook his hand, thanking him.

"'Caio,' he replied."

When Father Mike told me, I rejoiced. Steven's ring had been on the altar. Would now be the time the Blessed Mother would respond to our prayers?

On our last day, I went to confession. The message the Blessed Mother had been sending had been of prayer, of fasting, and of penance. Pilgrims like myself sought forgiveness and compassion, but the priest whose confessional I chose was stern and cold. Father Mike and I had come to the church together, he to hear confessions. Outside, before we'd entered, we'd seen the mystical Medjugorje sunset—the sun changing colors, moving towards us, then away, surrounded by a spinning white light—and I'd felt at peace, certain the presence of Our Lady was there.

The priest shattered my mood, telling me that my life wasn't as difficult as I'd felt, yelling at me in the most negative tones that I should be doing whatever I could for Steven, and trying harder not to get him upset. "I've been in war," the priest said, "and I've seen situations much worse than yours. You have to be a better wife to your husband, to act happy and be joyful even when that's not the way you feel.

"If you get upset," he continued, "go into the other room. Don't let him see it."

I left the confessional crying, looking for Father Mike. When I found him, he tried to console me. "Calm down," he said. "Don't worry. He had no right to say that. Those are the kinds of priests who make people not want to go to confession, and to church."

I knew he was right. The good from the trip—seeing the faith of thousands and thousands of young and old, a faith that prospered despite poverty and sickness—far outweighed any negative messages one man could give me. After dinner that night, Father Mike and I climbed the Hill of Apparition with several thousand other pilgrims. It was a cold and difficult climb, and at the summit we pressed close to the cross, lit by candles, where the Visionaries prayed. At 11:00 P.M., there was a stillness, a presence. We prayed, and Mary's words were translated as they'd been heard by Ivan and Marija. "I am happy you are here," she said, "and I know you are cold so I have touched you all on the shoulder to warm you. My son is delighted with the candles lighting up the cross. Pray for youth, they have so many problems. Especially pray for those who were never trained in faith. And pray for those who have the responsibility of youth."

I was at peace again. My healing had begun. What Steven and I would get, now and in the future, we would have to earn, I'd realized. For nearly three weeks, I'd been surrounded by men and women who were sick, or disabled, or emotionally wounded. I had no special claim to hardship and trouble. I had Steven and Conor to love, and whatever was worth loving was worth fighting for. Our struggle to live, I'd decided, would forever be colored by what I'd seen and heard here, at Fatima, and at Lourdes.

I was ready to go home.

Howard Beach, November 1988

The night Patti Ann came home we talked for hours about the trip, the shrines, the Visionaries. Before she'd left, I'd hoped she'd be touched over there by the Blessed Mother. So much had been taken from her, maybe something would be given back. And it hadn't, but I could sense she was renewed, that we both now had a stronger commitment to our relationship. I resigned myself that any healing would have to come later, in the days and months to follow. But my nights would improve. The house was alive again with the sound of her voice, and Conor's happiness. I wouldn't wake at three or four in the morning. I could sleep again.

* * *

We accepted an invitation for both of us to speak at an Advent prayer service at a church in Howard Beach, a white, middle-class Catholic Queens neighborhood that had been torn by racial violence a year earlier. A Brooklyn man and his passengers, all black, had been driving home on the expressway and had broken down just outside Howard Beach's small business district. They'd left the car and walked to a pizzeria, planning to call for assistance. At the restaurant, some local boys had words with them, and insults had escalated into assault. The Howard Beach kids outnumbered the Brooklyn men, who'd fled in panic. The locals chased them back onto the highway, where one of the stranded men had run into the traffic and been hit and killed by a passing car. In the aftermath, Howard Beach had been made a symbol, in the media, of racial hatred. The healing in that community was still going on, I knew, and the Advent service would be a part.

That afternoon, we'd posed for some family portraits and talked to a reporter about Christmas, and faith. "Christmas comes quicker as you get older," I'd joked. "But you always think back to Christmas past, and it's not the same. I'm thankful that I'm here, though. I'll take it any way." Going to Howard Beach, I said, would be a way to show that God exists, that Christ was alive. How? wondered the reporter. "Because if God hadn't wanted me to live in Central Park that July day," I said, "He wouldn't have shown those two cops where to find me in that wilderness. That's how God helped me."

When the writer and photographer left, Patti Ann and I got ready. Bob Dalia would drive. I asked Rose Garibaldi, the nurse, to shave me. As I lay back in the chair, shaving cream on my face, Conor snuck behind me, carrying a plastic toy garden hoe. With a swing Darryl Strawberry would have admired, he hit me as hard as he could on the top of my forehead. Rose looked at him with astonishment and took the hoe away. I sat motionless. The mark would still be there when we pulled up to the church.

"This is a free zone," said Bob, as he steered the van off the expressway. "You know who lives here? John Gotti." Gotti was reputed to be the Mafia's boss of bosses; I didn't expect to see him inside St. Helen's this night.

"See the Gulf station over there?" Bob continued. "The guy who died ran by there, then tried to cross the parkway we just got off."

In front of the church, a crowd of priests and officers, most of them auxiliaries, was waiting. "The regulars from the 106th Precinct aren't here," an officer named Bell from Community Affairs apologized. "We just found out about this the day before." I wasn't surprised; Mikhail Gorbachev was arriving that night too, and every available officer was assigned to midtown Manhattan. What did give me pause was the number of parishioners who spilled onto the sidewalk. I'd expected a small, church basement group, but I could see there were several hundred men, women and children. "Don't shut the engine off," I told Bob. "I don't want to get out right away."

I asked Patti Ann for a Bible, and as she held it in front of me, I reread The First Epistle of Peter. There are rich blessings for those who are sad, he'd written, because they suffer trials which are sent to prove their faith genuine. A message, I thought, for Howard Beach as well as me.

Outside, the priests waited. When I was ready, Bob and Patti Ann lowered me to the sidewalk and I puffed the chair into the church. They wanted me in front, but there was no ramp. Bob and an auxiliary tried to push me up the carpeted steps, bending one of the chair's footrests. As if I wasn't nervous enough. Now my foot would dangle, like a dummy's. "Pat," I whispered, "rest it on top of the other." Carefully, she did.

"To think," the priest began, "that a week ago we were wondering if anyone would be here. This gives us strength . . . God loves these two people on my left. They're a great inspiration to New York City, and to the whole world."

From where I sat now, I could see there were five hundred, maybe one thousand people jammed into St. Helen's. How could I ever have imagined I would be reaching people like these? "Officer McDonald will share his life with us," I heard the priest say. Then Patti Ann took the microphone and held it before my lips. "If I told you I was nervous," I began, "that would be an understatement. But coming through these doors, I felt your love. It's been a trying two years for all of us—your community and my family. That we've succeeded is proof our faith is real. I never thought our public life would come so far, and touch so many. When you're a police officer, you just do your job. You can go twenty, thirty years, and see no impact. I've seen it all in two and a half years.

"When I was shot, I asked God in a simple prayer, 'Please don't let me die.' I was found in the wilderness that's northern Central Park. I'm proof positive that God exists . . ."

Patti Ann began weeping, but kept the mike near my mouth.

"I know it looks bad," I said, "the way I am. You might say, what's to be thankful about. But if you could see my child . . . I should be dead today, with Chris Hoban and Mike Buczek, but I'm not. I thank God for the gift of life."

The parishioners stood and applauded. I smiled, grateful, eager to hear what Patti Ann would share with them. Wiping tears with one hand, she described my homecoming from Craig. "The reality hit home," she said, "when we moved into the house. I reached my breaking point. Go on a pilgrimage, I thought, and when you come back, everything will be off your shoulders. Prayer had always been so important, and when I was at my lowest, I'd say Hail Marys, light a candle, and talk to God. Then I went to Fatima, Lourdes and Medjugorje, and met the Pope. I saw Europeans who don't have half of what we have, yet they'd give you the shirts off their backs . . .

"My message to you is prayer," Patti Ann said. "Just prayer. It helps a lot."

A choir began singing. "Transform that which is ugly," the voices rang, "to that which is rich." A woman standing next to Bob said quietly, "Patti Ann's the closest person to a saint I've seen."

Our lives and our futures may have great limits on them, I thought, as scores of strangers approached to offer their prayers and wishes, but there will always be room for love and hope.

And in the Howard Beaches of the world, that could go a long way.

Malverne, January 1989

Occasionally, I'll hear that people are jealous of Steven and me. Jealous of *what,* I'd ask. The house? The media attention? If you want it, if you want to trade places with us, if you want our day-to-day lives, please . . . take them. Because I'd rather have what you have.

No, I'm not a widow. I haven't lost my husband, like some officers' wives have. I don't know that kind of loss. I still have Steven, thank God.

But others haven't had to face each day with their husband hooked up to that support system, watching him being taken care of. A six-two, stocky, robust man assisted in every aspect of his life. Every moving moment has been taken away. Others may have lost their son, or their husband, but they don't have to go through this every day. They don't have to see what I see.

Some days, I just have to leave the room because it hurts so much. And it wouldn't hurt as much if I didn't love him as much.

And Steven is the same man I've always loved. He's as handsome as he ever was. His personality and sense of humor are intact. He's a listener, a giver, a fine father. He's gotten lazy about getting off the respirator, about weaning himself as he was taught to do at Craig. But I still believe he will some day. I believe he'll do that, and he'll walk.

We follow spinal cord research closely. A Boston doctor recently told us about experiments he'd conducted where omentum tissue—the lining of the stomach—was transplanted to the cords of laboratory animals in order to stimulate blood vessel and tissue regrowth. The researcher had claimed success, but when we'd tried to confirm that with the Craig staff, we'd been told the jury was still out, that no results had been deemed conclusive. But people are studying and trying new things.

We haven't given up our hopes and our dreams. We're carrying on.

Malverne, January 1989

So George Bush won, and the PBA was invited to send a delegation to the Inauguration. The delegation didn't include me, and I wondered if my remarks on Joe Doherty and Northern Ireland have had anything to do with that. I wondered if the PBA had forgotten about me.

Before Christmas, I'd tried to bring Joe Doherty a card and a book. The guards stopped me at the door to the Corrections Center, and wouldn't let me leave the book. Ironically, it was the volume the Republican senate candidate, Robert McMillan, had given me, the diary of a Jesuit priest imprisoned in Russia. I wrote Joe to tell him what had happened, and he'd responded by saying he'd been put into solitary confinement. "The hole," he'd said. "We have a new prison administration," Joe wrote me, "that just wants to clamp down. Not allowing your visit is an example." Joe had said he'd celebrated his birthday that day.

"Thirty-four years young," he wrote, "still young at heart and will never let this torturing place take my sense of dignity."

With the New Year, I resolved to see him. As so many had given me the gift of hope and prayer, maybe I'd be able to help him, this Irish prisoner of war.

Another Christmas at home has passed, and Conor is nearly two. "Daddy," he can say, and he'll climb into my chair, and we'll ride through the living room, or into the therapy room. If he gets me a cookie, he knows he has to feed it to me. He's even trying to throw the football, though it slips off his hand as often as not.

God, how I wish I could throw it with him.

At night, upstairs, long before dawn, he'll call out, call to me, "Daddy, Daddy!" A nightmare, probably. Like mine? I wonder. Does he dream, as I did, of paralysis, of not telling the difference between hot and cold. I wake from whatever fitful sleep I've fallen into.

"Conor," I say, as soothingly as I can, "it's all right. I'm here."

But am I? Won't Patti Ann wake and take him into the other bedroom with her? Or won't the night nurse come upstairs and settle him down? *Whoop-whoosh,* the vent reminds me. You are Scrooge's Ghost of Christmas Past; I am your ball and chain. *Whoop-whoosh.* And yet I *am* there, as I was for Courtney at Craig, in the lonely darkness around our hospital beds. I'm accomplishing *something.*

The other day Bob drove me through Central Park, by the hill and the path where Shavod Jones shot me. The radio was on, and we picked up a call, a pursuit along West Drive. Bob flicked on the flasher, and we joined in. The perp hit a tree. We were the fourth or fifth vehicle on the scene. Someone opened the side door, and I watched the collar. I ached to be a part of it.

There are so many things I still want to do. Talk to Shavod Jones. Help injured officers. Talk to kids. Be a good father. When Thomas, my youngest brother, was five, at a time when my father was rarely home, I'd joined the Navy. Just before I left, Thomas and I watched a Christmas cartoon, "Magoo's Christmas Carol." In it, young Scrooge had been left at boarding school for the holiday, because his father blamed him for the death of his mother. "Two shoes, click to clack," he sings sadly, "I'm all alone, left in the world." The day I had to leave, Thomas handed me a drawing, a picture of two shoes.

There won't be two shoes for Patti Ann and Conor. I'll survive and get better. I'll find a role to play in the department. I'll find faith and hope in the inspiration that's Patti Ann's life. And I'll never forget the thousands who've given me their prayers and their love.

It's not evening now, just a beautiful, sunny early January afternoon. My mechanical chair is broken, and Bob Dalia's taken it to be repaired. Pat Dillon has pushed me out onto our back deck and angled me so that, when I tilt my head back, the full force of the sun falls on my face. A weak sun, not the burning Colorado disc that nearly peeled my face off. Like a junkie to his drug, I couldn't get enough of it. But, on these winter afternoons, what's the phrase . . . beggars can't be choosers?

The sliding door's open, and I can hear voices. Pat and Patti Ann. And Conor. He sounds so excited.

They must be . . . yes, they're putting together his new train set. They're gathered around, snapping the tracks together, and Conor's shouting with joy. Unintelligible, pure glee.

I'd drive to join them but . . . wrong chair. I'd shout, but then they'd have to stop and come and get me. Choices, bad choices. No, don't get down. We've come so far. We've been given so much.

Whoop-whoosh.

We have to be patient. There will be more to come.

Whoop-whoosh.

There has to be.

Epilogue

Am I, Steven McDonald, special? A hero cop, as the tabloids put it? No. I didn't think so before I was shot, I didn't believe it while I was hospitalized, and now, as we finish this book, I don't believe it either.

I wanted more than two years on the job. I'd read press clippings about my grandfather, and heard my father's stories. I knew about the good, and the bad, on the streets and inside the department. And I believed the good outweighed everything else.

I know now I was right. The selflessness and compassion I've seen since I was hurt, from other police officers and from the public, have been nearly universal. The city of New York has been heroic, not me. And every chance I've had to be exposed to another department or law enforcement agency, I've felt the same caring, the same understanding.

The oath I took in 1984 was to serve and protect. I'd take that oath again tomorrow. Being a cop is all I want. And the past two-and-a-half years have taught me that I made the right choice.

Whatever the consequences have been. And will be.

Many of us take too much for granted. Before I was injured, I sometimes took Patti Ann for granted. Now I value her love and appreciate her devotion more than anything in the world.

And a lot of us take a safe America for granted. But we must not!

Violent death comes too often in this country. Whether it's a teenage boy in the gutters of East New York, smoked lifeless by crack, or the flag-draped coffins of heroes: we cry.

Yet the cops and the kids of these United States deserve more than headlines and headstones. They deserve more than promises and proposals. A vest on every cop, an electric chair on every corner, or a stump speech on every channel will not breathe life into my slain Police Academy classmates.

We are a nation of sorrows. Mothers cry for their sons who kill and are killed. Black and white, we die slowly by needle and vial; we die quickly by Uzi and by knife.

And, so, today's heroes become yesterday's headlines. Today's drug victims become tomorrow's statistics.

But I won't accept that, and neither should you.

Now the future of this land is in our hands. The police and political leadership of America work as hard as they can to do what they can to stop the drug violence which promises to turn this republic into one long super highway of crack dens, shooting galleries and mortuaries.

It's time for all of us to stand up for our country, for our kids and for our cops.

We must begin today—not as self-appointed vigilantes or terrorists—not by carrying guns or torching buildings—but as responsible mothers and fathers, and as loyal sons and daughters, using the good sense God gave us and the system of laws for which Americans before us died.

Do we need tough laws and tough judges to sentence the drug killers the harshest way possible? Of course.

Do we need more help from the federal government, more border interdiction, more treatment centers? Of course.

But that's not enough. Young people need education: they need legitimate opportunity, and they need real jobs. They need true role models and responsible community leaders. They must understand that the genuine heroes are not the cash-carrying, BMW-driving, eighteen-year-old thugs who roam the city streets. The real heroes are the men and women of their community who work for a wage, worship on the weekend and catch the ballgame at night.

When you see crime, when you see drugs, pick up the phone from the security of your own home. Call the police and report what you see—whether you give your name or not.

Organize in your community. Let it be known that dope dealers are neither needed nor wanted in your neighborhood. Tell your elected representatives that, unless they begin to behave as if they actually live in the community, they can find some other line of work.

Every day, in every metropolis, families and friends grieve alone in small homes and in funeral parlors for the victims of drug crime. There are no headlines, no medals of honor, no honor guards for these victims.

So, too, do the centurions of our nation: the men and women in blue die without a legacy. As a boy, I remember attending the funeral of my father's partner. He was a strong, courageous man who died of a heart attack while he was breaking down a door during a police raid. His name was McGowan and, except for his family and friends, his sacrifice is mostly forgotten today.

That is what I fear. I'm afraid that a year from now, the names of our hero cops will be merely names on a precinct wall of honor, just convenient props in an election year.

The time for strife is over. It's time to stop fighting among ourselves. The drug dealers love that. It's good for their business.

Pick up the phone when you witness a crime. Call the police. If you don't want to give your name, call just the same, and tell the police that you're calling for Steven McDonald.

Then, and only then, will I be able to know that my time in this wheelchair will be spent as a worthwhile sacrifice, not as a life sentence.

Then, and only then, can we feel good about ourselves, our country, our kids and our cops.

Afterword

As quickly as a bullet turned our lives upside down, a phone call did the same. Shavod Jones was responsible for both. And as much as I believed I was, I wasn't really prepared for either.

Earlier this year, Shavod's grandmother, Lenora Jones, called Cardinal O'Connor and said she would like to meet me.

On a sunny Palm Sunday, we drove to the historic Convent Avenue Baptist Church in Harlem to attend services. I entered the church through a side entrance to avoid the reporters and photographers waiting for me on the front steps. On the wall was a painting of Jesus Christ, flanked on one side by a photograph of Abraham Lincoln and on the other side by a photograph of John F. Kennedy. I felt at home seeing this pantheon of personal heroes; the same pictures hang on the wall of my physical therapy room.

The church filled up with well-dressed black families who smiled at me, touched my arms and face as they walked by, and welcomed me to their place of worship.

An aging woman walked toward me as the choir sang.

"I'm Lenora Jones. I'm Shavod's gandmother."

"Hello, Mrs. Jones. I guess you know who I am. I'm hard to miss," I said, nodding to my wheelchair. Mrs. Jones put her head down, seemingly embarrassed. I think she felt guilty that I was sitting where I was.

I felt stupid making her feel guilty.

"I'm happy to finally meet you. You're a very fine woman."

She smiled briefly, then surveyed my entire body, from the top of my head to my feet bound up in the wheelchair. She shook her head ever so slightly and whispered, "Oh God." She smiled again and sat down next to me. From time to time throughout the service she looked over at me and nodded.

At the end of the service she said quietly, "Shavod's really a good boy. He needs help."

"Yes, I know," I answered.

"Can you help him?"

"I can try."

"Please try."

Dennis Breen pushed me down the aisle of the church. There was applause as I went by. A black boy, thirteen or fourteen years old, stood at the door; in his hand was a box of floppy disks.

"You like computers?" I asked.

"I love 'em," he answered. He held the box high in the air, as if it were a trophy.

"Keep loving them and you'll make it."

"Officer McDonald, thanks for being a good Christian."

"It's nice of you to think so."

Mrs. Jones and I parted, pledging to meet again. We did at the end of June. But something happened before that second visit that I will never forget.

It was mid-June and our house was as raucous as ever, with nurses, relatives and a rambunctious Conor scurrying about. We were running late, as usual, preparing to go to Manhattan for a fund-raising dinner on behalf of Covenant House, a legendary refuge for runaways and lost youths.

Just as Patti and I were out the door, the phone rang. Katie, Patti's sister, was at the house to babysit Conor and she answered it.

"Steven, there's a phone call for you."

"Take a message. I'll call back." The upcoming address distracted me.

"It's Shavod Jones," she said.

Everyone froze. I could see the contorted, anxious looks on the faces of everyone who stood around. Patti looked at me, white-faced and startled. You could hear a pin drop in the room. The only one undaunted was Conor, who watched us with childish wonder.

Shavod Jones was on the phone! If Katie had said it was one of my cop buddies I'd have told her to take a message.

But it wasn't.

"Officer McDonald?" the voice at the other end of the phone asked. In the background I could hear other kids screaming and the familiar New York sound of rap music.

I didn't say anything. The question was repeated again, milder and meeker this time. The voice sounded like that of a child lost in the park looking for the way home.

"Yup, this is Steve. Shavod, is that you?"

Another prisoner screamed in the background, "Give it up, Buddha. Off the phone now!"

"Are you okay to talk?"

"I'm okay."

"Shavod, what can I do for you?" I asked. As soon as the words came out I felt bad. Why should I put the poor kid on the spot? It must have been hard enough to call a cop from prison.

There was silence. Only the sounds of the shouts and the rap music. I said his name again.

"I don't really know how to say it."

As he hesitated I wondered if he had thought about this conversation as much as I had, each in our own prison.

"I'd just like to say that I'm sorry for everything that has happened."

Now I hesitated. What do you say to a person who tried to kill you and four years later tells you that he's sorry? Do you say, Ah, that's okay. Don't give it a second thought? Or I forgive you, but if you ever try it again I'll be very mad? I said neither. Instead I answered, "I understand, Shavod."

"What are you doing to keep busy up there?" Patti Ann looked at me as though I were insane. She shook her head and left the room. Maybe she was right. If anyone walked in at that moment it would appear I was shooting the breeze with an old Navy friend or a cop from the Central Park precinct.

"I work with my hands. They have a shop up here.

Some machinery. And I work with wood." He added, "But I'd rather be someplace else."

Like an innocent I asked, "What do you mean?"

"I'm getting along all right, but it's not like being home."

"You know your grandmother loves you. You know we've been doing some talking."

"I know," he whispered almost begrudgingly. Maybe he was embarrassed.

Patti Ann pointed to her watch, not so much because of the hour but because she thought enough was enough.

"Shavod, I'm gonna go now. I've gotta give a speech."

"Okay."

"But I want you to know that when you get out I'll be there for you. You've got some good family who want you to make it. And you've got me too."

"Thank you, Officer McDonald." He hung up the phone.

Patti Ann sat on the couch in the living room and she began to cry as I wheeled toward her.

"Come on, Pat, we'll be late." As I rolled past her, she touched my face with her soft hand, shook her head and smiled.

"That wasn't easy for him, you know," I said, almost apologetically. "And I know it wasn't easy for you."

"I love you, Steven. I love you."

A few weeks later the telephone rang again. The nurse who picked up mouthed the words of the operator on the other end, "Shavod Jones calling collect for Steve McDonald." I nodded yes from my bed and Jean Marie held the phone next to me.

"Mr. McDonald?"

"Shavod, is it you?"

"It's me. How ya doing?"

"I'm okay. How about yourself?"

"I'm doing better, Mr. McDonald. They had me in Elmira. Now they moved me to Cayuga Prison in Moravia. It's closer for my family. You know I've got two brothers and two sisters."

I didn't know. The McDonald and Jones families. Two sets of brothers and sisters hurt by what became of their brothers.

"I was wondering when you were gonna call me again. I hope this is not some big con job. If you're going to change your life it's going to take more than calling up a guy in a wheelchair."

He interrupted. "I know what you're saying. I gotta do it on my own. I've got plans when I get out of here. I'm getting my high school equivalency. I want to help the kids in the neighborhood. I want to make sure they don't make the same mistakes that I did."

All I could say was, "That sounds pretty good to me."

"My family sent me your book. I cried Mr. McDonald, I cried when I read your book."

"Thank you for reading the book, Shavod. But crying's not going to help either one of us."

"Yeah, I know, but I feel so bad."

I changed the subject. "You know Reverend Grant is getting ready to help build a new Boys Club in Harlem. You say you're good with your hands. Now's not a bad time to prove it."

"I want to help."

"It would make your grandmother happy."

"Is Patti Ann okay?"

Shavod had never mentioned my wife to me. It made me uncomfortable. It reminded me exactly who I was speaking to. I didn't respond.

"And your boy, Mr. McDonald?"

I did respond. "I love them more than my own life."

"Yes . . . well, I won't bother you any more now. Thanks for letting me call you. I'm going now."

"Goodbye, Shavod."

He hung up.

I don't want Shavod to spend the rest of his life in prison. I've forgiven him for what he's done. And I know that's easier for me than for those around me.

In some ways I feel good about Shavod. By calling me he's proven that he knows what he did and that it was wrong. Some people never come that far. Some never cry but only laugh at the pain they have inflicted on a stranger.

From our first meeting in Central Park, we will never again be strangers. Our lives and our names will always be joined whether we like it or not. Every achievement, every mistake we make, will reflect back to the day Shavod shot me. But what's done is done.

I am paralyzed. He's in prison.

I can't help but agonize over who has an obligation to whom? By virtue of his fateful act does he owe me and my family a debt? Should he be condemned to pushing my wheelchair, to suctioning my lungs, to helping me get my sneakers on? I don't think so.

He's paid his debt and now he says he's sorry.

But I can't help feeling guilty. I'm the person who

can't move but I feel guilty. Do I owe Shavod just as much as some people think he owes me?

Do I want Shavod to become Conor's friend, to be present at our family table for Christmas dinner, to go to our church, to join in our joy as a family?

Yes I do.

I don't know if it will ever happen or if it ever can. I'm not sure that it would be fair to Conor or Patti Ann to treat their father's and husband's would-be killer like a member of the family.

But I have a feeling that our relationship has only begun. I have a feeling that if Shavod can begin his life again, then maybe there's even hope for me.

Steven McDonald
with John Berry